Freeze Drying Mastery For Beginners Copy

Complete Guide To Long-Term Food Storage, Save Money, Reduce Waste and Ensure Your Pantry Is Always Stocked

HarvestGuard Publications

HarvestGuard Publications

Copyright © 2023 by HarvestGuard Publications – All rights reserved.

No portion of this book may be reproduced in any form without written permission from the publisher or author, except as permitted by U.S. copyright law.

This publication is designed to provide accurate and authoritative information in regard to the subject matter covered. It is sold with the understanding that neither the author nor the publisher is engaged in rendering legal, investment, accounting or other professional services. While the publisher and author have used their best efforts in preparing this book, they make no representations or warranties with respect to the accuracy or completeness of the contents of this book and specifically disclaim any implied warranties of merchantability or fitness for a particular purpose. No warranty may be created or extended by sales representatives or written sales materials. The advice and strategies contained herein may not be suitable for your situation. You should consult with a professional when appropriate. Neither the publisher nor the author shall be liable for any loss of profit or any other commercial damages, including but not limited to special, incidental, consequential, personal, or other damages.

Contents

Download Your Batch Log Booklet	1
Introduction	2
1. Understanding Freeze-Drying	4
2. Benefits and Uses of Freeze-Drying	11
3. Preparing Your Freeze-Drying Space	17
4. Must-Have Tools and Accessories	23
5. Setting Up Your Freeze Dryer	29
6. Food Preparation Techniques	37
7. Running Your Freeze Dryer	47
8. Packaging and Long-Term Storage	51
9. Consuming Freeze-Dried Foods	55
10. Maintaining Your Freeze-Dryer	62
11. Additional Tips, Tricks, and Resources	67
12. Freeze-Dryers' Favorites and Non-Food Items	71
13. Freeze-Drying Candy and Desserts and Top Tips for Success	77
Conclusion	85
Download All 104 Recipes in Color	87
Recipes	91
Batch Logs & Worksheets	196
About My Freeze Dryer	198
Rehydration Information	199
Rehydrating Your Food Sheet	200
Freeze Dryer Specs	201
How Long Does Freeze-Dryer Food Last	202
Oxygen Absorber Chart	203
Maintenance & Repair Log	204
Supplies	205

Recipe Freeze-Drying Sheet	206
4-Tray Batch Log Sheet	207
Candy 4-Tray Batch Log Sheet	208
Batch Plan Sheet	209
Freeze Dried Food Sheet	210
Freeze Dried Meals Sheet	211
Freeze Dried Candy Sheet	212
Freeze Dried Desserts	213
Freeze Dried _____	214
Publisher	215
Resources	216

FREE DOWNLOAD

THE ULTIMATE BATCH LOG BOOKLET

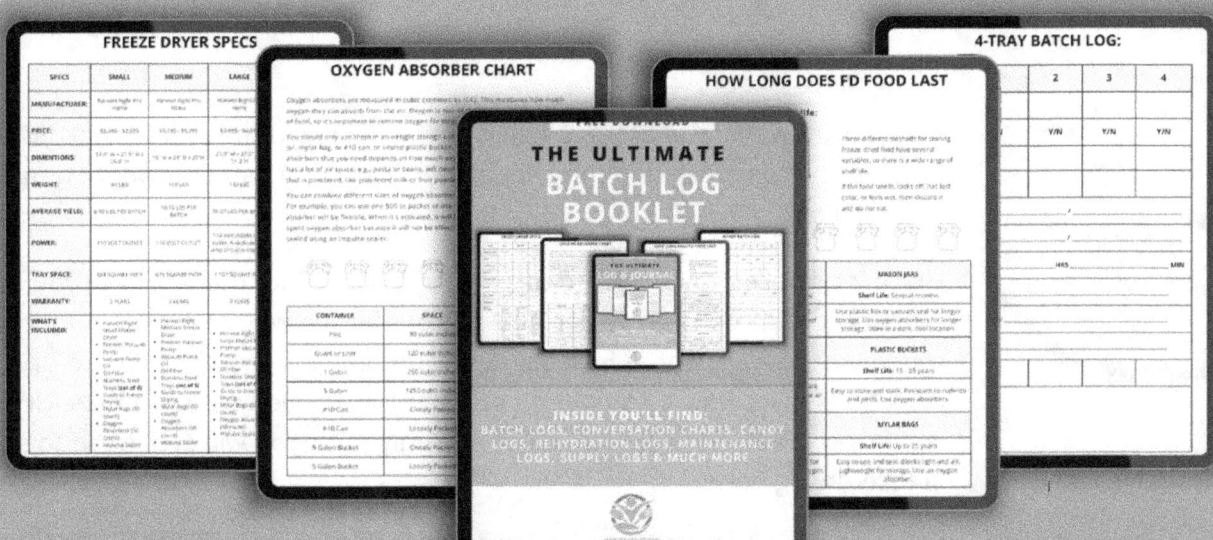

Introduction

Did you know that the average American family of four throws away $1,500 in wasted food per year, and the annual food waste in America is approximately $161 billion?

Since food prices have reached their highest point since the 70s, have you ever wondered if there is an easier and more effective way to preserve food for when you need it? There is absolutely a better way. It's called freeze-drying! This book gives you a complete and comprehensive guide to freeze-drying your own food at home. This will be the only book you will ever need to start freeze-drying now!

I was skeptical when I first heard about freeze-drying food, but I quickly realized that it could save me a lot of money and prevent waste in the long term. I initially bought a home freeze dryer during lockdown because, like everyone else, I freaked out, thinking, this was it, the beginning of the end and I figured I better be ready for it. While everyone else was hunting for flour to bake bread, I started freeze-drying food for my family and my pets. My dog has always been incredibly fussy, and I realized I could save money by freeze-drying leftover meat that she was more likely to eat than the store-bought variety, not to mention it was 100% natural. Not only did I know the exact ingredients in what they were eating, but I no longer had a surplus of dog food bought in bulk that she had eaten for two days and then no longer touched.

Once I realized that freeze-dried food didn't need to be refrigerated, the initial outlay of funding a home freeze-dryer was very quickly validated. I no longer had to worry about expensive food becoming spoiled, and the cost of living crisis became a thing of the past.

How often have you had to throw food away because plans changed and you didn't use it when you thought you would? Have you ever felt guilty about throwing away spoiled food when costs are constantly rising? Not to mention that my two teens are so annoying when it comes to leftovers. They wouldn't eat the same food twice, and I can only eat it so much before I get sick of it. So what's the option? Stare at it sitting in the fridge and watch it go bad or freeze it and then remember that I froze it months later when its freezer burned and ready to be thrown in the garbage.

The best thing about freeze-drying food is that it doesn't affect your food's **nutritional value** or **taste**. You have complete control over your ingredients, and it couldn't be easier.

This book is a comprehensive guide to freeze-drying, which will walk you through every step of the process.

You will discover:

- How freeze-drying works
- The benefits and uses of freeze-drying
- How to prepare your freeze-drying space
- Must-have freeze-drying tools and accessories
- How to set up your freeze-dryer
- Freeze-drying food preparation techniques
- How to run your freeze-dryer
- How to package and store your freeze-dried foods long term
- Tips for consuming freeze-dried foods
- How to maintain your freeze dryer
- Other freeze-drying tips, tricks, and resources
- You will get over 100 recipes
- You will learn how to make freeze-dried candy

…. and so much more.

Once you have read this book, you will completely understand everything you need to freeze-dry your food at home. You will not only learn about the versatility of freeze-dried food but how much fun it can be, and you will never struggle with waste again. This I promise you!

Without further ado, let's dive into the wonderful world of freeze-drying. It is a fun hobby and a sustainable and sensible way of preserving your food. In the first chapter, we will examine how freeze-drying works and why we should all be doing it.

Chapter One

Understanding Freeze-Drying

How Freeze-Drying Works

Put simply, freeze-drying removes moisture from foods to preserve the texture, flavor, freshness, and nutritional value of perishable ingredients, giving them a longer shelf-life and making them easier to transport. In simple terms, you can freeze food to prevent it from spoiling. It can then be dried in a vacuum for a few days under carefully controlled heat to remove the water without affecting the food structure and taste.

The fancy science behind this is sublimation, which converts solids into gasses without going through the liquid stage. As the food is dried, the molecules are pushed out of the liquid until they're all gone. Water sublimes from a solid to a gas (ice to vapor) when the molecules have sufficient energy to break away, but the conditions aren't conducive to forming a liquid.

There are three stages to freeze-drying:

1. The freezing phase

2. The primary drying phase (Sublimation)

3. The secondary drying phase (Adsorption)

Freezing Phase

The freezing phase is the most critical part of the process and must be done quickly. First, you freeze the food to well below 0°F. You can do this in several ways, but the colder the freezing phase, the more successful the drying phase will be. You can put your food in a freezer or a shelf in a freeze-dryer.

You can even put the food in an ice bath. However, to remain safe, you must ensure the temperature reaches 41°F in 1-4 hours or less. If you are not sure you can do this accurately, putting foods in a freeze-dryer is the best option. Foods must be frozen below their triple point to ensure that sublimation occurs rather than melting. Otherwise, the food structure will be affected.

Using large ice crystals is an excellent way to freeze-dry food, but they may break the cell walls if they are too large, meaning the food may not be preserved effectively. The freezing is undertaken rapidly to avoid this problem.

Primary Drying (Sublimation) Phase

The drying phase is precisely as it sounds. The pressure is lowered, and heat is added to the food for the water to sublimate. The vacuum speeds up this process by drying the food under controlled heat, and the water vapor solidifies on the cold condenser (2). The condenser protects the vacuum pump from the water vapor.

During this phase, about 95% of the water is removed. Only residual moisture should be left over if this has been done correctly. The drying phase should be slower, as too much heat too quickly can alter the food structure.

Secondary Drying (Adsorption) Phase

The final stage of the process is the adsorption or secondary drying phase. The temperature is higher than in the primary drying phase, and the bonds between the food and water molecules are broken. Although the food may appear dry, there is still about 7-8% residual moisture at this point.

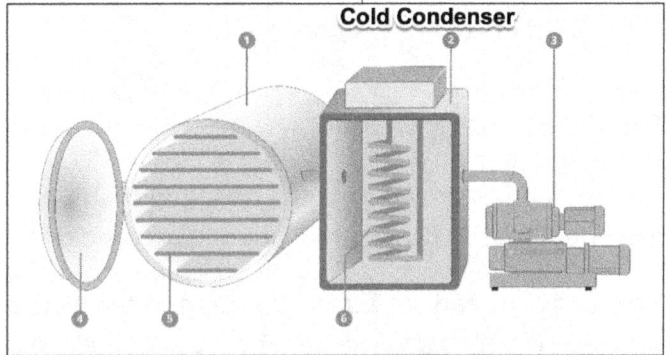

Image Credit www.proFoodworld.com

Once this stage is complete, the food should be dried to 1-5% residual moisture. You will know that the food has been freeze-dried successfully if the food is crispy in texture. Foods with a high sugar content may be malleable but not sticky.

It is important to remember that freeze-drying does not kill bacteria, so food must be handled safely.

Manifold Method

The manifold method is a good starting point for beginners because it isn't overly complicated. Vials or flasks are directly attached to the ports of a drying chamber. This process can be used only for small amounts of food.

The product may be frozen in a freezer or a chilled bath. The pre-frozen food is then attached to the drying chamber, and the vacuum is created quickly to avoid it warming up. The low temperature of the food must be maintained throughout.

Manifold drying is advantageous because the flasks are attached individually onto the drying chamber, which means each vial or flask has a direct path to the collector. This is more efficient, and drying time is considerably quicker than other methods.

Several flasks can be attached to a manifold system, meaning different foods can be dried simultaneously. Once drying is complete, each flask can be removed from the manifold separately without interrupting the drying process of the other foods. Drying efficiency is maximized because the flasks are close to the collector.

Batch Method

This method places several similarly-sized flasks or vessels containing the same food products in a tray dryer. The food will typically be pre-frozen on the shelf of the tray dryer. Unlike the manifold method, this method allows you to maintain precise control over the temperature and the amount of heat you apply to the food as it is dried.

This system is designed to treat all food products the same way. However, temperature variations can occur, causing differing conditions in certain parts of the tray and residual moisture to remain in some of the products at the end of the drying time.

In the batch method, the flasks are all closed off with stoppers simultaneously, meaning each vessel is subject to the same atmospheric conditions and will have the same shelf life in storage. Batch drying is used to prepare large numbers of one product.

Bulk Method

This method is similar to batch drying in that it is carried out in a tray. However, the food is not placed into individual vessels but poured into one pan and dried out as one unit.

The food is spread out across the tray and can be the same thickness as the food dried in individual vessels, but the absence of space between the mass of the product limits the input of heat, which comes directly from the tray.

Unlike batch and manifold drying, this method cannot seal products under specific conditions. The food product is typically removed before closure and quickly packaged in airtight containers. Because of the limitations of this method, the bulk method is not used for products that are over-sensitive to moisture and oxygen.

Freeze-Drying Compared to Other Food Preservation Methods

Many presume freeze-drying and dehydrating are the same. Still, although both methods are used for food preservation, they have subtle differences. The most obvious is the length of time they have been around.

Dehydrating has been in practice since as far back as 12,000 BC. Ancient civilizations realized that moisture was the culprit for spoiled food, and we know that the Romans would typically use fire to dry out their fruits and vegetables to preserve them. In contrast, freeze-drying is quite a modern concept. During World War II, it was used to preserve medicines, plasma, and food for the soldiers.

Removing moisture from food prevents it from growing mold and bacteria and increases its shelf life. However, this needs to be done without altering the food structure so that it retains its taste, texture, and nutritional value. Both freeze-drying and dehydrating remove water from foods, but you have more variety with freeze-drying, allowing you to extend almost any product's shelf life by years.

Depending on the quality of the dehydrator, it will remove between 70–80% of the moisture in foods, but the food will only stay fresh for a few months. Most dehydrated foods will have a shelf life of up to one year. In contrast, the shelf life of freeze-dried food can be extended by as much as 15–25 years!

Freeze-drying food removes approximately 99% of the moisture content while maintaining up to 97% of its nutritional value. The cold vacuum process that extracts the water does not disrupt the food structure. In contrast, dehydrated food often contains only 60% of its original nutritional composition because the heat cannot be carefully regulated and causes the breakdown of minerals and nutrients.

Freeze-dried foods weigh much less than their dehydrated counterparts. It is beneficial for storage and transportation and good news for hikers who want to carry plenty of calorie-rich foods without the added weight in their backpacks.

Unlike dehydrated foods, the freeze-dried variety will not look or taste any different when rehydrated. You could freeze dry a complete Christmas dinner with all the trimmings, ignore it for 15 years, and, once rehydrated, it will still taste the same as if it had been freshly made.

You can freeze dry practically any food, and when I say *any* food, I am not kidding!

Meats, fruits, vegetables, dairy, eggs, cottage cheese, and even soured cream are all fair game. Entire meals and desserts can all be freeze-dried and rehydrated quickly. You don't need to refrigerate the foods you would have previously stored at low temperatures once freeze-dried. When you freeze dry food, you catch it at its best and lock in all the nutrients and flavor. You can freeze dry practically any food and retain its texture, color, and original shape, which is not the case with dehydration.

On the other hand, canned food has been around for a long time and is still a widely used method of food preservation today. It is a much cheaper option than freeze-drying, is readily available, and cans are airtight and animal-proof. The downside of canned goods is that the heat required to preserve the contents destroys much of the nutritional and mineral content, and the contents don't remain fresh for as long as freeze-dried foods. They are also cumbersome, so they are not ideal for backpacking or camping trips or for anyone with storage space issues.

In addition to this, they have been known to explode if exposed to severely cold temperatures, so they are not the best choice for winter excursions. You need a can opener to get into them unless you carry pop-top cans, which are less durable than regular, sealed cans. Although a bit more expensive, freeze-drying is much more flexible than canning. Foods retain their nutritional value and are much more portable.

Freezing is an excellent way to preserve food. As the composition of food is mostly water, freezing prevents harmful bacteria or microorganisms from growing because they cannot feed off the frozen water, and most cannot survive the cold. Freezing slows down the enzymes that cause food to spoil and enables you to store food for longer periods of time that otherwise would have gone bad in the refrigerator if you didn't use it in time. You can store your favorite foods in the freezer for up to a year.

The main difference between freeze-drying and freezing food is that freeze-drying doesn't alter the composition of your food. Freeze-dried food will taste better than frozen food because the moisture has been gradually removed, but its structure hasn't been compromised. You can also store freeze-dried food for much longer than a year.

The main differences between freezing and freeze-drying food are as follows:

- **The process**: When freezing food, its temperature is lowered below the freezing point of water, whereas freeze-drying involves removing the water from the food by sublimation.

- **Equipment required**: Freezing can be done using a standard household freezer, but it's much easier using specialized equipment, such as a freeze dryer or lyophilizer. While it is possible to freeze-dry foods in a home freezer, it can take much longer and you run the risk of freezer burn. You could be waiting a long time for a tray or two of freeze-dried vegetables, so it's not the most practical method.

- **Time needed**: Freezing is a relatively quick process. Food can be fully frozen in an hour or two, whereas freeze-drying can take more than a day to complete.

- **Cost**: Effective freeze-drying is more expensive than freezing due to the processing time and equipment. However, it will save you thousands of dollars in the long term, and many manufacturers offer payment plans for freeze-drying machines.

- **Shelf life**: Freeze-dried products have a much longer shelf life than frozen products because most water has been removed to preserve it.

- **Weight**: Removing the water from freeze-dried products makes them much lighter than frozen products.

- **Storage**: Removing the water from freeze-dried products means they have a lower weight and volume and take up less space.

- **Nutritional value and quality**: Freeze-drying food preserves the nutritional value of most foods better than freezing, as the food is kept at a lower temperature and exposed to heat for a shorter period.

- **Rehydration**: Freeze-dried products must be rehydrated before consumption, while frozen products can be quickly thawed and eaten.

- **Usage of frozen/freeze-dried foods**: Frozen foods may taste slightly different once thawed because freezing food expands the cell walls and causes damage. Freezing can also cause freezer burn if food is improperly stored, and if you thaw frozen food too quickly, it can have a peculiar texture. In contrast, freeze-dried food will taste exactly the same years later as it did on the day it was freeze-dried. The downside is that it must be rehydrated before it can be eaten.

Shelf Life and Nutrient Retention of Freeze-Dried Foods

Freeze-drying preserves food's natural vitamins and minerals. If they are stored in airtight packaging at a consistently low temperature, most freeze-dried foods can last between 25 and 30 years as long as they are sealed from moisture, heat, and light and stored in a cool, dry place.

You can freeze-dry most foods, but vegetables, fruit, meat, and whole meals are some of the best options for long-term storage. Unfortunately, foods with high-fat content, such as butter, cream, and oils, or high-water content like lettuce, watermelon, or cucumber don't freeze-dry well.

Freeze-Dried Vegetables

If you freeze-dry vegetables at peak freshness, they can last up to 25 years with minimal preservatives for extended shelf life.

Freeze-Dried Fruits

Freeze-dried fruits will have 25 years of shelf life and can be rehydrated to use in recipes or eaten as a snack straight out of a bag.

Freeze-Dried Meats

Freeze-dried meat has the same nutrition you'd expect from fresh meat, and you can use it in soups, stews, or any other recipe just by adding water. If stored correctly, freeze-dried meats have 25 years of shelf life.

Nutrient-Dense Meals

With a 25-year shelf life, nutrient-dense whole meals are ideal for family camping trips, or home use when food prices go up. They are handy for emergencies where you need lightweight, filling food. They offer a completely balanced meal and are an excellent option for long-term storage and food on the go. These balanced meals often contain various proteins, vegetables, and grains. All you need to prepare them is a small amount of water.

We have looked at how we can eliminate food waste through different forms of food preservation. In the next chapter, we will further explore the benefits and uses of freeze-drying.

Chapter Two

Benefits and Uses of Freeze-Drying

As with all methods of food preservation, freeze-drying has benefits and limitations. Let's explore these in more detail and look at the different uses for freeze-drying.

Benefits of Freeze-Drying

Freeze-dried foods are your ticket to buying inexpensive seasonal food and preserving it for the same produce when prices go up in the winter. Instead of buying cookies and candies, why not freeze dry fruit to provide your kids with healthy snacks or add them to yogurt for a tasty, cost-effective and healthy dessert all year round? If you are going on a family day trip, you can pack a mix of lightweight freeze-dried snacks and fresh food to ensure your little ones are getting balanced nutrients instead of processed foods.

The potential savings from freeze-drying food versus wasting uneaten food can vary significantly depending on several factors. The example below takes under consideration savings for an average family of four:

- The initial cost of a freeze dryer
- The cost of electricity to run the freeze dryer
- The cost of the food that would otherwise be wasted
- The cost of vacuum-sealed bags or canning jars for storage

Assumptions:

1. A home freeze dryer costs around $2,500 and has a lifespan of 10 years. So, the annual cost would be $250.

2. The cost of running a freeze dryer is around $1 per batch, and let's assume you run it once a week. That's an annual cost of $52.

3. The average American family of four wastes about $1,500 to $1,800 of food per year.

4. The cost of vacuum-sealed bags or canning jars for a year is around $50.

5. Here is a simplified chart to compare the costs:

Below is a chart that compares the potential annual savings when freeze-drying food versus throwing it out. The assumptions remain the same as mentioned in the previous example.

Criteria	Freeze-Drying (USD)	Throwing Food Out (USD)	Savings by Freeze-Drying (USD)
Freeze Dryer Depreciation	250	0	-250
Electricity	52	0	-52
Cost of Food (if wasted)	0	1,500 - 1,800	1,500 - 1,800
Storage Materials	50	0	-50
Total Annual Cost	352	1,500 - 1,800	1,148 - 1,448

In the "Freeze-Drying" column, the costs are those associated with freeze-drying your food. This includes the depreciation cost of the freeze dryer, electricity, and storage materials. The cost of food is not included here since we are assuming it's being saved rather than wasted.

In the "Throwing Food Out" column, the costs are the estimated costs of the food that would have been thrown out. No costs for a freeze dryer, electricity, or storage materials are included, as we're assuming the food is simply wasted.

In the "Savings by Freeze-Drying" column, the values are the differences between the two scenarios. A negative value means an additional cost for freeze-drying, and a positive value means a saving.

According to this model, freeze-drying could potentially save you between **$1,148 and $1,448** per year compared to throwing food out. Keep in mind that these are approximate values, and actual savings could vary.

A Few Limitations of Freeze-Drying

Effective freeze-drying requires specialist equipment, so at-home food preservation was not viable until the recent innovation of home freeze-dryers. While these have increased in popularity, they are an investment. You can find them second-hand for much cheaper and in perfect condition. Remember, this is a one-time expense and as long as you follow the maintenance instructions, you will have your freeze-dryer for life.

It's a Slower Process, and a Small Amount of Water is Needed

The average freeze-drying cycle can take at least 24 hours, which is slower than other food preservation methods such as freezing but it lasts for much longer. Due to their water content, a batch of plums, peaches, or nectarines could take up to a week to freeze-dry correctly, so it's bad news for those who are impatient. Unless you are rehydrating simple foods such as snacks, you will also need a small amount of warm or cold water.

What is Required For Effective Freeze-Drying

While it is possible to freeze-dry food in your freezer at home, you need special equipment for the most effective freeze-drying, and that's not always possible. However, using your standard freezer is not the most practical choice, as food needs to be spaced out on trays. Freeze-drying in your freezer can take up a lot of space, and while many people will try to convince you it can happen in two weeks, you are realistically looking at months to freeze-dry anything using this method. It's also worth mentioning that the shelf life of your foods will be considerably shorter using this technique. Using a home freezer, you can't reliably get as much moisture out of food, so it's more of a stop-gap measure than a solution.

Unless you buy expensive shop-bought freeze-dried foods, you are better off buying your own equipment. This is great because you will significantly decrease food waste at home, but, being a relatively modern innovation, it means you are looking at an initial outlay of a minimum of $2,000 for the most basic at-home freeze-drying machine. Having said that, your freeze-dryer will pay for itself within a year with the savings you will make on groceries.

Airtight Containers are Needed for Long-Term Storage

This is not a huge problem, but it does mean stocking up on airtight Tupperware or good quality ziplock bags to store your freeze-dried food. You will also need space to house it because the size and shape of the food are not affected by freeze-drying. Alternatively, you can invest in a vacuum sealer to save on buying lots of airtight containers and space, but this is another cost you will need to budget for.

What Foods are Best for Freeze-Drying?

If you are trying to decide whether you can justify the price tag of a freeze-drying machine, it might help to know just how many options are available to you. It may surprise you to know just how many foods you can save from being needlessly thrown away because you didn't manage to use them on time.

There is little point in freeze-drying foods your family is unlikely to eat. However, since you have a 20 to 30-year shelf life on a lot of foods, there is a chance that stocking a wide range of preserved foods will come in handy in the future, so it's an excellent opportunity to try something new.

Fruits

When it comes to fruits, the freeze-drying world is your oyster. You can freeze-dry almost every fruit, but some taste better than others. This is subjective and requires some trial and error to know what suits your taste buds best. Just be aware that if you freeze-dry fruits with a high water content, they will take slightly longer. Peeling and slicing fruits into smaller pieces will make the process significantly quicker.

I slice peaches before freeze-drying them and enjoy them with my oatmeal. You can hydrate these with milk or water. Freeze-dried grapes taste better than candy and are much better for you. I'd recommend slicing them in half before freeze-drying them to speed things up. Remember, the smaller the pieces, the quicker they dry.

You can even freeze-dry avocado! Just remember that, much like when it meets the air, avocados will discolor during the freeze-drying process. Applying lemon juice to the flesh beforehand will keep it nice and green.

Vegetables

Some vegetables don't appreciate the freeze-drying treatment, and you must treat others with special care. Again, you will need to test it out and see what works best for you, but it will be fun to find out.

Asparagus is one of my favorites, but exercise caution when rehydrating it. If you rush the process, it will become soggy. Corn can be freeze-dried, but only once removed from the cob. You will have ready-made freeze-dried potato chips if you slice up and preboil potatoes!

Meats and fish

You can freeze-dry most meats, but remember to remove as much fat as possible before you start so it doesn't go rancid over time and spoil. Beef, pork, fish, sausages, bacon, and poultry are all fair game, but low-fat cuts are the best options.

While you can freeze-dry raw, I think it's safer to ensure all meats and fish are cooked or blanched to avoid the risk of food-borne illnesses. I then slice them into thin strips once they have cooled.

You can then arrange the pieces of meat on the freeze-dryer trays, ensuring they are not touching each other. This process will take between 24 and 48 hours, depending on the cuts and thickness of the meat or fish.

Dairy products

It's surprising how many dairy products can be freeze-dried. Yogurt, cream cheese, and even milk can be freeze-dried! However, you may notice a small change in taste and texture with dairy products. I would advise grating hard cheeses before freeze-drying as it helps them to dry out more evenly.

Eggs

You can whisk eggs and freeze-dry them to make an egg powder, which can be a less messy option in baking. One top tip is to pour whisked egg mixture into ice cube trays before placing them on the drying tray. It's a bit like creating weaning foods for babies in small quantities!

Meals, soups, and stews

Soups and stews have a higher water content than other foods, so bear in mind that they will take longer to freeze-dry. You can freeze-dry meals partially or entirely, but remember that different ingredients may respond better to the process than others. It's also vital to remember that meals with higher sugar or fat content will have a shorter shelf life than those without.

Having a supply of ready meals can be a godsend when life is busy and you have no time or inclination to cook. Pasta and casseroles respond well to freeze-drying, and the cooking process is much the same as usual, except that you will need to cut them into bite-sized pieces once cooled before spacing out the pieces on the freeze-drying trays.

Grains, breads, and dough starters:

Rehydrating grains, breads, and dough starters require patience, and bread, in particular, will be a bit different once it has been freeze-dried. Many people find it has an odd taste and texture no matter how slowly they rehydrate it.

If you find you are one of those people, you can still use freeze-dried bread for bread crumbs or croutons. I find that it's okay if you rehydrate it slowly with humidity, but you might be disappointed if you want fresh, soft bread at the end. In the end, do what makes your taste buds happy.

If you plan to freeze-dry rice, it works better if you pre-boil it first.

Sourdough starters freeze-dry well, and freeze-drying is a great way to preserve your starter if you pause and leave it for whatever reason and don't want to give up on your hard work to keep it going.

Candy and desserts

The key takeaway here is that although you can freeze-dry candies and sweets, they will only last in storage for about 5–10 years. In my opinion, that's still pretty good. Their high fat and sugar content makes them a bit trickier to freeze-dry successfully, but it's possible if you cut most of them, such as cheesecake and caramels, into small pieces.

Cheesecake can be rehydrated slowly in a humid place, or you can eat the pieces as they are. They make for a crunchy snack, and they taste so good! You can freeze-dry marshmallows, small cubes of Jello, and even Skittles, although these tend to expand, and the shell will crack down the middle to give you super-sized, inflated Skittles! Yum! Check out the end of the book for amazing candy recipes that I experimented with and have to say, the kids love them!

Herbs and spices

Herbs and spices can be freeze-dried but they break down into powder afterward. It's easier to deal with a powder than picking little leaves off the trays, and the flavors remain potent for your cooking. Just remember to thoroughly clean your machine before putting fruits or desserts in after you've freeze-dried garlic, or they may absorb the smells and flavors and it will change the way your desserts taste.

How to Use Freeze-Dried Foods

Though you may need to rehydrate certain foods after freeze-drying them, many foods can be eaten as they are straight after the freeze-drying process. Did you know that you can also cook and bake with freeze-dried foods? We will look at that in more detail later on!

Freeze-dried food can be enjoyed in various ways. You need to use your imagination and practice what works and what doesn't.

Meats, fruits, vegetables, and meals can all be rehydrated to bring them back to their original state. For cooked meats, you need to use warm water. It must be warm rather than hot or boiling, or you will overcook your meat. Bear in mind that less is always more. A small amount of water will return the food to its former state. Use too much, and you will end up with a plate of soggy mush! You can expect a few failed experiments and that's ok. Remember, you are getting used to this process and all foods are different. Our instinct is to want to add more water to speed up the process, but a little goes a long way when rehydrating freeze-dried foods.

Freeze-dried fruits and vegetables can be eaten as they are without adding water. They are a healthy snack that can be eaten straight out of a bag. These are a perfect alternative to a bag of potato chips for your children. They have far more nutritional value; kids love them because they taste great! They are also a great addition to your cereal in the morning.

If you cook a meal with a high water content, such as a casserole, you do not need to worry about rehydrating ingredients before using them. Put them into the pot, and the moisture will deal with it for you.

Interesting and Unique Uses for Freeze-Drying

There are plenty of exciting foods you might not have considered viable choices for freeze-drying, but you'd be surprised. You may have heard about astronauts enjoying ice cream in space, and this is possible because of freeze-drying. If you want to try this at home, use small scoops and ensure you've put your freeze-dryer on a freezing setting at the get-go so the ice cream doesn't melt. The texture of freeze-dried ice cream may be more like meringue than the soft scoop, but the taste will be the same and kids love it!

Much like ice cream, you might think Greek yogurt is too messy, but it can also be freeze-dried. It's best to choose plain yogurt to avoid the sugar and fat content. You can either freeze-dry it as it is or create bite-sized healthy snacks by placing the yogurt into a piping bag and squeezing small circular dots directly onto the freeze-dryer tray. It can also be turned into a powder and added to smoothies.

You can also freeze-dry scrambled eggs and add them to your all-day breakfast while camping or in a hurry. Simply add some water to return them to their original state.

Mushrooms are one of the best vegetables to freeze-dry. They are incredibly versatile and can be rehydrated in different ways. You can even turn them into powder to add to soups.

Artichoke hearts might not be a staple or even something most people would consider buying, let alone freeze-drying, but it's proof that just about anything can be freeze-dried. If this is something you are interested in trying, drain them and space them out on parchment paper-lined trays. They will freeze-dry down to a powder and can be added to other meals or dips. Honestly, the sky is the limit.

My parents grow rhubarb and always seem to have an inexhaustible supply. I used to store it in my freezer, but I was overwhelmed with the stuff! I wasn't sure what to do with it, so I just chopped it into pieces without blanching it and popped it into the freeze-dryer. Once rehydrated, this was far too tart for me, and although freeze-drying suggests avoiding sugary foods, I recommend putting rhubarb into a sugar water solution overnight or roll it in in brown sugar. However, like many other things, it can be successfully freeze-dried and it's delicious!

Why don't you experiment with a few things you wouldn't usually try or use my recipes at the end of the book as a starting point for new ideas? Some of the recipes are from a few of my Facebook friends. They are tested and true. You will love them.

Now that we've looked at some of the benefits and uses of freeze-drying let's look at how to set up your freeze-drying space.

Chapter Three

Preparing Your Freeze-Drying Space

Choosing the Right Freeze-Dryer Model

Freeze-drying can be more pricey at the onset, but when faced with climate change and a cost of living crisis, more and more people are finding ways to preserve their food, and science shows us that freeze-drying is a much healthier option than canning or dehydrating your food.

I've tested a few of the top models to examine the advantages and disadvantages of each, so you don't have to! Here you go.

The Stay Fresh Standard Freeze Dryer

This machine comes in one size and is a perfect starting point for someone new to freeze-drying, as it has a pre-programmed algorithm to assist as you learn how to use it. The price of this machine is $2,999 (as of October 2023) and has become so popular that there is a waiting list of two months to get your hands on it.

It has a pre-programmed candy program for those with a sweet tooth or kids and can freeze-dry up to 12 pounds of food in 30 hours. It has four trays as standard, with the option of adding additional trays to your order. This will easily feed a family of four.

The Stay Fresh Standard has a responsive touchscreen with straightforward controls and customization opportunities. It has everything you need to get up and running, including an oil filter, an impulse sealer, and 50 mylar bags. Love this deal!

Image Credit:
www.stayfreshfreezedry.com

The Blue Alpine Freeze Dryer

Image Credit:
www.bluealpinefreezedryers.com

This machine has a simple but stylish design, and there is the option to purchase it in blue! This medium freeze-dryer is roughly 25% larger than its smaller counterparts.

The company has tried to address all the typical teething problems customers have faced with other brands, such as increasing the longevity of the vacuum pump life, installing a circulating fan to blast-freeze food with more efficiency, and using barbed rather than crimped fittings which were prone to vacuum leaks. They also offer a 2–12 month payment program to purchase it in installments.

There are recipes programmed into the machine to optimize usage, and the trays they use are a standard size, meaning customers can buy more from their local stores instead of having to order specific sizes from the company. This machine has all the usual starter equipment: sealer, vacuum pump and oil, 50 mylar bags, and 50 oxygen absorbers. It is $2,895 and again, due to popularity, there is a 3–4 month waiting list.

The Harvest Right Small Freeze Dryer

 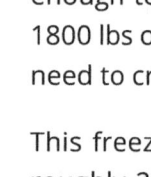

Image Credit:
www.HarvestRight.com

This is the smallest freeze-drying machine at 91 lbs and the most affordable option that Harvest Right offers. At $2,295, it offers the best bang for your buck! It comes with the standard vacuum pump, four trays, oil filter, and oil. It is small enough to fit on your countertop but allows you to freeze-dry approximately 1800 lbs of food a year! Remember that although the machine is small, you will need to create space for the external pump and drain hose.

This freeze-dryer has four trays and can hold 7 lbs of food, but it will take roughly 20–40 hours to freeze-dry it. It comes with a guide, 50 mylar bags, 50 oxygen absorbers, an impulse sealer, an oil filter, and oil. Unfortunately, although they are the market leaders, these machines have been prone to vacuum seal leaks, faulty parts, and malfunctioning touch screens. They come with a 3-year warranty but have received mixed reviews. However, Harvest Right is updating and upgrading its machines all the time. While this machine is suitable for small spaces, it is a little noisy to run.

The Harvest Right Medium Freeze Dryer

Same look as above, this machine is a slightly bigger version of its smaller counterpart but will still fit on a kitchen surface, provided you have room for the external pump and drain hose. At $2,895, this freeze-dryer can produce up to 3,000 lbs of food a year and is a suitable option for those who have a small distribution channel or want to supplement their income with sales of freeze-dried meals at farmers' markets. I'll be honest, I wish I had bought the medium right from the start. I ended up swapping it for a medium after.

It comes with all the same startup equipment as the small freeze-dryer, but you also get an additional tray. Unfortunately, the oilless pumps have been known to malfunction, so I recommend sticking with the standard variety. Harvest Right also offers a payment program where you can pay as much as you want with zero interest as long as you pay $250 upfront. That's a good deal.

The Harvest Right Large Freeze Dryer

Harvest Right is the only company offering large and extra-large freeze-dryers. This model will set you back $3,595 and can produce up to 5,000 lbs of food per year. According to their website, their extra-large version provides up to 10,000 lbs of food a year for $4,995, but neither of these options would be suitable for someone who is freeze-drying for themselves as a hobby. These products are aimed at people using them on an industrial scale as a primary means of income.

If you are looking for a freeze-drying machine that can run all day, every day at capacity, this is the one for you. The large size comes with six trays and the extra large comes with seven. It includes all the same starting equipment as its smaller counterparts, and weighs in at 143 pounds, so it won't fit on your countertop like the others. It does give you a lot for your money, though, and there is the usual layaway option if you want to avoid paying for it all at once.

Freeze-Dryer Electrical and Space Requirements

Harvest Right provides a handy FAQ section on their website to give customers an indication of the capacity of each batch of food and what each machine can hold, as well as how much food can be freeze-dried each year according to the size of the unit you choose. It also provides information regarding the size and weight of each machine and a rough idea of how much it will cost to run.

As a rough idea, most small and medium units can be plugged into a standard 110-volt outlet and will cost between $1.25 and $2.80 per day, depending on prices in your area. Large and extra-large freeze-dryers may need a 110-volt NEMA 5-20 outlet and will cost between $2.00 and $3.00 per day, depending on prices in your area.

While specifications will vary according to brand, and customers will need to check the exact specifications of the model they are planning to purchase, the following information from the Harvest Right website is a helpful starting point:

Small and medium machines will generally fit on a kitchen countertop, but the larger machines require more space (Harvest Right, 2019).

SIZE	DIMENTIONS	WEIGHT
SMALL	16.5" W x 18.5" D x 25 H"	91 lbs. Stainless: 98 lbs.
MEDIUM	18" W x 21.25" D x 28.5" H"	119 lbs. Stainless: 127 lbs.
LARGE	20.25" W x 23.75" D x 30.75" H"	143 lbs. Stainless: 150 lbs.
X-LARGE	23.25" W x 33.7" D x 35.6" H"	N/A. Stainless: 258 lbs

Preparing Your Surrounding Area and Environment

Before purchasing a freeze-dryer, it is a good idea to consider where you plan to put it. Not only are freeze-dryers renowned for being noisy during the drying stage of the process, but they also give off quite a lot of heat, and where you put them could affect their longevity and functionality.

We know freeze-drying machines are expensive, so to get the best out of them, we need to ensure they are placed in a well-ventilated area such as a laundry, utility room, garage or your basement if you have one.

You must also ensure that freeze-dryers are never exposed to extreme heat or cold. These machines do not respond well to temperature fluctuations, so barns and sheds are a no-go, especially in warmer climates. Garages are also subject to temperature changes, so you should only store freeze-dryers in garages if you live in a colder climate or if your garage is climate controlled.

Pick a Well-Ventilated Space and Raise the Machine off the Floor

The pump at the back of a freeze-drying machine gets very hot during a cycle. Much like a standard freezer, it needs space around it to prevent the buildup of heat and humidity. You also need access to the pump and power switch on the back of the machine, and the machine needs to be raised slightly from the floor so the drainage tube can run into a bucket below it.

The machine's functionality will be impaired if the environment gets too hot. If you don't have any choice but to store it in a small room, you need to consider airflow and ventilation. Ensure it is near an open window while running, or has a fan running close by to circulate the air.

Given the size and weight of these machines, a sturdy table or countertop is usually the best surface to put them on. However, ensure that all the vents are clear.

Control the Temperature and Humidity of the Space

Locating your freeze dryer next to any other appliances that give off heat, such as a freezer or tumble dryer, is a bad idea. It's a good idea to put your freeze-dryer in an environment with a temperature between 35 and 90 degrees Fahrenheit, so dig out those thermometers and ensure you are giving your machine the ideal spot to run efficiently.

While humidity won't affect the functionality of your machine, it may harm the food you are trying to freeze dry. The whole point of freeze-drying food is to remove the moisture and preserve the lifespan of the food. If you put your machine in an area with high humidity, the food will instantly absorb the surrounding moisture when removed, completely negating your hard work.

Consider the Power Source

There is little point in putting your freeze-dryer in an ideal environment if you do not have the correct power setup. You must use the correct plug for your unit and have enough amperage to run the freeze-dryer and anything else on the same circuit. Otherwise, the power draw will likely be too much, and the circuit will blow a fuse.

Ideal Locations

You don't need to live in a huge mansion to have a freeze-dryer, but it's a good idea to think about cool, spacious areas and consider ways to create the ideal temperature and ventilation if the area is not as cool and airy as you'd like.

The following are all good locations for your freeze-drying machine:

- A well ventilated laundry room
- A storage room or workshop
- In an unoccupied bedroom (with an open window in a warm climate)
- The basement

Unsuitable Locations

In light of the need for spacious, well-ventilated areas for your freeze-dryer, there are some places where you should NEVER put one. Remember that freeze-dryers should never be exposed to fluctuating or extreme temperatures, direct sunlight, or other elements, so they do not belong outside. Exposure to the elements will undoubtedly shorten the lifespan and functionality of your machine.

Unless you have a large, temperature-regulated shed with a decent power outlet, you should never put your freeze-dryer in one. Most sheds are cramped, poorly ventilated, and tend to house a lot of other clutter, which could impair the dryer's functionality and the food quality. The same applies to garages and barns unless you can regulate the temperature all year round or live in a cool climate. Even if you live in a cooler place, the temperature in your garage or barn will fluctuate from humid and hot in the summer to cold and damp in the winter.

It would be best not to put your freeze-dryer on a porch. Even if you have an enclosed porch with a watertight door, your dryer will be subjected to changing temperatures and direct sunlight throughout the day. Freeze dryers do not work if they are too hot, so direct sunlight should always be avoided.

Small closets and cupboards are not suitable locations for freeze-dryers. Even small freeze-dryers give off a lot of heat, which could be a fire hazard. You also won't be able to access the back of the machine if the machine is in cramped conditions.

Now that we've determined the ideal environment for your freeze-drying machine, let's have a look at some of the freeze-drying tools and accessories you can buy to complement your freeze-drying journey.

Chapter Four

Must-Have Tools and Accessories

Most freeze-dryers come with a few standard components included in the purchase, but it depends on which model you decide to purchase. In this chapter, we will look at some of the essential tools you will need and some desirable items you can add to your freeze-drying toolkit later.

Must-Have Tools for Freeze-Drying

Vacuum Pump

A vacuum pump is necessary to remove moisture from your processed food. A basic oil pump is included with each freeze-dryer as it is essential to get started. These pumps are reasonably cheap if purchased separately. However, you must factor in the servicing costs as they need to be drained and filtered regularly. You can filter and reuse oil at least once, but you will need replacement oil ready for your first oil change.

The oilless pump is considerably more expensive but only requires occasional cleaning. Before servicing, you will get ten batches of freeze-dried food out of an oilless pump. It is down to personal preference as to which will work better for you, but you may find that a basic oil pump is more cost-friendly overall, even with the purchase of additional oil.

Bucket

A plastic bucket is necessary to drain the water from food after the freeze-drying cycle. A 5-gallon bucket is slightly bigger than you need but offers peace of mind that it won't overflow.

Replacement Pump Oils

Having at least 32–64 ounces of additional pump oil in stock is a good idea to keep you from running short. It also makes sense to use the oil specific to the brand of freeze-dryer you have bought so you know it will work well.

Stainless Steel Trays

Freeze dryers usually come with a few trays, but you may need more if you have a lot of food to freeze-dry. That way, you can work on a stock rotation basis and have trays of frozen food ready to place in the dryer following the defrosting cycle of the previous batch.

Helpful Freeze-Drying Accessories

A heavy-duty steel cart with wheels

Depending on where you store your freeze-dryer, a heavy-duty cart with wheels could be helpful if you decide to move it for whatever reason. Make a note of the size and weight of your freeze-dryer beforehand. Freeze dryers can be pretty heavy, so it's worth purchasing a cart that will be big enough to hold the vacuum pump on the same level and with storage underneath for the bucket or other tools.

Extra trays

Unless you purchase a Blue Alpine freeze-dryer, which has standard-size trays that you can buy at any thrift store, you may choose to buy more sets of trays than the minimum supplied with your freeze-dryer. If you want to avoid the expense of specific freeze-dryer trays, you can buy cheap trays from any store that won't fit your freeze-dryer but can be used to pre-freeze food in your freezer, ready for the next freeze-drying batch!

Image Credit: www.HarvestRight.com

Silicone molds or mats

Silicone molds are useful for freezing small amounts of produce, such as candies or other foods you want to store in small portions. The silicone mats can be helpful to place under the stainless steel trays to make it easier to remove sticky foods that might otherwise weld themselves to them. They wash very easily if you are freeze-drying foods such as bananas or runny foods.

Oxygen absorber packets

If your freeze-dryer does not come with a vacuum sealer, oxygen absorber packets will remove any remaining oxygen inside a self-seal plastic bag. Remember that some sealers won't remove the remaining oxygen before sealing your food inside the bag.

Image Credit: www.HarvestRight.com

Mylar bags or self-sealing freezer bags

These are alternatives to food storage that take up less room than jars or Tupperware. These bags can help you decide how much you want to store in each for individual or family use. You can place oxygen absorber packets into these. As a general guide, 1 x 300CC size packet will suffice for a 1-gallon Mylar or self-seal bag.

An impulse sealer or vacuum sealer

Impulse sealers create a seal for Mylar bags, which can be opened up and re-sealed under the original seal. In contrast, vacuum sealers remove the remaining oxygen from the bag before the food is sealed inside.

Some people use oxygen absorber packets for both to be on the safe side. Vacuum-sealed food will last from a few months to several years, depending on what you are storing. Impulse-sealed food will also have long-term storage as long as you remember the oxygen absorber packets.

Mason jars

These are great for foods you will either snack on or use in the near future. Foods stored in these will have a short shelf life, so they are ideal for things like dried fruits and vegetables that you will add to cooking and baking regularly.

Pantry inventory tracker

It's always a good idea to note what you freeze-dried and when so you know what you have in storage. If you are anything like me, you will find things in the freezer that you labeled last year sometime and completely forgot about, so this will assist with storage and stock rotation.

Moisture meter

A moisture meter is a handy tool for checking that your foods have been appropriately freeze-dried before being stored. It's not always easy to tell if foods are as dry as they should be, and you don't want to open up a bag of spoiled food in 20 years.

Scale that reads grams

Before the freeze drying process begins, it's important to weigh the product. This initial weight helps in calculating the amount of water to be removed during the freeze drying process. Accurate weighing ensures that the right drying parameters are set, which is crucial for maintaining the quality and integrity of the product.

Storage bins

Storage bins are optional but handy for your peace of mind, depending on where you store your Mylar bags of food. One of the benefits of canned goods is that they are animal-proof. Your freeze-dried food will be protected from moisture and light in the bags but may only last for a while if mice and other small animals get to it first!

Funnel

As most freeze-dried foods will be on trays, it can be quite helpful to have a funnel to transfer foods into the bags, Tupperware, or mason jars once ready.

Tray dividers

Dividers are an excellent alternative to separating foods if you aren't using silicone molds. These are especially useful if you are freeze-drying foods like candy, which may puff up, such as Skittles.

Tray stackers

Depending on the size of your freezer, tray stackers help save space. They are plastic risers that fit onto the trays' corners and separate them. They prevent the food in the tray underneath from getting squashed.

Tray lids

Using tray lids, which are explicitly designed for freeze-drying, may be even better than the stackers, provided the level of the food does not sit proud of the top of the trays. You can then place the trays in your freezer without them all having to be in one stack.

Kitchen Equipment and Supplies

Hot pads/mitts

Much like you need oven gloves for cooking, you might find the addition of hot pads/mitts useful for freezing to protect your hands from freezer burn. A freeze-dryer will keep the food below zero in the dryer until it is turned off, and the trays will be too cold to touch with your bare hands.

Rubbing alcohol

If you opt for a basic pump, you shouldn't have to worry about this, but oilless pumps tend to develop a build-up of residue and fine metal shavings over time. You can remove this by pouring a small amount of rubbing alcohol through the hose while disconnected from the freeze-dryer.

Large metal spatula/scraper

Runny or liquid foods such as sour cream or yogurt will freeze-dry into a congealed mass. A large spatula or scraper can help loosen and remove the food in pieces and avoid crumbling before it is placed into bags or other storage containers.

A plastic tote

Once you become more accustomed to freeze-drying, you may find that your equipment starts to grow. A large tote can help organize your supplies, and if you decide to purchase a heavy-duty cart, you can keep all your accessories on the same shelf as the drainage bucket if there is room.

Cherry and olive pitter

If you are a fan of freeze-drying fruits, a cherry and olive pitter will make the removal of pits and stones a lot easier and quicker, with the bonus of leaving the fruit intact afterwards.

Apple slicer

Not just for freeze-drying fans, this tool should be an accessory in your kitchen anyway. It makes coring and slicing apples a piece of cake by cutting them into eight equal slices and removing the core and seeds simultaneously.

Cup slicer

Perfect for freeze-drying smaller fruits such as strawberries, tomatoes, or kiwis, the cup slicer will chop these fruits into perfect rounds evenly so they can be freeze-dried with minimal fuss.

Kernel Cutter

This tool is a must-have for anyone who wants to freeze-dry corn but is struggling to separate the corn from the kernel. This tool will remove your corn from the cob without damage so you can get on with the freeze-drying process.

Rapid prep mandoline

This tool is brilliant for multitasking. It will prepare various fruits and vegetables for the freeze-dryer. It will shred, chop and slice julienne to save you time.

Strawberry corer

This may be a tool you have never heard of or thought you needed, but it's a great way of de-coring your strawberries with minimal fruit waste. It's not exclusively for freeze-drying, either. You can use it when whipping up desserts or making strawberry preserves.

Snack bar maker

Did you know that you can buy a tool to help you make your own snack bars? This can be used as a mold to make and freeze your own bars without any mess. It comes with a lid to freeze-dry your snacks without the risk of freezer burn.

While many of these tools are not essential, you can see why they would be useful, particularly if you enjoy freeze-drying and plan to prepare a lot of food to freeze-dry in bulk. These tools will take the time and effort out of chopping, and you can slice food quickly and uniformly, making the freeze-drying process more successful. You don't need all of these immediately, but you may be tempted to try them once you get used to the process.

Please take a moment to leave your review on Amazon and share your story. How has this book impacted your approach to freeze-drying? In what ways has it simplified your life? Your journey could be the very sign that someone else needs to take the first step towards mastery in freeze drying.

The next chapter will cover how you should set up your freeze-dryer.

Chapter Five

Setting Up Your Freeze Dryer

Unboxing Your New Machine

Image Credit: www.HarvestRight.com

I will walk you through what you will receive if you buy the most popular freeze-dryer. Harvest Right is the leading manufacturer of freeze-drying machines, and the starter equipment is the same for each size of machine apart from differences in the type of pump you can purchase and the number of trays provided with each product according to its capacity. The power cable is also slightly different if you buy one of the bigger machines. Most freeze-dryers of any brand come with essential accessories included with the purchase to get you started.

Whichever size machine you choose, your freeze-dryer will be delivered on a pallet, with a box holding the pump and accessories required to get started. The freeze-dryer will be protected with plastic wrap, and the pump will be securely packed in a box with cardboard and plastic wrap around it for protection.

You can choose three different vacuum pumps for your freeze-drying machine, regardless of whether you opt for the small, medium, or large size. You can opt for the Standard, Premier, or Oilless pump.

Standard Pump

The Standard pump will be included with the purchase of your freeze-dryer if you decide not to upgrade to a higher specification. It will last for years with proper care and maintenance, but you must drain and filter the oil in the pump after every 4–5 batches of freeze-drying.

This is a very straightforward process. All you need to do is open a valve, drain the oil into the top of the oil filter provided, wait a few moments for the oil to filter through, and then pour it back into the pump.

Premier Pump

At the time of writing, the upgraded Premier pump is included with every Harvest Right freeze-dryer purchase, so the Standard pump may be phased out in favor of a more user-friendly version.

The Premier pump still requires oil to run but has a gas ballast feature, so it rarely needs to be changed or filtered because the water doesn't stay in the oil. Due to this feature, the oil in the pump should remain clear and clean even after 20–30 batches of freeze-drying, but it will only take about two minutes to change the oil when required.

Oilless Pump

The final vacuum pump upgrade does not need oil to run. The clue is in the name! This pump requires no regular user maintenance. However, it is an expensive investment, and you must send it in for servicing at an extra cost every two years or so. If you hate changing oil all the time, this is a better option for you, but you will need to factor in the extra cost for maintenance and shipping.

High Vacuum Pump Oil

If you are using a pump that requires oil, using the specific oil brand for your machine is crucial. Suitable brands are listed on the manufacturer's website and in the freeze-dryer manual. You will receive one bottle of oil with your freeze-dryer purchase. If you use the wrong brand of oil, you could damage the seals in the pump and end up with leaks or an expensive repair bill.

½ Gallon Mylar Bags, Oxygen Absorbers, and Impulse Sealer

The Mylar bags are where you will store your food. You will receive a pack of 50 8" x 12" clear bags with space to write the contents and the date you freeze-dried the produce. You will also receive 50 x packs of oxygen absorbers to remove any excess oxygen in the bags before you seal them. Harvest Right provides a complimentary impulse sealer as part of your purchase to seal your bags of food when you are ready.

Trays

You will receive a set of freeze-dry machine-specific, heavy-duty trays that fit in your machine when you buy your machine according to the number of shelves in your freeze-dryer.

The small machine includes four trays, the medium includes 5, the large includes 6, and the extra large includes seven trays.

Vacuum Hose, Drain Hose, and Power Cord Connector

On the right side of your freeze-dryer, as you look at the front, is the connector that links the vacuum hose to the top of the pump. The vacuum hose is a heavy-duty, garden-style hose.

On the left side of the rear of your freeze-dryer are the on/off switch and two plug sockets.

This is why it is a good idea to set up the freeze-dryer on a cart with wheels so you can rotate it to get to the cabling and switches. One of the sockets is for the power supply (looks much like a computer plug socket), and the other is a plug that your vacuum pump plugs into.

If you have bought a small or medium freeze-dryer, the power cord will be for a standard 110-volt outlet. If you have bought a large or extra large freeze-dryer, the power cord will be for a 20-amp plug with two horizontal plugs and one vertical. You cannot use a large or extra-large machine without the appropriate power supply. While most modern kitchens have both, you need to be sure that you have a dedicated 20 amp circuit for the large and extra large machine. However, this is a reasonably straightforward job for an electrician if you want to use larger machines.

On the left side of your freeze-dryer is the drain valve. This will be protected with removable plastic when it arrives. The drain hose is attached to the ball valve. When the valve is flush with the tube, it is open, and when you flip it to a right-angled position, it is closed. When you've finished freeze-drying, you can open the valve to release all the water, and the water will drain into your bucket below.

Oil Filter

Harvest Right provides you with an oil filter to drain and filter your oil if you've opted for the Standard or Premier pump.

Manual, Freeze-Drying, and Troubleshooting Guides

You will also receive a user manual, a troubleshooting guide to help you with any issues, and a freeze-drying guide.

Initial Tasks and Checks

When unboxing your new freeze-dryer and accessories, ensure you check that all of the equipment listed on the box is present and correct and that there is no damage. Don't worry if you feel any residual moisture from connection points like the drain valve. This will likely be due to manufacturer testing rather than faulty seals but check around the whole unit to ensure there are no dents or scratches.

Before assembling your freeze-dryer, take everything out of the box and ensure you have everything you need to get started, including all cables and trays for your machine.

TASKS & CHECKS

I have provided a brief checklist below with descriptions to make this easier:

- **Harvest Right Home Freeze-Dryer** - the main freeze-drying unit (check specifications to ensure it is the right size)

- **Vacuum pump** - an oil-free pump is a small black unit which looks a bit like a fan whereas the other pumps are green in color with a black handle

- **Power cord** - a black cord that plugs in at the wall and the freeze-dryer

- **Vacuum hose** - a heavy-duty, clear garden hose that connects the dryer to the pump

- **Vacuum pump oil** - a bottle of branded vacuum pump oil

- **Shelving unit** - this sits in the main section of the freeze-dryer to house the shelves

- **Food trays** - there should be enough trays to sit in the shelving unit

- **Owner's manual and freeze-drying guide** - brochures with instructions

- **Black insulator door pad** - removable insulation (for cleaning) around the freeze-dryer door similar to the insulation around a washing machine door

- **Oil filter** - clear jug with a filter to clean your oil

Read the manual to familiarize yourself with safety precautions and operating instructions before you use the machine.

Basic Freeze-Dryer Controls

Most freeze-dryers will allow you to customize various functions and settings according to the produce you are using.

Adding Time

If you want to check on your cycle earlier or later than usual, you can override the freeze-dryer's customized times. Regardless of brand, most freeze-dryers can customize the freezer's temperature and time before you start or adjust the countdown time while the machine is running.

The Harvest Right dryers have a default setting of two hours' additional drying time. This is incredibly useful if you are freeze-drying something with a high water content, such as peaches or nectarines, to ensure you remove every last bit of moisture before storing your freeze-dried produce.

Managing the Heating Cycle

If you are short of time or want to avoid checking your freeze-dryer cycle when your machine runs at antisocial hours, you can customize the drying time by increasing or decreasing the time. Freeze-dried food is less likely to absorb moisture from condensation if it ends on a heating cycle, and a longer heating time may help to give freeze-dried food a longer shelf life.

You can increase the heating time by pressing the up arrow, and you can do the same in reverse if you want to decrease the dry time. If you think the food is ready and you want to stop it, press the down arrow until the timer reaches zero, and you can manually override the setting.

Managing the Freezing and Vacuum Cycle

There is the option to adjust the freeze timer in the customization menu. You may see a warning message to let you know that this is a pre-set program and does not require adjustment, but certain foods require extra freezing time such as thicker joints of meat. You can add time by clicking the up arrow on the right side of the freeze timer. The machine will start freezing when you click the 'Custom Start' button.

Ensure you don't add pre-frozen food to the dryer until it reaches freezing point, or it may begin to thaw. If you need to adjust the timer again, click the up arrow while the cycle is in progress. If you want to shorten the freezing cycle, it is precisely the same process in reverse. Click the arrow that points down to reduce the freezing time.

Ending a Cycle

On occasion, you may want to stop the cycle early. It could be that the food requires less time, or you don't want to over-dry it. You can end a cycle on the cold setting if the food is already pre-frozen before putting it in the dryer. Pre-freezing your food is a good time-saver if you freeze-drying in bulk.

You can load batches into the dryer while preparing another batch for freeze-drying in the freezer. There is a risk that your food is more likely to absorb moisture if you end the cycle on the cold setting, as it will meet warm air when it comes out of the dryer.

If you want to end the drying cycle on warm earlier than expected, ensure you check your food regularly. You can either bite into a thick chunk of food to check for moisture or try to snap it in half. If it doesn't split cleanly in half, there is still residual moisture in the food, and you must begin the drying process again.

Where possible, cutting your food into small pieces will make the freeze-drying process faster as the dryer cycle will remove the moisture more quickly. A good rule of thumb is to check the thickest piece of food for moisture before storing your food and try to end cycles on warm where possible to avoid condensation putting moisture back into your freeze-dried food.

Setting up for Your First Test Batch

You've unboxed and assembled your freeze-dryer, and you're ready to go... almost. Here's a step-by-step checklist for running your first test batch without hiccups!

1. Place your freeze-dryer in an appropriate, well-ventilated spot close to a wall outlet. Do not be tempted to plug your machine into an extension cord, which could cause the refrigeration compressor to malfunction. The freeze dryer should be the only device on the circuit; the vents should be clear, and it should be placed on a flat surface.

2. Remove the gasket seal from the dryer's door, connect the electrical connectors at the edge of the tray rack, and install the rack. Reinstall the rubber door seal.

3. Fill the vacuum pump with oil by removing the oil cap and filling the oil to the middle of the window between min and max. If you have an oilless pump, you can disregard this step!

4. Connect the hose to the dryer and the pump. You can tighten this by hand. Don't be tempted to use tools, as it won't be necessary and might damage the seal. The O ring should be tight enough without additional tightening or tape around the joins.

5. Insert the drain tube into the drain hose and place the open end into a 5-gallon bucket to catch the water.

6. Plug in the power cord and turn on the dryer. The "0" is the off position, and "I" means it is switched on. If all is connected correctly, the screen should light up.

7. Close the door and check it seals fully against the gasket.

8. Select the 'functional test' setting and press the 'on' icon to start the freeze-dryer on a test run. This should take approximately 30 minutes. Once complete, the pressure should read below 500 mTorr. If the reading is not below this, double-check all the connections and seals again, and ensure the drain valve is set to the closed position. If the reading is as it should be, you can press 'done' on the dryer, and you are ready to go!

Before you start freeze-drying everything in sight, the manufacturers recommend that you freeze-dry a batch of moist bread. Not only will this reassure you that everything is working as it should, but it will help to remove the factory smell of your new machine.

Running Your First Test Batch

1. Slice and prepare your food, ensuring the slices are no thicker than ½" (13mm), or you may end up with pockets of moisture in the center of foods that slow down the drying process or never fully dry. Remember that some foods take longer than others, and you must exercise patience with food items that contain more water.

2. All food items should be placed as flat as possible on the trays and placed apart. Overcrowding the trays increases the freeze-drying time.

3. Load food tray(s) into the machine and press start on the home screen. Ensure the drain valve is set to the closed position. Otherwise, the pressure buildup could cause a leak.

4. Leave your machine to do its magic. The freeze-drying process will take about 8 hours unless you have customized your settings.

5. Check the food at the end of the cycle by slowly opening the drain valve to bring the pressure down so you can open the dryer door. If the food snaps, it is ready. If not, it needs further time in the dryer. You

do not need to re-freeze the food, but you will need to set up the dryer cycle again if the food contains moisture.

6. Remove the trays from the machine and store the freeze-dried food for later.

Remember to defrost the accumulated ice on the walls of your freeze-dryer. You can do this by opening the drain valve and using the tray rack to heat the chamber and speed up defrosting. You can then dry off any remaining water with a cloth.

Be prepared to have a few failures while you get used to what your new machine can do, and don't be afraid to experiment.

Now that we have covered how to set up your freeze-dryer and get started on the basics of freeze-drying food, we will look at the various food preparation techniques for freeze-drying.

Chapter Six

Food Preparation Techniques

Food Safety Guidelines

You must take steps to learn the food safety basics and handle, cook and store foods carefully to prevent food poisoning. Unfortunately, you cannot taste, smell, or see bacteria that might cause foodborne illnesses, so you must follow the guidelines to keep your food safe during food preparation. This is especially important when it comes to freeze-drying. Although the process slows down and inhibits the growth of harmful bacteria as it removes the moist environment in which they thrive, it does not destroy it.

Image Credit: www.HarvestRight.com

There are four basic guidelines that you need to remember when handling food. These are as follows:

Clean

Wash hands and surfaces frequently to stop germs from spreading. Always wash your hands thoroughly for at least 20 seconds with soap and water before, during, and after preparing food.

Be extremely vigilant about this after handling chicken, poultry, seafood, eggs, flour, and uncooked meat. After every use, sanitize cutting boards, utensils, and cookware with hot, soapy water. Fresh fruits and vegetables should be rinsed under cold, running water before use.

Separate

Don't cross-contaminate foods. Keep raw meat and eggs away from cooked foods, raw produce, and surfaces/cookware you will use for these items. Keep raw meat and their juices separate from other foods when grocery shopping. Raw or marinating meat, eggs, seafood, and poultry should also be kept separate from all other foodstuffs in the refrigerator.

Raw meats should be placed on the bottom shelf and kept in secure, airtight containers to avoid leakage. Do not wash raw chicken before cooking it, as this can spread germs to other areas in the kitchen. Use separate chopping boards for raw meats and fish and separate boards for fruits, vegetables and other foods that won't be cooked.

Cook

Cook foods to the correct temperature and check them with a food thermometer to ensure the internal temperature is as high as it should be. You might be able to check by sight if something looks cooked (you can tell from the color of fish), but you cannot guess whether meat has been cooked to a temperature high enough to kill the harmful microorganisms unless you check it. It is vital that you place the thermometer in the food correctly to get an accurate reading.

Generally, this should be in the thickest part of the food, away from bone, gristle, or fat. Read the instructions first, as there is little point in taking the temperature of the wrong part of the food.

Chill

Refrigerate foods promptly. Don't leave them sitting out on the counter even if they are still warm. If foods are left out in the danger zone between 40°F and 140°F, bacteria can rapidly multiply. Ensure your refrigerator is at 40°F or below and your freezer is at 0°F or below. If you don't have an integrated thermometer, you should have an appliance thermometer inside the fridge to test the temperature.

Packaging warm or hot food into shallow containers in the refrigerator is safe if you want to chill them faster. All perishable food should be refrigerated within two hours. This will reduce to one hour if the food has been subjected to higher temperatures, like being stored inside a hot car. Food can be thawed safely in cold water inside the refrigerator or slowly heated in the microwave. Never let food defrost at room temperature, as this provides a perfect breeding ground for bacteria when parts of the food warm up.

Food needs to be cooked to the correct temperature and appropriately stored afterwards. Below is a comprehensive chart which shows the safe minimum internal temperature chart for cooking.

Food	Type	Internal Temperature (°F/°C)
Beef, bison, veal, goat, and lamb	Steaks, roasts, chops	145°F (63°C) Rest time: 3 minutes
	Ground meat and sausage	160°F (71°C)
Casseroles	Meat and meatless	165°F (74°C)
Chicken, turkey, and other poultry	All: whole bird, breasts, legs, thighs, wings, ground poultry, giblets, sausage, and stuffing inside poultry	165°F (74°C)
Eggs	Raw eggs	Cook until yolk and white are firm
	Egg dishes (such as frittata, quiche)	160°F (71°C)
	Casseroles (containing meat and poultry)	165°F (74°C)
Ham	Raw ham	145°F (63°C) Rest time: 3 minutes
	Precooked ham (to reheat)	165°F (74°C) Note: Reheat cooked hams packaged in USDA-inspected plants to 140°F (60°C)
Leftovers	Any type	165°F (74°C)
Pork	Steaks, roasts, chops	145°F (63°C) Rest time: 3 minutes
	Ground meat and sausage	160°F (71°C)
Rabbit and venison	Wild or farm-raised	160°F (71°C)
Seafood	Fish (whole or filet), such as salmon, tuna, tilapia, pollock, bass, cod, catfish, trout, etc.	145°F (63°C) or cook until flesh is no longer translucent and separates easily with a fork
	Shrimp, lobster, crab, and scallops	Cook until flesh is pearly or white, and opaque
	Clams, oysters, mussels	Cook until shells open during cooking

Image Credit: Assistant Secretary for Public Affairs (ASPA), 2023.

Below is a cold food storage chart which shows how long you can refrigerate or freeze specific foods and how long they will keep. Always store foods properly in the fridge or freezer before freeze-drying them.

Food	Type	Refrigerator [40°F (4°C) or below]	Freezer [0°F (-18°C) or below]
Salad	Egg, chicken, ham, tuna, and macaroni salads	3 to 4 days	Does not freeze well
Hot dogs	Opened package	1 week	1 to 2 months
	Unopened package	2 weeks	1 to 2 months
Luncheon meat	Opened package or deli sliced	3 to 5 days	1 to 2 months
	Unopened package	2 weeks	1 to 2 months
Bacon and sausage	Bacon	1 week	1 month
	Sausage, raw, from chicken, turkey, pork, or beef	1 to 2 days	1 to 2 months
	Sausage, fully cooked, from chicken, turkey, pork, or beef	1 week	1 to 2 months
	Sausage, purchased frozen	After cooking, 3-4 days	1-2 months from date of purchase
Hamburger, ground meats and ground poultry	Hamburger, ground beef, turkey, chicken, other poultry, veal, pork, lamb, and mixtures of them	1 to 2 days	3 to 4 months
Fresh beef, veal, lamb, and pork	Steaks	3 to 5 days	4 to 12 months
	Chops	3 to 5 days	4 to 12 months
	Roasts	3 to 5 days	4 to 12 months
Ham	Fresh, uncured, uncooked	3 to 5 days	6 months
	Fresh, uncured, cooked	3 to 4 days	3 to 4 months
	Cured, cook-before-eating, uncooked	5 to 7 days or "use by" date	3 to 4 months

	Fully-cooked, vacuum-sealed at plant, unopened	2 weeks or "use by" date	1 to 2 months
	Cooked, store-wrapped, whole	1 week	1 to 2 months
	Cooked, store-wrapped, slices, half, or spiral cut	3 to 5 days	1 to 2 months
	Country ham, cooked	1 week	1 month
	Canned, labeled "Keep Refrigerated," unopened	6 to 9 months	Do not freeze
	Canned, shelf-stable, opened Note: An unopened, shelf-stable, canned ham can be stored at room temperature for 2 years.	3 to 4 days	1 to 2 months
	Prosciutto, Parma or Serrano ham, dry Italian or Spanish type, cut	2 to 3 months	1 month
Fresh poultry	Chicken or turkey, whole	1 to 2 days	1 year
	Chicken or turkey, pieces	1 to 2 days	9 months
Fin Fish	Fatty Fish (bluefish, catfish, mackerel, mullet, salmon, tuna, etc.)	1 - 3 Days	2 - 3 Months
	Lean Fish (cod, flounder, haddock, halibut, sole, etc.)		6 - 8 Months
	Lean Fish (pollock, ocean perch, rockfish, sea trout.)		4 - 8 Months
Shellfish	Fresh Crab Meat	2 - 4 Days	2 - 4 Months
	Fresh Lobster	2 - 4 Days	2 - 4 Months
	Live Crab, Lobster	1 day	Not recommended
	Live Clams, Mussels, Oysters, and Scallops	5 - 10 Days	Not recommended

	Shrimp, Crayfish	3 - 5 Days	6 - 18 Months
	Shucked Clams, Mussels, Oysters, and Scallops	3 - 10 Days	3 - 4 Months
	Squid	1 - 3 Days	6 - 18 Months
Eggs	Raw eggs in shell	3 to 5 weeks	Do not freeze in shell. Beat yolks and whites together, then freeze.
	Raw egg whites and yolks Note: Yolks do not freeze well	2 to 4 days	12 months
	Raw egg accidentally frozen in shell Note: Toss any frozen eggs with a broken shell	Use immediately after thawing	Keep frozen, then refrigerate to thaw
	Hard-cooked eggs	1 week	Do not freeze
	Egg substitutes, liquid, unopened	1 week	Do not freeze
	Egg substitutes, liquid, opened	3 days	Do not freeze
	Egg substitutes, frozen, unopened	After thawing, 1 week or refer to "use by" date	12 months
	Egg substitutes, frozen, opened	After thawing, 3 to 4 days or refer to "use by" date	Do not freeze
	Casseroles with eggs	After baking, 3 to 4 days	After baking, 2 to 3 months
	Eggnog, commercial	3 to 5 days	6 months
	Eggnog, homemade	2 to 4 days	Do not freeze
	Pies: Pumpkin or pecan	After baking, 3 to 4 days	After baking, 1 to 2 months
	Pies: Custard and chiffon	After baking, 3 to 4 days	Do not freeze
	Quiche with filling	After baking, 3 to 5 days	After baking, 2 to 3 months
Soups and stews	Vegetable or meat added	3 to 4 days	2 to 3 months

Leftovers	Cooked meat or poultry	3 to 4 days	2 to 6 months
	Chicken nuggets or patties	3 to 4 days	1 to 3 months
	Pizza	3 to 4 days	1 to 2 months

Image Credits: Assistant Secretary for Public Affairs (ASPA), 2023a.

How to Freeze-Dry Food Safely

Freeze-drying your food is safe, provided the cycle's freezing and vacuum drying stages are done correctly. The freezing process needs to be quick, and the food needs to reach 41°F within 1–4 hours if not already refrigerated or frozen beforehand.

The drying process needs to remove as much moisture as possible. Anything which does not contain a high sugar content should be crisp and breakable, whereas fruits can be malleable but not sticky if dried correctly.

What You Can and Cannot Freeze-Dry

Most foods can be freeze-dried successfully. However, as freeze-drying works by removing moisture from produce, most oil-based, fatty foods do not respond well to this method. The same is true of foods with a high sugar content.

Some foods, such as avocados, prove the exception to this rule, but most foods with a high-fat content cannot be successfully freeze-dried. However, you can freeze-dry foods with sugar or oil-based ingredients in them.

The following foods **can** be freeze-dried:

- Fruits
- Vegetables
- Meat and fish (raw and cooked)
- Eggs (raw and cooked)
- Dairy products
- Whole meals, soups, and stews (including leftovers)
- Desserts, snacks, and candy
- Some drinks
- Herbs and spices
- Grains, bread, and dough starters
- Pet food

The following foods **cannot** be freeze-dried:

- Butter
- Honey
- Jam (including preserves and jellies)
- Mayonnaise
- Peanut butter
- Syrups
- Pure chocolate
- Water
- Alcohol
- Nuts
- Sodas

Sublimation does not work well with oil-based food because these foods leave behind the oil content, and you end up with a sticky mess! The same applies to juice concentrates or very sugary liquids, which can get rather explosive if you don't dilute them. It's just not worth the clean-up afterwards. Foods like nuts may seem fine to freeze-dry but are not reliable, as there is always the risk of the fats going rancid at a later date.

Prepping Foods for the Freeze-Dryer

While you do not have to pre-freeze food before placing it into the freeze-dryer, I have discovered that it can be very beneficial to do this, particularly when freeze-drying anything liquid. The back of my freeze-dryer sits slightly lower than the front, even on a flat surface. This is so the excess water can drain towards the back and out of the drain tube. While this makes perfect sense, it means the freeze-dry trays are also at a slight angle, so anything too liquid will slowly make its way out of the back of the trays and make a horrible mess. You will only need to make this mistake with yogurt once, and you won't repeat it!

Pre-freezing is also helpful for using shaped silicone molds such as stars or animals to make yogurt bites. If these don't go into the freeze-dryer already frozen, they will begin to thaw and lose the shape of whichever silicone mold I have used.

I pre-freeze things like fruit and vegetables while drying several batches of food at once, and I can't keep fresh produce as fresh as I'd like while waiting for space in the freeze-dryer. Putting it into the freezer provides a short-term storage solution. You can either keep it on the trays until you are ready or, if you're short of room, transfer it into freezer bags until there is space in the dryer. Pre-freezing also speeds up the freeze-drying cycle. It minimizes the risk of germs getting into the food and the amount of freeze-drying time, and you can process more food. Win-win!

Before putting food in the freeze dryer, you need to follow these steps:

Step 1

Cook the food (if applicable). Wash fruits and vegetables thoroughly. You can do this with plain water or use vinegar, salt and baking soda if you are worried about dirt or bacteria on fresh foods.

Step 2

Remove the excess water with a paper towel. This minimizes the likelihood of bacteria getting into the food. You can also use a salad spinner to remove any residual moisture.

Step 3

Chop your food into small, uniform pieces (if applicable) to ensure even drying. If the pieces are too thick, you will end up with moisture pockets, which may mean you must repeat the drying cycle. It's a good idea to remove the rind or peel as these don't freeze-dry very well, but if you'd rather keep the outer skin for storage and flavor purposes, ensure you allow maximum airflow between the pieces of food and consider piercing the rind/peel before freeze-drying.

Portioning and Tray Arrangement

Tray dividers have made the art of freeze-drying uniform portions of foods so much simpler. You can turn your trays into grids and freeze-dry up to 40 identical portions of whatever you like, be it eggs, milk, or yogurt. These are particularly useful when you are freeze-drying liquid foods that you cannot cut into portions and do not want to use silicone molds.

The tray dividers have been designed to work with all the other freeze-drying products so that you can use the tray stackers, silicone sheets and parchment. They are perfect for creating snack bars or dessert squares, and the versatility does not end there.

The interlocking grids are made from high-density polyethylene, which will last forever. It will not only handle the temperatures of the freeze-dryer but is malleable, so it won't break if it gets slightly warped and can be bent back into shape. Each set of interlocking grids has a knife edge on the bottom of the plastic so that you can push it down to cut the food in the tray into portions of equal size. As all of the interlocking sections are removable, you can adjust the size of each section if you want some sections to be bigger than others. The possibilities are unlimited.

When freeze-drying foods, ensure that you group similar food items on the same tray. Doing this prevents cross-contamination and the risk of foodborne illnesses. It's a good idea to get into the habit of using baking sheets on your trays to make washing up easier. Then, any mess from freeze-drying attempts that aren't hugely successful can be thrown away with the parchment. Ensure you thoroughly wash the trays and the dryer between cycles and practice good food hygiene.

Finally, avoid being tempted to overcrowd your trays with food. Ensure the food is cut into small pieces and laid as flat as possible. The freeze-drying cycle can take a long time, and getting as much food in there as possible can be tempting, but be mindful that more food means it will be a longer process to remove all the moisture. Keeping the food separated will also enable good airflow, which is key to successful freeze-drying.

Now that we've explored safe food preparation and setting it up correctly for pre-freezing and freeze-drying, we'll look at how to run your freeze-dryer.

Chapter Seven

Running Your Freeze Dryer

Operational Phases and Timelines

We've talked about the three different phases of freeze-drying, but now we'll explore what happens in your freeze-dryer during each of the three stages and how long you should expect each part of the cycle to take.

The freezing phase

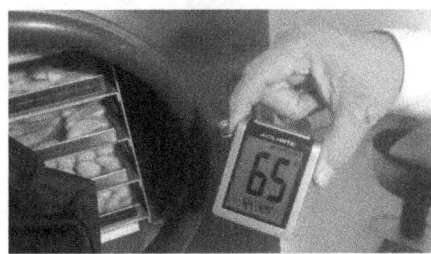

This stage takes approximately nine hours, as this is plenty of time to freeze most food items. However, suppose you are freeze-drying foods such as pineapple or ice cream. In that case, I recommend freezing the food for another hour or two to account for the high water and sugar content and the fact that people cut their food into different thicknesses. During this time, your food will be frozen to about -30°F.

Image Credit: www.HarvestRight.com

The primary drying (sublimation) phase

The vacuum pump will turn on automatically once the freezing cycle is complete. The vacuum pump will pull a reliable vacuum down to 500 mT in minutes. The freezer drops even colder at this stage, to about -50°F or even lower. Once the vacuum reaches 500 mT, the heaters will come on automatically, and the sublimation process will begin. During this stage, the ice is changed from a solid to a gas as it comes out of the food.

The produced water vapor freezes to the side of the freeze-dryer chamber. The pressure in the chamber will rise to 700–800mT, and the heaters will turn on and off according to the pressure in the chamber until most of the water has been removed from the food. This part of the process can take anywhere between 6 and 15 hours, depending on what you are freeze-drying. It all depends on the sugar and liquid content of the food. Foods with a higher volume of moisture will take longer to freeze dry.

The secondary drying (absorption) phase

Once the vacuum pressure gets below 500 mT and remains there consistently, the heaters will come on and stay on for a pre-programmed time of 7–12 hours. This is designed to wring out every last bit of residual moisture from the food. This final drying stage can be customized according to what you are freeze-drying. If you are drying a batch of pineapple, peaches, or ice cream, I recommend adding 2–3 hours to your drying time to ensure the most success.

A Step-by-Step Guide to Your First Run

Are you excited to get started? Here is a comprehensive step-by-step process for running your freeze-dryer for the first time.

Step 1: Place prepared raw or cooked food on trays as instructed. Most foods can be put directly onto freeze-dryer trays in whatever form is convenient for you. Products with skins should be chopped in half and placed cut side up on trays so the moisture can be removed more easily.

Step 2: Load the trays into the freeze-dryer, taking care not to spill anything with a high liquid content if you haven't pre-frozen it. For foods with a high liquid content, it is best to insert the freeze-dryer tray ¾ of the way into the dryer before pouring the liquid into the tray. This should prevent it from tipping, but it's often easier to pre-freeze it.

Step 3: Press start on the machine. Most machines ask if your food has been pre-frozen or not. Select the appropriate option.

Step 4: Run the machine.

Step 5: Allow the machine to run its course. Get comfy. As you can see from the above operational times of the different stages, this takes a while!

Step 6: Unload the trays from the machine.

Step 7: Promptly store the freeze-dried product in sealed bags/containers. If using an impulse sealer, place oxygen absorbers in the bags or jars before closing them.

Common Freeze-Drying Mistakes and How to Avoid Them

Freeze-drying is a learning curve, and you may need to do a bit of trial and error to work out what works well and what doesn't, but I wanted to include a list of common mistakes people make when they first start freeze-drying and what you can do to avoid them.

Freeze-drying large chunks of food

The larger you cut your pieces of food, the longer they will take to dry. If you are freeze-drying meat, cutting the pieces into small chunks is crucial, as larger pieces are more likely to go rancid due to the fat content.

Cross-contamination

It's okay to combine different foods with similar flavors, such as various fruits in the freeze-dryer simultaneously. However, you should exercise caution when freeze-drying raw meat. Don't combine raw meats with any other product.

Not cleaning your dryer after each cycle

To maintain the functionality of your freeze-dryer, you must clean it after every use with a soft cloth and mild soap. Not only is this necessary for good hygiene, but it will prevent clogs in your dryer.

Avoid using anything abrasive to clean the inside of your machine. If you struggle to remove strong scents, you can eliminate most odors with a vinegar, lemon, and water solution. You can freeze-dry a batch of bread, which manufacturers recommend to remove any lingering smells.

Overloading trays

Avoid the temptation to stack up food on your trays. More produce means more drying time, and not leaving sufficient airflow space on trays could render the whole process unsuccessful. If you are likely to freeze-dry big batches of food, you would be better off getting a larger machine with more space and extra trays. Filling the freeze-dryer with too much food creates more ice and makes it much harder for the machine to finish the drying cycle efficiently.

Freeze-drying foods high in fat and sugar, and storing them for a long time

We've touched upon the fact that foods with a high fat or sugar content do not do very well in the freeze-dryer, but you can freeze-dry other foods with these ingredients inside them. However, you must remember that these foods will have a shorter shelf life as fats can go rancid over time, so you will need to use them more quickly. If you are freeze-drying cooked meats, drain as much fat from them as possible before putting them in the freeze dryer.

Not using a liner

Using baking or parchment paper makes cleaning your freeze-dryer trays much more straightforward. Liners protect the trays from grease and other food flavors and prevent your freeze-dried foods from getting stuck.

Putting different strong-smelling/tasting foods in the same batch

If you don't mind your fruity yogurt bites tasting like curry, then, by all means, freeze-dry your madras alongside them. If you have slightly more discerning taste buds or prefer your food to smell as originally intended, it's a good idea not to combine foods with dissimilar flavors.

Expecting quick drying in hot weather

Freeze dryers have to work harder when the ambient temperature rises, so you should avoid placing them in a location subject to direct sunlight. Higher temperatures can add hours to the freeze-drying process, so either ensure your dryer is placed in an air-conditioned environment or avoid using it in sweltering temperatures. This is less of a problem in colder countries, but use common sense and consider running the machine when it is less hot and humid.

Freeze-drying fruit with tough skins whole

Tough skins or rinds are exceptionally good at containing water. Freezing dry fruit whole will massively extend the drying time and will likely be unsuccessful, as moisture pockets will remain in such large pieces of food. By chopping the fruit into smaller pieces, you give the moisture an exit route and significantly reduce drying time.

Mixing food sizes

While this isn't the end of the world, food that is not chopped into uniform pieces will take different lengths of time to freeze-dry, meaning you could end up stopping the cycle too early and having some foods that have not thoroughly dried out, or you end up running the cycle for much longer than is needed for a few different things, so, maybe invest in a good quality food cutter.

The same is true when you overload your trays and stack foods on top of one another. The top layers of food will prevent sublimation of the lower levels, so adequate space between food portions is vital.

Filling trays with liquid before loading them into the unit

If you must fill the trays directly with liquid, you need to limit how far the foods travel in the tray so you don't have to clean milk or yogurt off other surfaces. It's much easier to pour the liquids in after the trays have been placed in the freeze-dryer, but if you don't want to do it like this, make sure you load liquid foods while you are standing right next to your freeze-drying machine, so you don't have to carry it across the length of your kitchen.

So, now we know how long it takes to complete each stage of the freeze-drying process and how to avoid common freeze-drying mistakes. The next chapter will explore how to package and store freeze-dried foods effectively.

Chapter Eight

Packaging and Long-Term Storage

Enemies of Long-Term Food Storage

Preparing food for long-term storage takes a bit of time and effort. It is a valuable investment for those who want to save money, and it puts you ahead of the game regarding adequate supplies in an emergency. However, there are a few enemies of long-term food storage that can shorten the shelf life of your food or even ruin your hard work.

Overly high and low temperatures

In an ideal world, your freeze-dried food should be stored at a constant temperature between 40 and 70°F (5-20°C) and doesn't fluctuate too much within that range. If your food is subject to hotter or colder temperatures, it will likely lose color, taste, texture, and nutrition.

High levels of moisture and humidity

Bacteria and mold love moist conditions, so food needs to be vacuum sealed or sealed with oxygen absorber packs. If any moisture gets into your stored food, it will cause it to spoil. In addition to this, if you are storing your food in bags, moisture can damage the packaging, which exposes the food to further deterioration.

To prevent your food from coming into contact with moisture, protect it from humidity and pack it into storage bags with desiccants and oxygen absorbers. The ideal storage location for your foods should have a humidity level of 15% or less.

Sunlight

Exposure to natural sunlight and artificial lights can cause your food to degrade over time. Studies have shown this is most noticeable in proteins and vitamins such as A, D and E, which may lose color, nutrition and flavor. You can avoid this by storing your food in Mylar bags in a cool, dark space.

Oxygen

While it is something we all need for survival, oxygen can be problematic when storing food. Over time, fats in food will oxidize and become rancid. We can prevent this with oxygen absorbers or vacuum-sealed food bags.

Rodents and other pests

Oxygen absorbers will prevent pests such as bugs from feasting on your food, as they cannot survive in the sealed bags without air. However, rodents will have no problem munching their way through. If you are storing your food in bags rather than mason jars, be wary of anything in your location with sharp teeth that might get to your stored food before you do. You should consider some barrier between your food and small animals looking for some free lunch.

Best Practices for Packaging

Choosing a suitable airtight container is critical to storing your freeze-dried food successfully. While Mylar bags may take up less room than other options, you may need to consider a more heavy-duty storage bin to protect your packaging from animals and moisture. Ensure the food is completely dry before sealing it in an airtight container. If you aren't completely happy that your food contains only residual water when packing, you can put it into the oven or a dehydrator to dry it out.

The best place to keep your freeze-dried foods is in a cool, dark pantry away from sunlight and temperature variations. If you do not have space in your pantry for all your freeze-dried foods, a similar indoor location such as a large closet, cold basement or even underneath a bed will suffice. Ensure your foods are kept away from sinks or bathrooms where they will be exposed to humidity and moisture. While they may have plenty of storage, garages and garden sheds are not ideal locations unless you can control the ambient temperature and keep pests away from your produce. There's a good reason why people built cold storage in basements before the invention of refrigerators!

To ensure that you are using the oldest food items last, you should label your foods carefully with the contents and the date they were placed in storage so you can rotate your stock and use it in the correct order. Organizing your food by type of produce in different plastic bins or storing it on labeled racking can make locating what you are looking for easier.

Containers and Sealing Equipment

Packaging is one of the most essential parts of the freeze-drying process because you will undo all your hard work if you get that bit wrong.

Jars (airtight)

Jars are perfect for storing freeze-dried products. You must ensure they are thoroughly sanitized beforehand and remember to put an oxygen absorber in with the food. You can use a vacuum sealer to remove all the oxygen from the jars, but it's difficult to remove it all, so it's a good idea to add an oxygen absorber to be on the safe side.

Jars are advantageous in that you can see exactly what is inside them, and they can also be reused repeatedly, which is more cost-effective than having to keep buying bags. They take up space, however, and must be stored somewhere dark so they are not exposed to sunlight.

Cans (airtight)

Cans are brilliant for food storage because they are airtight and don't allow any sunlight to get through, meaning you can be slightly less concerned about where they are stored. They should still be kept in a cool environment, though. The downside of cans is that you can only use them once as they cannot be resealed, so you need to think about what you store inside them.

If you decide to use gallon-sized cans, you could find yourself with a lot of food that needs to be used straight away. You might even end up wasting it, which defeats the whole point of food preservation. You can use smaller cans or portion your food into smaller packets inside them to ensure the food gets used before it goes off.

Mylar bags

Mylar bags are the simplest way to pack your freeze-dried food, and since you get a supply included with the purchase of your freeze-dryer, it makes sense to start with these. They are designed to block out light and air, but you must remove as much oxygen as possible before sealing them, and remember the oxygen absorber if using an impulse sealer.

Mylar bags are lightweight, portable, easy to store, take up less room and can be washed out, reused and resealed. They are the best storage choice in an emergency when you need to carry as much food as possible. However, most animals and other small animals would have no trouble getting their teeth into them, so they need to be placed somewhere inaccessible or protected by a more hardy container.

Plastic buckets

Plastic buckets are an economical storage solution and are the perfect choice for preventing exposure to light and moisture. You can store large amounts of food, such as grain, or house several Mylar bags inside them to protect them. They are also stackable. The downside to buckets is the amount of room they require.

Specialized food storage containers

Many freeze-drying companies provide specialized food storage containers, which have been created specifically for the long-term preservation of food. These containers are often quite large, so they are not ideal for people with limited storage space. As products such as this tend to be branded, you may also find yourself out of pocket, and companies that sell them often tie them in with the purchase of other products, so you can't buy them cheaply.

Vacuum packing machine and vacuum-sealed plastic bags

A vacuum packing machine can be an absolute godsend when removing excess air from jars, cans, buckets and bags before you seal them. However, it is almost impossible to remove all of the oxygen, and because the bags tend to be made from clear plastic, oxygen and moisture can eventually get through to the contents. These machines are great if you want to store foods for 2–3 years, but jars and cans are better options if you are looking for longevity.

Smart Labeling for Longevity

Labeling your freeze-dried food is an excellent idea, so you know exactly what you've got in your packaging, whether it is cooked or raw, and the date it was preserved. However, labeling the food with its pre-freeze-dried weight is also a good idea. When you go to the grocery store, foods are labeled with the number of servings per container, determined by weight.

However, this is harder to ascertain with freeze-dried food as the weight is very different once the moisture is removed. Therefore, you need to weigh your food before freeze-drying to determine how many servings you will have once it is rehydrated. Once you have done this, you can either note the different weights before and after freeze-drying or write down how many people each container will serve.

Labels can make finding foods on the shelf much more manageable, particularly if you color code different produce. For example, you could have green for vegetables, red for meats and proteins, pink for fruits, purple for desserts/candy, blue for whole meals and gray for other items/miscellaneous foods. You can leave a space on each label for the name of whatever food you are storing, the date it was freeze-dried, its pre-freeze-dried weight, and any directions/ instructional notes.

Consider including information such as serving sizes and whether vegetables are blanched, raw, or cooked. If making labels for meats, you can include whether it is raw, cooked, or seasoned. The more precise your labels, the easier it will be to find what you are looking for and the state it was in when you preserved it. If you are anything like me, you won't remember the rhubarb you put in the freezer last year, so these pointers help to remind you what you need to do with foods once they've been rehydrated.

Now that we have learned how to package and store your freeze-dried foods for the long term, we will look at consuming freeze-dried foods.

Chapter Nine

Consuming Freeze-Dried Foods

Rehydrating Your Foods

It's all very well learning the ropes of freeze-drying, but you might feel stumped when you open your first batch of freeze-dried food and wonder what on earth you are supposed to do with it. We all know that food is meant to be consumed, but how do you rehydrate the foods so they are ready to eat again?

Fruits and vegetables can be eaten in their freeze-dried state as a healthy snack straight out of the container and can be used as they are if you are baking. Other foods, such as raw, freeze-dried meat and whole meals, must be rehydrated before you consume them. If you are planning to cook your freeze-dried food in a sauce, there is no need to rehydrate it first. You just need to add slightly more water than the recipe of whatever you're making suggests. The same process can be used when you are baking.

It's a good starting point to use a 1:1 ratio for rehydrating. However, this is no such thing as one-size-fits-all, and different foods require different amounts of water depending on their state and environmental factors. You may experience a few challenges when you try to rehydrate certain foods. It's a learning curve, but I will list some top tips to get you started.

Equipment Needed:

   1. A digital scale with at least 0.01-gram accuracy.

   2. Notepad and pen, or a digital device, for recording weights.

Instructions:

Before Freeze-Drying:

Calibrate the Scale:

- Ensure your digital scale is calibrated according to the manufacturer's instructions for accuracy.

Prepare the Trays:

- Arrange your products evenly on the freeze-drying trays.

Weigh Each Tray:

- Place one tray at a time on the scale.
- Record the weight (including the weight of the tray and the product).
- Repeat this for each tray.
- Make sure to note down the weight against each tray number or identifier to avoid confusion later.

After Freeze-Drying:

Remove Trays After Process:

Once the freeze-drying process is complete, allow the trays to come to room temperature to avoid condensation affecting the weight.

Weigh Each Tray Again:

- Place the same tray back on the scale.
- Record the new weight (post freeze-drying).
- Repeat for each tray.

Calculate Water Loss:

Subtract to Find Water Loss:

For each tray, subtract the post freeze-drying weight from the pre-freeze-drying weight. This gives you the weight of the water removed.

Water Loss per Tray = Pre−Freeze − Drying Weight − Post−Freeze−Drying Weight

Total Water Loss:

- Add up the water loss from all the trays to get the total water removed in the process.

Example:

If Tray 1 weighed 1000g before freeze-drying and 800g after, then the water loss is 200g.

Final Steps:

Record Keeping:

- Keep a detailed record of these weights and calculations for future reference and for monitoring the consistency of the freeze-drying process.

Analyze the Data:

Use this data to assess the quality and efficiency of the freeze-drying process. Large variations in water loss between batches may indicate an issue with the process or the initial product preparation.

By accurately measuring and calculating the water loss in each tray, you can gain valuable insights into your freeze-drying process, enabling you to make necessary adjustments for optimal results.

Spritzing

You can rehydrate fruits and vegetables via spritzing, an excellent way to determine how much water they need without accidentally adding too much and ending up with a mushy mess. To use this method, place your fruits and vegetables on a tray or in a bowl and spray them with room-temperature water, stirring them as you go. The idea is to ensure every surface of the fruit and vegetables gets covered in some of the water. Once all the produce has been spritzed, stop and check if further rehydration is required before spraying any more.

Soaking

To use this method, fill a bowl with the freeze-dried food you want and add just enough cold water to cover the bottom, ensuring the liquid level does not cover your fruit and vegetables and make them soggy. Stir the food in the bowl until everything has been rehydrated. This method has more room for error, as some foods may be in the water longer than others. Be mindful that you cannot leave the foods in the water for too long, or they will be reduced to mush.

Rehydrating meat using water or broth

The 1:1 ratio works well for rehydrating freeze-dried meat. Be mindful that thicker chunks of meat may take a bit longer, and if you rehydrate shredded or ground meat, you will likely need less water. Shredded chicken, in particular, absorbs water rapidly, so handle it with care. You can add more water if you rehydrate raw meat, but check whether the meat is fully rehydrated before adding more to cooked meats.

The temperature of the water should be cold when you rehydrate raw meats to prevent your food from being overcooked. You can use warm or even hot water when rehydrating cooked meats, though many people avoid hot water to avoid overcooking the meat. You can also use broth to rehydrate meats if you want a tastier option and don't want to consider extra seasonings.

Rehydrating freeze-dried meals

If you are rehydrating whole meals you have freeze-dried yourself, starting with a 1:1 ratio of food and water is best. If you think the food will require less water, you can start with less and add it in gradually. Getting this technique down to a tee takes some practice, but you'll soon get the hang of it.

If you are rehydrating packaged meals, they usually come with instructions on the packet. Most freeze-dried meals require adding hot or boiling water and waiting a few minutes before consuming.

Tips for not over-hydrating your food

Take care when soaking food so that you do not over-hydrate it. Always watch it during rehydration because it may take less time than you think. You can check the texture of food at intervals to see if it is ready. Some small fruits can take only a few seconds or minutes to rehydrate, whereas thick slices of meat may take over an hour.

It is also prudent to mention that when you drain away the water used to rehydrate your freeze-dried foods, you also drain away many water-soluble vitamins, which defeats the point of retaining all the nutrients during the freeze-drying process.

Cooking and Baking with Freeze-Dried Ingredients

If you are making foods such as sauces or soups, you won't need to rehydrate the freeze-dried vegetables in advance. Put them all in a pot, add the required amount of water, and leave it to simmer. The same applies to fruits that you are making into a smoothie. Add them all and blend with the liquid you are using. You only need to remember that foods prepared this way will require approximately 3–4 more tablespoons of liquid than you would typically need for your recipe.

You can sauté freeze-dried vegetables without rehydrating them. You add a bit of oil and treat them exactly as you would if they were fresh. The only difference is that the vegetables will cook more quickly, so you must add whatever cooking stock or liquid you are using earlier to prevent burning.

If you are freeze-drying fruit at home, you can use whole dried pieces in baking, but you can also grind fruits into a powder with a food processor or a pestle and mortar to add flavor to your bakes. You can mix these powders into pretty much anything. Frostings, batters, doughs, and buttercreams can all be used to add tangy flavors, and you can use as much or as little as you like according to color and taste. Fruits such as blueberries, strawberries, raspberries, and cherries are the best fruits to add bold colors to your baking.

One of the best things about adding freeze-dried fruits to your baking is that you don't have to consider the moisture content of fruits that generally make your buns or cookies soggy. You can stir in freeze-dried pieces of fruit to add flavor while maintaining the texture of your crunchy and yummy cookies.

Snack and Quick Meal Ideas

If you're sick of forking out good money each week on the snack aisle of the grocery store, to feed your constantly starving little ones, you will find freeze-drying highly beneficial from a health and cost perspective. Ditch the processed cereal bars and use your new toy to create a variety of after-school snacks that will fuel your little darlings through Jiu-Jitsu, swimming, or gymnastics but will save you time and money.

You can also feel smug about the fact that you are providing healthy snacks rather than high-sugar options, which are full of preservatives. Freeze-dried snacks offer variety, do not require refrigeration, and you have complete control over their ingredients, so you don't have to worry about allergies.

I have included some favorite snack ideas for you to try below.

Apple and oatmeal bites

It doesn't get much more straightforward than this. You only need to whip up a batch of oatmeal and stir in chopped apples about an inch in size. You then spoon dollops of the mixture onto the freeze-dryer trays and run them through a standard drying cycle. They are the perfect size for little hands and are full of protein and slow-release energy to keep kids going until dinner. Top tip: use parchment paper on the trays to prevent them from sticking.

Yogurt drops and fruit

Fill a ziplock bag with yogurt and cut a small hole in one corner. Use it like a piping bag to create small yogurt rounds on the parchment-coated trays. It's a good idea to start your freeze-dryer about half an hour before you start piping these so it's nice and cool when they go in. For the healthy fruits to go with them, chop up some favorites and add them to the tray. These food items can go in the fryer simultaneously on a standard cycle.

Veggie chips

Any vegetables can be made into a healthy snack with a spray of oil and a spot of seasoning. Vegetables have a lovely, yummy, crispy texture and a strong flavor. It's a great way to introduce your kids to vegetables if they aren't keen on the texture of the fresh version, and is a much healthier option than potato chips. Making these couldn't be any simpler. Just slice up your favorite veggies, put them in the freeze-dryer, and sprinkle with whatever seasoning takes your fancy. Freeze-dried sweet potatoes are a thing of wonder!

DIY trail mix

Chop up and freeze-dry some bananas and strawberries and combine them with pistachios or almonds and a small amount of dried coconut. You can change the ingredients if you aren't a fan of these nuts and fruits, but the nuts and coconut provide healthy fats and protein, and the fruit provides a bit of energy.

Dark chocolate bark with berries

To make this delicious treat, you will need 10 ounces of dark chocolate, 1 ¼ cups of freeze-dried Berry De-lite Blend (or your home freeze-dried sliced fruits), and 2–3 tablespoons of honey or maple syrup (optional). Melt the chocolate and stir in ¼ of the De-lite Blend or your own berries and honey and pour into a tray lined with parchment paper. Smooth out the chocolate to determine how thick you want the bark to be, and then sprinkle the rest of the berries over the top evenly. Put the tray in the freezer for half an hour or until the chocolate solidifies. You can use tray separators to portion these up or use a knife to cut them into similar sizes afterward.

Blueberry energy balls

Shop-bought granola bars are a sugary snack dressed up as a healthy treat. However, you can make these blueberry balls to give you healthy energy instead. You will need the following ingredients:

- ¾ cup rolled oats
- ¼ cup unsweetened, shredded coconut
- 4 tbsp chia seeds
- 4 tbsp nut butter (peanut & almond if possible)
- 4 tbsp maple syrup
- ¼ cup coconut oil
- ⅓ cup freeze-dried blueberries

Add the nut butter, syrup, and coconut oil to a bowl and blend until well combined. Mix the dry ingredients separately (oats, chia seeds, coconut, blueberries). Pour the nut butter mixture into the bowl of dry ingredients and mix well. Cover the bowl in a dry towel and let it rest for half an hour. Make small balls of the mixture and place them in a container. These can be stored in the refrigerator for up to 2 weeks.

Banana strawberry s'mores

Delight your taste buds with this freeze-dried sensation that can be enjoyed all year round. You will need the following ingredients:

- 6 halved Graham crackers
- 6 ounces of dark chocolate chopped into 6 chunks
- 12 marshmallows
- ¼ cup of freeze-dried strawberries
- ¼ cup of freeze-dried banana slices

Preheat your oven to 400°F. Use one half of each Graham cracker as the bottom layer and set the other aside for the top. Put them on a large plate and top them with the freeze-dried strawberries and banana slices. Place the chocolate chunks on top of the fruit.

Place the marshmallows on top of a parchment-lined tray and cook them in the oven for 3–5 minutes or until they begin to turn brown. Rotate the marshmallows so they don't burn. Once roasted, remove them from the oven and put them on the fruit and chocolate. Add the other Graham cracker to the top of each s'more.

Now that we've looked at rehydrating your freeze-dried foods and discovered some of the cooking options and healthy, yummy snacks you can make, we will look at the importance of freeze-dryer maintenance to get the most out of your machine for years to come.

Chapter Ten

Maintaining Your Freeze-Dryer

Regular Cleaning and Upkeep

Before we get into cleaning and caring for your machine, it's important to mention that each machine IS different and there are some nuances that you will just have to try for yourself as you are getting to know your machine. *Please consult the owners manual for the exact steps to properly care for your freeze-dryer* as it is a significant investment and you want to do this right. If you look after it well, it will serve you for a lifetime. One of the best ways to maintain your machine is by cleaning it properly after each use. A quick two-minute clean could save you from costly repairs caused by clogs, leaks, and the build-up of 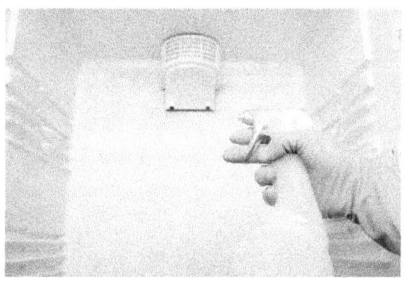 dirt and debris over time. You must remove any standing water after each freeze-drying cycle, as this will cause rust to accumulate on the freeze-drying trays or damage the other components. You also risk mold developing in your machine if you don't clean it after each use.

It's a good idea to have some supplies designated for cleaning your freeze-drying machine. As a minimum, you should clean the chamber and door of your machine with a white vinegar solution and wipe it down with microfiber cloths after every use.

Still, you should also give your dryer a deep clean every couple of weeks, even if it appears to be clean, as the vacuum phase of the cycle can cause food debris to float around and stick to the inside of the chamber. It is handy to have a long bottle cleaning brush to get to the parts of the machine you cannot reach and remove any residual food. An old toothbrush is also valuable for efficiently removing food spills on the trays.

Avoid using abrasive cleaners like Windex or bleach on your machine's door, as it can cause damage. If you use bleach to clean your machine, dilute it to 1 tablespoon per gallon of water.

Step-By-Step Guidance to Cleaning Your Freeze-Drying Machine

1. Before cleaning anything, turn off the freeze-drying machine and unplug it.

2. Fill a spray bottle with white vinegar or diluted bleach. These options are not only cheaper than branded

cleaners, but they are also less abrasive.

3. Spray the door with white vinegar or diluted bleach and wipe down thoroughly inside and out with a microfiber cloth.

4. Remove the black rubber gasket around the chamber's circumference and wipe it clean.

5. Remove the trays. Remove the rack system inside by unplugging it from the back and removing it from the chamber.

6. Remove any debris from the chamber and condenser area.

7. Thoroughly clean the inside of the chamber. Spray it with white vinegar or diluted bleach and scrub it with a microfiber cloth. Use isopropyl alcohol and a toothbrush to remove any stubborn food residue or spills that are smeared inside the chamber.

8. Wipe the chamber's interior and the condenser area with a clean cloth using clean water. Then, dry out the inside of the chamber with a clean, dry cloth.

9. Next, clean the racking system and trays. Spray the surfaces with white vinegar or bleach, and clean every surface with microfiber cloths. Persistent stains or food residue on the trays can be removed with a toothbrush and hot, soapy water.

    > Do NOT spray the heating elements within the tray setup, as this could damage them. Clean out the heating elements with air dusters.

    > Use the long bottle cleaning brush to clean between the racking system levels. Use isopropyl alcohol to target any stubborn food residue. Wipe down the rack system with clean water.

10. Wipe down the outside of the machine with a dry cloth.

11. Flush the drain line to ensure it has no debris stuck inside it. Replace the drain line if necessary.

12. Reinstall the rack system back into the chamber. Plug it back into the housing and replace the trays in the rack. Replace the rubber gasket around the chamber, ensuring the seal is flat.

13. Plug in the machine, and you're all set to go again. Remember to leave the door open for airflow in case there's any trace moisture left in the chamber, as this will minimize the chances of mold growth inside. It's also a good idea to leave the door of your freeze-dryer open when the machine is either defrosting or not being used if there is any moisture in the machine (no matter how little); sealing it in will increase the risk of mold growth.

Software Updates and Troubleshooting

To keep your machine running as it should, you must ensure its software is updated. However, before performing any updates, you need to know your current version, as some of the newer updates are incompatible with the older software on models that have been around longer.

Installing an update that is not compatible could cause irreparable harm to your freeze-dryer, and there is no support available to revert to an older version, so you must check this first.

Don't panic if your machine is older and incompatible with the newer firmware. There is no reason why it cannot continue to function perfectly well as long as it has the most up-to-date version of the software that suits your model.

Newer models will show you the version number in the top right corner of the dryer home screen, whereas older models may show it in the middle or the bottom of the right-hand side.

The only way to find out whether or not your machine is ready for an update is by checking the Harvest Right website to see if there is a newer version than the one you have. If you have subscribed to Harvest Right's mailing list, you may receive an email informing you of these updates (Starr, 2023).

Before installing any new updates, check the following:

- Ensure the compatibility of the update with your machine
- Download the update
- Make sure the freeze-dryer is turned off
- Have an empty USB thumb drive at the ready

The installation process may vary slightly between different makes and models, but here are step-by-step instructions for the downloading and updating process.

Step 1: Prepare and download the update files

Depending on the update, there may be one or several files, so make sure your thumb drive has nothing else stored on it. A small thumb drive is handy if you are trying to put the drive into the port and your unit is in a cramped space. Download the update file(s) to the root of your thumb drive rather than a folder. Leave the file naming conventions such as .hff, .hfw, or .hrf as they are.

Step 2: Install the updates

Put your USB into the port on the unit. Turn the freeze dryer on once you've done this, and it should install any updates automatically. Once this has been done correctly, you will see the new version number on your home screen. If the update fails to install, turn off the dryer, reinsert the thumb drive, and try again. If you still have issues, you will need to contact Harvest Right's customer support team to guide you through troubleshooting.

Step 3: Restart the machine and start recalibration

Once you have installed the software, you can begin recalibrating it. Manual recalibration is not usually required, although you may need to do this for the touch screen if it needs to be fixed. Turn the freeze-dryer off and on, after which the screen should turn white, and you should press the center of it.

Step 4: Press the flashing circle

The machine will make a sound, and a flashing circle will appear. You should call customer tech support to investigate if this doesn't happen. Press the flashing circle. It will then move, and you can press it again to triangulate its positioning.

Once you have pressed the circle enough, you can 'write' on the screen with your finger for approximately 20 seconds to check the touch screen is working correctly. Once this stage is complete, your start menu should load onto the screen, and all the buttons should register your touch. If this doesn't happen, tech support can offer advice.

Step 5: Reset the freeze-dryer

To reset your freeze-dryer, turn it off and on again. You shouldn't need to do this except when recalibrating, but it's a good starting point for resolving glitches that might occur, such as a frozen screen. It may resolve problems without you having to contact customer tech support.

Machines occasionally require a spot of technical TLC. With this in mind, Harvest Right has put together a Freeze Dryer Problem Diagnosis Guide, complete with troubleshooting videos offering help and guidance in dealing with some of the most commonly reported issues (Harvest Right, 2023).

Here, you will learn what to do if any of the following problems occur:
- **Vacuum errors:** epoxy plug leaks/replacement and replacement of drain valve or vacuum sensor
- **Refrigeration issues:** Frost pattern, condenser fan, and relay board problems
- **Drying issues:** Faulty heater wires or relay board
- **Touchscreen issues:** White, frozen, or black screen and recalibration
- **Power issues:** What to do if the power receptacle shorts out

Maintenance Schedule and When to Seek Help

Keeping on top of your freeze-dryer's maintenance schedule is the best way to ensure longevity so you can enjoy your machine for the next 20–30 years. Get into the habit of defrosting and draining your dryer after every use, wiping it down, and giving it a deep clean every fortnight. The chamber must be neutralized if you have placed anything acidic or used chemicals in your freeze-dryer.

Those with an oilless pump do not have to worry about this, but the vacuum pump oil needs to be changed whenever it begins to darken in color. As a general rule of thumb, the oil in the pump should be okay for about 100 hours of use, but it largely depends on what you are running in the machine. Keep an eye on the color and change it when it is required. It's better to drain the oil and filter it when it is warm, as it will flow more easily. Use an oil filter to remove any debris.

Keeping the vacuum pump debris-free and clean ensures your freeze-dryer pulls sufficient vacuum. Regular oil changes will help to extend the life of your vacuum pump. If your drain valve is not fully closed, this could be the culprit for any vacuum error messages. You can tighten the valve with a screwdriver. Hose connections could also be a problem if your vacuum is not behaving as it should. Check the O rings are forming tight seals around connector hoses and the door gasket is sitting flush against the door. You can also run a dry vacuum test to check it is functioning as it should before contacting a technician to look at it.

Suppose you have unresolved issues with the following functions after going through the troubleshooting checklists and videos. In that case, it's time to contact customer support and have a technician look at your machine.

- Power issues
- Touchscreen issues
- Drying issues
- Refrigeration issues
- Vacuum error

Now that we have looked at cleaning and general maintenance of your machine, we will explore some additional freeze-drying tips, tricks, and resources.

Chapter Eleven

Additional Tips, Tricks, and Resources

Freeze-drying will save you a lot of money in the long term, but what about the short term? Many people are going through hard times economically, and it can be hard to get started when you factor in the cost of the machine and the food storage you will need. However, you do not need to buy everything at once, and every time you freeze-dry food, you are preventing food wastage and knowing that you've put more meals in storage for a rainy day.

The wonderful thing about freeze-drying is that you will have a surplus of food if/when times get hard in the future, and you need to keep an eye on the purse strings. Here are some valuable tips for those on a tight budget or just starting out on their freeze-dry journey.

Buy food when it's on sale and buy it in bulk

It may seem scary when money is already tight, but buying as much as possible when food is on sale is a good idea. Buying food in season is generally much cheaper than getting hold of it when it isn't. Stock up on your strawberries in the summer, and then you can enjoy them whenever you like once they've been freeze-dried.

I generally have a weekly menu plan to ensure I only buy what I need, but I break this rule when food is on sale because I don't want to miss an opportunity. To keep tabs on my spending, I will switch out whatever I have in mind and replace it with whatever is on sale. So, if I was going to buy pasta, but soup is on sale, I would buy the soup in bulk and get the pasta next time.

Keep track of how much you're spending on food

Work out your budget for groceries and stick to it! It's a good idea to note the prices of things you buy regularly at different stores to give you a baseline to work from. I know it's not the most exciting way to spend your time, but knowledge is power. That way, you can keep up with rising costs and consider shopping elsewhere or buying cheaper brands. Don't get sucked in by reasonable offers without checking the unit price. Bigger containers aren't necessarily the cheapest.

Share food with friends

If you have friends struggling to make ends meet, it's a great idea to club together. If you both adopt a deep pantry approach to food storage, you can buy food in bulk and share it. The same can be said for buying food storage containers. If there is a bulk offer, you can split the cost and the shipping on items you both need.

Grow Your Own Food

Growing your food is a fantastic way to save costs. Even if you are short on space, there are many small-space gardening ideas on the internet. You could even make your own basic hydroponics kit, which only requires a windowsill worth of space and some sunlight. You could save money on water costs by collecting rainwater, saving water from the bath, or even your condensing tumble dryer.

Making an Income with Your Freeze-Dryer

We know that a freeze-dryer will pay for itself within a year, but have you considered the additional money you could make if you start your own freeze-drying business? You can either sell the produce or rent out the unit to make money and how much you charge is up to you. Private owners usually rent out a freeze-dry tray for $5.

If the person wants to rent the entire freeze-dryer for their own use, a standard charge is about $60 per cycle. You could even sell food containers for people to take away their freeze-dried food. Consider all of your production costs and the cost of store-bought freeze-dried food before setting your prices.

According to author Sara Wells, a medium-size freeze-dryer can make about $10,000 worth of food each year. If you have a large freeze-dryer, you could rent out some space in your dryer while running it for yourself. You likely won't make big bucks doing this, but you could cover the annual running costs of your freeze-dryer, which would save a lot of pennies over time (Wells, 2022).

If you're planning to go into a freeze-drying business, buying a large or extra large machine or several small to medium units makes sense so you can run them at different times for peak productivity. Even if you aren't running your own business, a larger machine is a good investment for people who grow their own produce. Growing your food saves a considerable amount of money, but it takes a lot of time and effort, and a large machine will ensure that you can freeze-dry everything you grow without fear of wastage.

Before you launch yourself into business, check the laws of the state you live in to ensure it's allowed. Some places require simple vendors' permits and adherence to health and safety standards, but rules are more stringent in other places. Check to see if you have a Farmers Market Network, or do a broader search of the U.S. Department of Agriculture's site to find food directories for farmers markets local to you. Farmers' Markets are a great place to sell your goods. You can also sell online, although this will require further permits and rules.

Once you have established that you are allowed, you need to familiarize yourself with basic laws that apply to any business.

- **Food handling laws and regulations -** Food is being handled safely for human consumption

- **Business laws and regulations -** Specific rules you must adhere to in your location
- **Rules, regulations, laws, and covenants -** Regulations determined by the federal government that you must follow in your city/town/state
- **Cottage industries -** Ensure your state allows these and look into whether or not you need a permit to sell foods at Farmers' Markets without a commercial kitchen

In addition to these laws, there are basic laws in every state relating to food hygiene to which you should adhere.

- **Food storage -** Adequate storage facilities must be provided for fresh and dry foods
- **Cleanliness -** If you run a freeze-drying business from your kitchen, you should ensure it is kept clean and that pets are not allowed in the vicinity. If this is unworkable, putting your freeze-dryer in an inaccessible area to pets might make sense. Basements are often better choices for the location of freeze-dryers as the ambient temperature is cooler.
- **State and city business license/other permits -** You will need a permit even if you are only a vendor at a Farmers' Market. Check your government website to see if you can get an application form there. You should be able to find other required permits and zoning clearance certificates (where applicable) on the government website. Remember that even if you only rent out the space in your freeze-dryer, you still run a business and may require a permit. Unless cottage laws mean you are exempt, you may also be subject to kitchen inspections.

Freeze-dried foods are high in demand, not only because of their long shelf life, intense flavors, and health benefits, but because they are portable, lightweight foods perfect for day trips, hiking, travel, and busy midweek evenings when you'd rather not bother cooking. They are an excellent choice for busy moms who want to ensure their children are getting healthy snacks, health-conscious people who want healthier foods such as ready-to-eat fruits and vegetables without additives and chemicals, and elderly citizens who require access to a nutritious, balanced diet that they can prepare themselves. You can even buy freeze-dried food for your pets, meaning there is a considerable market for setting up your business.

If you are selling food at a Farmers' Market, there will usually be food packaging guidelines. Provided all freeze-dried produce is protected from sunlight, air, and water, you can be creative with your packaging and develop your own branding. Mylar bags are a good, lightweight option, and the customers can continue to store whatever they buy from you in these when they get home. If you want to be more fancy, use mason jars with oxygen absorbers inside them and a branded sticker on the side. You can opt for Mylar bags with a window in them so that customers can see the produce before they buy. You can also use clear plastic bags, but these are not recommended because the light will degrade the food over time.

Community Resources and Support

Freeze-drying has been hugely beneficial in terms of providing community support. With the invention of smaller, residential freeze-drying models, community grant programs have had access to a more cost-effective solution to providing tasty, healthy foods for those in need without the hefty price tag that comes with commercial freeze-drying. Non-profit organizations can now purchase smaller machines to provide freeze-dried fruits and vegetables for hungry children. They can also freeze-dry some of the donated produce with a shorter shelf-life that food banks cannot donate before it spoils. Freeze-drying has enabled food banks to provide fruit and vegetables all year round, meaning families who depend on free school meals or heavily reduced food can still get the nutrients required for a balanced diet.

Freeze-drying is also a valuable means of delivering aid in emergencies. However, some natural disasters or places decimated by war require a lot more assistance, and those with a home freeze-dryer can come together to support organizations working hard on the ground.

The Harvest Right website offers suggestions on how to help people in need. There is something so rewarding about coming together to help people worldwide with a freeze-dryer, knowing that your preserved produce could travel hundreds of miles and be used wherever it is most needed (Harvest Right, 2017).

Now that we've explored the potential for beginning your own home business and the rewards of helping others, we will look at 111 of the most popular foods for freeze-drying.

Chapter Twelve

Freeze-Dryers' Favorites and Non-Food Items

Freeze-drying is not limited to those who want to save money on groceries or set up a freeze-drying business. Celebrities have also jumped on the bandwagon to create delicious freeze-dried foods for people and animals in challenging circumstances.

Heston Blumenthal

When astronaut Tim Peake went to the International Space Station in 2016, celebrity chef Heston Blumenthal was tasked with creating his bonus food supply. Not only did he have to ensure the food met the most stringent European Space Agency safety criteria, but he also needed to make it taste, look, and smell as appetizing as possible. In the early days of space travel, space food was primarily considered a means of survival rather than something to be enjoyed. However, it has come on in leaps and bounds compared to the unrecognizable and unappealing freeze-dried cubes, food paste in tubes, and bread pieces coated in gelatine from the first space flights. Astronauts require the correct amount of calories and nutrients a day to remain healthy in space, but food needs to be lightweight, compact, and have a long shelf life without the help of cooking or refrigeration. In addition, they have a bonus food allowance, usually selected from a menu and intended to boost morale.

Blumenthal wanted to create a more interesting bonus food supply because he believes food profoundly impacts people's emotional and mental well-being, particularly when isolated in space. While basic food will ensure survival, he wanted to create recipes that would offer more than a simple existence and would provide a nostalgic source of comfort in a harsh environment. The challenge was to create recipes, some of which were freeze-dried, which would remind Peake of his childhood, family, and home life to lift his spirits when the going got tough. Although freeze-dried foods do not lose their taste, nutritional value, or texture, being in a zero-gravity environment affects the body's senses. Therefore, food created on Earth can taste bland when eaten in space.

To recreate the conditions in which Peake would eat his food, Blumenthal created his recipes in zero-gravity conditions and carefully monitored acidity, sweetness, salt thresholds, and moisture levels. He also worked closely with Peake to establish his likes, dislikes, and reactions to specific tastes.

While he faced many challenges along the way, including overcoming excess liquid without compromising the taste of one of the dishes and having to use cans rather than pouches to store the food, Blumenthal managed to create seven new space food recipes, one of which was the first bacon sarnie to be eaten in space.

Katherine Heigl

In August of 2022, actress Katherine Heigl launched her own pet food brand for dogs. The Badlands Ranch pet food brand, named after the ranch she owns, offers medical care, obedience training, and homes for pets in need. It utilizes freeze-dried methods of high-quality canine-friendly ingredients to develop its pet foods for exceptional nutrition. The dog food can be served dry in its packaged form or rehydrated with warm water to boost moisture.

Badlands Ranch also offers a single-ingredient dog treat made from freeze-dried raw beef liver, providing dogs with high-quality protein. Heigl's pet products do not contain any fillers, preservatives, or artificial ingredients, and the funds raised from feeding your dogs with her exceptionally nutritious foods go towards helping other animals in need on the ranch.

Gwyneth Paltrow

Opinions are divided on the new trend of companies that offer to freeze-dry breast milk under sterile conditions. Actress Gwyneth Paltrow recently invested $400,000 and took a 20% stake in the Texas-based company Milkify, which offers to safely freeze-dry breast milk as she felt it was a product that would "give such agency to moms, to working moms" to store their breast milk safely. Milkify uses a patent-pending process to freeze-dry each breast milk bag individually, without any contact with equipment or utensils. It is ideal for parents with limited freezer space who do not want their breast milk to expire. It is also beneficial for working parents, those who plan to move house, or need to travel.

As freeze-dried breast milk powder is 90% lighter than frozen milk and requires no refrigeration, it is ideal for moms returning to work after maternity leave who want to continue providing their own milk for their babies. Some daycare providers refuse to accept frozen breast milk but will allow powdered breast milk because it is like formula. It doesn't need to be thawed before use or kept in particular conditions so that it won't spoil. You just need to add water to rehydrate it to its almost original form.

Meals in a Jar

Creating "Meals in a Jar" is a remarkably easy and efficient method of food preservation that has gained popularity among various groups of people, from busy families to outdoor enthusiasts. This innovative approach to meal preparation not only simplifies the process of preserving food but also offers a fun and creative way to prepare meals ahead of time.

After the freeze-drying process is complete, the meals are ready to be sealed. This step is crucial as it ensures the longevity of the food. Properly sealed freeze-dried meals can last for years, making them an excellent option for long-term food storage. This feature is particularly appealing for those interested in emergency preparedness or reducing food waste.

Using the meals is just as easy. When you're ready to eat, simply add water to rehydrate the contents, and within minutes, you have a meal that's as good as fresh. This convenience is invaluable for those who enjoy outdoor adventures, as it allows for lightweight and nutritious meals on the go. For families, it means having quick and healthy meals on hand for busy days. You can try any of the soups I included. Simply measure out the ingredients and put them in a jar for storage.

Freeze-Drying for Other Purposes

Freeze-drying is not just limited to the preservation of foods. There are many other things you can freeze-dry either for longevity of life, reduced storage, travel purposes, or just as a cool experiment with the kids. Freeze-drying non-food products is just as beneficial as freeze-drying food items. It reduces their weight, makes them easier to store and transport, and prolongs their shelf life. Freeze-drying favorite products will also enable you to stock up if products are discontinued, and the process has proved to be incredibly beneficial to extending the life and effectiveness of medication and vaccines.

Listerine mouthwash

There are various video trends on social media sites where people send suggestions of things to freeze-dry, and those with access to a freeze-drying machine and plenty of time on their hands comply by posting videos of their results. Listerine transforms into an impressive blue glass-like solid you can chew rather than gargle with!

Toothpaste

There are videos on TikTok where people have taken it upon themselves to freeze-dry various toothpaste brands in different patterns. One experimented with Colgate Total, Arm & Hammer with Baking Soda, and Aquafresh. Colgate Total was the only one that freeze-dried successfully, creating a solid toothpaste that foamed up when water was added. Arm & Hammer remained chewy in consistency, and Aquafresh looked particularly appealing, as it had been freeze-dried in swirls. The result was reminiscent of strawberry and cream marbled sweets, but it didn't taste very good. Freeze-drying toothpaste and mouthwash may be handy for travel, as this renders them solids rather than liquids.

Flowers

Freeze-drying edible flowers is one thing, but did you know you can freeze-dry real flowers to preserve them? Many companies are now offering this service to preserve bridal bouquets, which, given the cost and sentimental value, is proving to be a very popular service for decorative purposes or a cherished keepsake.

Unlike air drying, freeze-drying keeps your flowers in perfect form, meaning the petals will not fade or change shape over time. You can freeze dry almost any flower, as it is a very delicate process, and the foliage won't fall apart. The only word of warning is to avoid placing poisonous flowers in your freeze-drying machine, as toxic chemicals may be left behind after use.

Plants

Powders can be made from freeze-dried plants for skin, medicinal, and home remedies. Things such as Echinacea Tea and Aloe Vera have been proven to have health benefits. Mixing Aloe Vera powder with water to rehydrate it will provide a potent, healing salve for your skin.

Shampoo

Shampoos are primarily water-based and, therefore, freeze-dry well. They are also easy to rehydrate, but the freeze-drying process will turn it into a soap bar. You could use a silicone mold to shape it into a more uniform bar shape or an animal-shaped mold if experimenting with children. While rehydrating the bar back into its original liquid form is a lot of fun, leaving it as a solid bar would be a great option when traveling.

Conditioner

Much like shampoo, conditioner works well when freeze-dried. I suggest using a mold for it, and the rehydration process can be very messy, but leaving it in a bar form is a handy travel tip if you are adhering to restrictions on liquids.

Makeup

Since products containing a lot of water are a breeding ground for bacteria, waterless makeup is on the rise. For many years, products have been made longer-lasting and seemingly more profitable using water as a filler, but this is neither good for our skin nor the environment. The cosmetic industry has adopted freeze-drying processes to preserve products without additives. Freeze-dried makeup doesn't dry out our skin and is better for the environment because it requires less water and packaging. It's also more concentrated, less prone to oxidation, and has a much longer shelf life.

Insects

Yes, you read that correctly. For those who keep reptiles as pets, freeze-drying insects is an excellent way to preserve them. I would put them on a separate tray so as not to contaminate anything else you might be freeze-drying at the same time. However, more and more people are baking with insects as a sustainable source of protein, fiber, and essential nutrients.

Paints

This can be another fun experiment to do with the kids. It's a bit messy, and the results may be mixed, but it makes sense to freeze-dry large quantities if you do this. If you want to create a paint sample, it's more practical to write down the name and number of the paint. Then, you can paint a bit on the card and let it dry.

Adhesives

As a general rule, adhesives don't freeze dry very well because they contain solvents that aren't water-soluble. Water-based glues will do better in the freeze-dryer but are unlikely to rehydrate back to their original state and may be tricky to use.

Water-soluble, homemade adhesives should freeze-dry, provided you don't add any solvent into the mix before freeze-drying. If you need to add a solvent, wait until you are about to use it before adding it.

Chemicals

Not all chemicals are freeze-dry friendly, but some cleaning products can be freeze-dried. It would help to avoid anything with a high alcohol content, like disinfectants or sanitizers, as they will likely evaporate during sublimation.

There's a bit of trial and error required for these products. Liquid soaps and some detergents work well, but it largely depends on the brand. I will save you the bother of experimenting with laundry pods, and don't attempt to open them to see if the liquid inside will freeze-dry. It's a waste of effort!

Freeze-drying has proved incredibly valuable in the field of Biomedical products and Pharmaceuticals. While I recommend leaving this to the experts, it is a testament to how beneficial the freeze-drying process can be. Storing frozen pharmaceuticals is expensive, and a power cut could ruin the products. In contrast, freeze-dried pharmaceuticals are not at the mercy of environmental factors, provided they are packaged and stored correctly.

Medicines

Even with the option of freezing medicines, products such as insulin cannot be stored long-term and do not freeze well. Freeze-drying offers a solution to this problem, but care must be taken to ensure the medicine retains its original potency when rehydrated.

Antibiotics are sensitive to environmental factors, so freeze-drying is a perfect way to preserve them, with the bonus that, once freeze-dried, they are easier to transport as they no longer require refrigeration.

Vaccines

Not all vaccines can be freeze-dried effectively, but those that can are much easier to ship around the world, making them more accessible to those in need without the need for refrigeration.

Supplements

Freeze-dried supplements are becoming more advanced, and probiotics and natural enzymes can also be preserved through freeze-drying. The nutraceutical industry has recently incorporated freeze-dried lamb hearts and liver into some products.

Blood Plasma

Blood plasma must be frozen within 6–8 hours of collection, and this temperature must be maintained to preserve its quality. Freeze-drying blood plasma is a much better option, as it is much more cost-effective. It can then be stored, transported at room temperature, and rehydrated before transfusion. Freeze-drying removes the water from blood plasma but preserves the proteins that allow clotting.

Tissues

Because they are very delicate, freezing tissues can affect them structurally, so they must be stored with Cryopreservation, a freezing process using liquid nitrogen. Freeze-drying tissues simplifies this complex process and makes storage and transportation easier.

Cells

Much like tissues, cells can be freeze-dried instead of undergoing Cryopreservation.

Now that we have looked at some of the weird and wonderful non-food items you can freeze-dry, we will explore top tips and advice from seasoned freeze-dryers who have shared stories to give you further insight into your freeze-drying journey.

Chapter Thirteen

Freeze-Drying Candy and Desserts and Top Tips for Success

We know that freeze-dried candy and desserts don't last as long in storage as other foods because of their high sugar and fat content, but don't let that put you off. It is worth experimenting with because some candies and desserts freeze-dry successfully, and some of the effects can be very surprising. It is fascinating from a scientific point of view and a rewarding hobby that can lead to some tasty and lucrative results.

If you are freeze-drying candies to sell, consider the ingredients and texture beforehand, as some fillings, such as caramel, can undergo moderately vigorous reactions in your machine. While this doesn't matter if you are freeze-drying at home for fun, it might make for something other than the most visually appealing merchandise to sell. Thankfully, many videos on YouTube show other people's experimentation with all kinds of candies and desserts, so you can check those out before wasting your time freeze-drying batches of candies that might not deliver the desired results.

Generally, candies with simple ingredients and a solid texture freeze-dry more successfully than others. Still, there are endless possibilities for making your own delicious freeze-dried candy recipes.

Preparing Candy and Sweet Treats for Freeze-Drying

You can save yourself a lot of time by freeze-drying unwrapped candies, but if you are attempting to freeze-dry something like Starburst, removing the wrappers first is advisable. Consider the time required to do this before you start! Some freeze-drying experts have experimented with leaving wrappers on or opening them slightly to achieve different results. However, if the candy is sticky, you may find it easier to remove the wrappers when the product is at room temperature. However, if you are freeze-drying a product with a high caramel content, try experimenting with one wrapped and one unwrapped sample to see how different the result can be.

When freeze-drying anything with high sugar or fat content, it's a good idea to use parchment paper or some silicone mats. While you can throw the parchment paper away and save time on a clean-up mission, it is more cost-effective to invest in silicone mats, which are easy to clean and can be used repeatedly. These are particularly handy when experimenting with new things, as you're likely to find that at least some of your experiments will result in a sticky mess. Candies should be placed in a single layer on the freeze-dry trays and spaced apart like any other food product. Freezing your candy before freeze-drying helps to prevent it from becoming too sticky.

Unlike other freeze-dried foods, which retain their flavor, size, and texture, some candies and desserts can expand in weird and wonderful ways. Aside from the expansion, one of the most noticeable changes in candies is the effect that freeze-drying has on their texture. Many sweets develop a crunchy or melt-in-the-mouth sensation similar to the texture of Cheetos. It is also impossible to rehydrate most sweets as, depending on the ingredients, they tend to dissolve as soon as they touch water. If you want to freeze-dry a large amount of candy, you can get cost-effective deals by buying in bulk from places like Costco.

While I'm sure you cannot wait to start experimenting with freeze-drying your candies and sweets at home, I have described some of the reactions you can expect from the most popular brands and desserts in this chapter and included some pictures. However, if you'd like to see real-time visual results, a quick Google search will bring up many videos from influencers who have freeze-dried everything from Sponge Bob Square Pants-branded candies to Saltwater Taffy.

Freeze-Drying Candy

Skittles

Image Credit: HarvestRight.com

You may have seen some of the more popular freeze-dried candies for sale online. Skittles are a firm favorite because they tend to expand and crack fairly uniformly, giving them a striking visual appearance, not dissimilar to balls on a pool table. The crispy shells crack with the expansion of the molecules when the moisture inside the candy freezes, but they retain their flavor. If anything, the flavors become more concentrated when the moisture is removed. They are slightly bigger, which is a win-win situation for anyone who loves Skittles. They have been described as Skittles popcorn. The interior melts in your mouth, but the crispy exterior shell remains the same.

Starburst

Freeze-drying Starburst requires time to prepare due to the wrapper removal. Starburst candies retain their flavors but become slightly hardened in the freeze-dryer. On the DIY Freeze Dry YouTube channel, there is a suggested hack that you can warm the Starburst in the oven at a low temperature for about 10-15 minutes before freeze-drying to make them slightly melted and chewier before the freeze-drying process. Still, the result would suggest no scientific merit in doing this. The freeze-drying process leaves them crunchy regardless.

Image Credit: www.shopify.com

Gummies

Image Credit: www.etsy.com

Gummies are one of the most fun things to freeze dry because they react dramatically. There are various examples of videos online where people have experimented with a selection of different-sized gummy worms and candies, such as Haribo Cherries. All gummies expand massively after the freeze-dryer treatment. The gummy worms can grow up to three times their normal size, and the Haribo Cherries swell up into giant bubbles, giving them a stained-glass effect. Depending on the size of the original piece of candy, the texture changes from chewy to crispy, like a puffy potato chip. Small gummy worms remain chewy inside, but larger ones become entirely crispy.

Gummy Bears

These are a childhood favorite, but plenty of adults enjoy them too. Like other gummy candies, freeze-drying causes them to expand into a light and airy tasty snack, much like Cheetos in consistency. The air bubbles in them expand until the candy explodes, and the original shape is stretched beyond recognition. You can also purchase giant gummy bear sweets, which become huge in a freeze-dryer.

Image Credit: www.shopify.com

Milky Way

Image Credit: www.etsy.com

The nougat becomes very crunchy when you freeze-dry a Milky Way candy bar. If you leave the wrapper on when you put it in the freeze dryer, the liquid cannot escape, and the caramel is held in place. However, if you remove the wrapper before freeze-drying, the caramel swells up into a crunchy, styrofoam texture and takes on a taste and texture that is similar to honeycomb. This is much like the texture of the large freeze-dried gummies, but the caramel dissolves in your mouth the second it hits your tongue.

Saltwater Taffy

Saltwater Taffy expands dramatically in the freeze-dryer, with aesthetically pleasing results. If you leave it in the wrapper, it retains a reasonably uniform shape, although it will try to escape! If you unwrap it and allow it to expand fully, it puffs up and changes from small, chewy candy to meringue-like spheres. Visually, the different colors can give taffy the appearance of colorful bath bombs. People have likened the taste and texture to cotton candy when it meets any moisture because it disintegrates in your mouth. If you were to drop it into a bowl of water, it would dissolve in seconds.

Image Credit: www.etsy.com

Turkish Delight

Image Credit: www.etsy.com

Turkish Delight starts off gummy and maintains its appearance after going through the freeze-drying process. It doesn't expand but becomes more solid in texture. You can see air bubbles beginning to develop inside the candy, but nothing much else happens besides the jelly-like texture changing to a more solid one. Perhaps the reason for this is the cornstarch on the outside acting as a barrier and preventing the moisture from escaping.

Marshmallow Fluff

Although you can successfully freeze-dry marshmallows to preserve them, they do not change in appearance much in size or taste. However, marshmallow fluff expands a lot. It grows into a large, light, and fluffy meringue after the freeze-drying treatment and is well worth trying as an experiment with the kids. Much like taffy, this will dissolve quickly when it meets moisture, so it will melt on the tongue but disappear quickly if placed in water.

Image Credit: www.etsy.com

Mentos

Image Credit: www.etsy.com

Mentos are much like Skittles: sugary shells over chewy interior, so I expected them to react similarly in the freeze-dryer. Interestingly enough, the fruit Mentos expanded and puffed up like Skittles, but the mint Mentos didn't change except for the outer shell's slight cracking. I don't know which ingredients cause these shelled sweets to puff up, but it was interesting to note the difference. It would be rude not to try the Mentos and Diet Coke challenge once they've been in the freeze-dryer, so I decided to include the results of that experiment here in case you want to try it at home.

For anyone living under a rock, Diet Coke reacts dramatically when you add Mentos to a bottle. If you drop a Mento or two into the neck of the bottle, the Coke fizzes up and overflows. The mint sweets offer a surface for the gas bubbles in the Coke to cling to, and, as the bubbles of gas in the Coke are lighter than the liquid, they quickly shoot to the top of the bottle as the bubbles of gas get larger. Although the mint Mentos didn't appear to change much in the freeze-dryer, there was a noticeable difference between freeze-dried and non-freeze-dried Mentos when added to the Diet Coke. Both provided a dramatic reaction, but the freeze-dried Mentos had a much quicker effect and then stopped, whereas the non-freeze-dried Mentos produced a slower reaction, which lasted longer.

Jolly Ranchers

Jolly Ranchers are one of the most satisfying candies to freeze-dry because they look fantastic. Like Skittles, they are a very popular freeze-dried candy to buy online. If you are marketing these, I suggest placing them in window bags, as they are very aesthetically appealing. Hard candies are one of the best options for freeze-drying as they have a low moisture content, meaning they are less likely to become sticky and gooey or lose their texture. The candy pops when the vacuum and the heat hit the freeze-dryer, causing it to transform from a hard, boiled sweet into a fluffy, sugary ball. They are visually appealing because they puff up into what looks like brightly colored styrofoam balls and have a very pleasing light, airy, and crispy texture. Jolly Ranchers are very easy to freeze-dry, but the time devoted to removing the wrappers can be lengthy. One way to speed this up is to chop the sweets in half with a sharp knife to make the removal of the wrappers easier. It also means you will have a larger supply of freeze-dried candies at the end of the process. If you have time to freeze the candy in the freezer before putting it in the freeze dryer, this will remove any residual stickiness and prevent them from clumping together.

Image Credit: www.etsy.com

These examples are just the tip of the iceberg when it comes to freeze-drying sweet treats and candies. You can try other chocolate bars such as Snickers, Mars, Rocky Road, and other chewy sweets like Fruit Salad and Fruitella. There is a huge variety of sweet and sour gummies with many different flavors, so there is plenty of fun to be had. At the time of writing, freeze-drying your own candy is cheaper than buying it online.

Now, let's look at what happens to some desserts when you freeze-dry them.

Freeze-Drying Desserts

Fat Boys/Ice Cream Sandwiches

Image Credit: www.etsy.com

The original space/astronaut ice cream, Fat Boys, tends to freeze dry more successfully if you remove it from the wrapper. You can freeze-dry ice cream sandwiches without taking them out of the packaging, but they will freeze-dry more efficiently if you rip the wrapping open slightly and place them on the tray with the slit facing up. You may need to leave them in the machine longer than other candies and desserts to ensure no moisture is left in the center of the ice cream. If you don't leave them long enough, you will find a pocket of fluid left in the center.

Chocolate Mousse

The best way to freeze dry mousse-like desserts is to either spread them out on parchment paper or silicone trays to about half an inch thick or place small scoops onto the tray if you want to try a small amount. Depending on the type of chocolate mousse you freeze dry, you may find that the top of the mousse is slightly different in texture from the underneath. Still, once freeze-dried, it will have a crumbly texture, which you could sprinkle over other desserts like ice cream or eat as a chocolate snack. The best part about freeze-drying desserts is that you can take them with you if you are traveling and don't need to worry about refrigeration. They also taste divine.

Image Credit: https://www.youtube.com /@TheKingofRandom

Lemon Meringue Pie

Image Credit: www.FreezeMania.com

Judging from the freeze-drying experiment on YouTube's The King Of Random (TKOR) channel, Lemon Meringue Pie doesn't fare well in the freeze-dryer. The once gooey meringue takes on a solid consistency and becomes much like freeze-dried marshmallow fluff. The lemon curd solidifies and becomes tasteless, according to the presenters. You never know until you try, but this might be one to avoid! You can freeze the pie in a regular freezer, or this might be a dessert to make fresh as and when you want to eat it.

Cheesecake (all varieties)

The best way to freeze dry cheesecake is to cut it into smaller pieces. It has a very high fat and sugar content and might be too dense. It will work, provided the pieces aren't too large, and it will retain its flavor perfectly. However, the texture will be very different from what you'd expect. Many people describe it as a cookie that tastes like a cheesecake.

Image Credit: www.shopify.com

Oreos

Image Credits: www.etsy.com

Imagine my joy when I realized I could freeze-dry the world's favorite sandwich cookie. It's important to remember that freeze-drying will remove most of an Oreo's moisture content, but some of the oil will remain, meaning these can only safely be consumed within a few weeks. Oreos rarely make it into the freeze-dryer in our house before the kids have inhaled them, so there's never going to be an issue with consuming them before they spoil, freeze-dried or not. The real challenge will be getting them into the freeze-dryer before they are eaten.

Fudgesicles

Freeze-drying Fudgesicles is about as effective as freeze-drying marshmallows. You can freeze-dry both of them successfully, but nothing changes except they get crunchier. On their TKOR YouTube channel, Nate Bonha describes the taste as "not really pleasant" because it leaves a film on your teeth. Interestingly, fudgesicles still look frozen once they've been freeze-dried, but they are no longer cold, just crunchy. They could work better as a prop on a film set than a tasty treat, a frozen treat that won't melt!

Image Credit: www.shopify.com

Popsicles

Image Credit: www.youtube.com/TKOR

Again, Nate Bonham carried out this experiment on the TKOR channel. Only try this at home if you're willing to accept a clean-up mission. Due to the water content, you would assume that this might not be a very successful item to freeze dry, but Nate commented on its high sugar content, causing it to "expand more than almost anything else we've put in the freeze dryer." The visual effect is quite impressive, and it is an interesting experiment. Like the fudgesicle, it is confusing for the brain because it's not frozen, but the flavor is more concentrated than the popsicle in its original form, even if it is no longer juicy.

Top Ten Tips For Sweet Freeze-Drying Success

Freeze-drying candy and sweets is great fun, but without wishing to put a dampener on your experimental kitchen recipes, there are things you should consider beforehand.

1. You can freeze-dry candy that contains fruits or nuts no problem. I've had a couple of occasions where nuts and fruits went bad despite being frozen, and it spoiled the whole batch. If the fruit has already been cooked before going in the freeze dryer, it will be totally okay. Sweets such as chocolate bars with fruits and nuts in them are great to freeze-dry.

2. Check the expiry date of whatever you intend to put in the freeze dryer. Suppose you're starting on a candy freeze-drying venture. In that case, the chances are that you will buy everything brand new before you start, but resist the temptation to start rifling through the cupboards and digging out last year's Halloween gummies that you'd forgotten about. Even sweets containing preservatives with a high sugar content are not necessarily safe to eat. It's also a waste of time and energy preserving food already past its best. Throw them away and know that, now you have a freeze-dryer, you won't ever waste any food again.

3. Check the surface of your candy before you freeze-dry it. Even if it is within the expiry date, if it has a grainy or sticky surface, it has likely gone bad. A change in texture means the candy has spoiled due to temperature abuse. I am not talking about a change in texture after the freeze-drying process, as we expect this to happen. Ensure it looks normal before you put it in the freeze-dryer. If it smells strange or appears discolored, it's not worth bothering to freeze-dry it.

4. Avoid freeze-drying honey unless it is a component ingredient in something else. Honey becomes explosive when freeze-dried, and although it looks solid when it comes out, it will dissolve the second it makes contact with water or your tongue. From the various online experiments I have seen, it doesn't taste great either. It's not worth your time and effort.

5. Always make sure you separate your candy according to size and ingredients. For example, we know that caramels and toffees are likely to behave unpredictably, so make sure they are well-spaced on freezer trays and keep them away from your gummies. Once the candy has been freeze-dried, ensure you store it separately, too. You wouldn't put gummies in with Skittles or Jolly Ranchers, as you want to avoid mixing flavors or having everything stick together. Different candies have different freezing points; separating them allows a longer shelf life for your sweet treats. It also makes sense to separate them from a space point of view.

6. Ensure your freezer trays are dry before you assemble your sweets, and line them with baking parchment or silicone liners. This is particularly important when freeze-drying hard candies, as they tend to stick when the moisture is extracted.

7. Surprisingly, cheap vanilla ice cream tastes better than the posh stuff once it has been freeze-dried. This could have something to do with different flavors reacting strangely or the moisture content. Anything with a caramel content will likely bubble up and take on a crispy texture. The presenters on the TKOR YouTube channel did an experiment where they freeze-dried cheap Walmart ice cream, fancy cookie and caramel ice cream, and American gelato. While the expensive ice creams tasted better before the freeze-drying process, the Walmart brand was the clear winner afterward. The fancy ice creams tasted like freeze-dried milk/yogurt bites, which didn't go down well!

8. Where time permits, always pre-freeze your candy before freeze-drying to remove stickiness and prevent candies from welding themselves together.

9. When freeze-drying desserts with powdered sugar on the top, such as lemon bars, it's a good idea to blow the excess off before placing them in your freeze dryer. You won't be able to remove all of it, but powdered sugar has a tendency to blow around your machine during the freeze-drying process. Not only can this cause clogs, but it can also contaminate anything else you are freeze-drying in the same batch.

10. If you are freeze-drying ice cream bites, a melon baller is a perfect kitchen tool to ensure all the pieces are the same size and shape. A standard ice cream scoop is too big, and a melon baller will give you perfect bite-sized rounds to accompany whatever dessert you fancy. Having a container of boiling water on hand also helps you scoop out the ice cream easily.

I hope some of these tips will help you on your freeze-drying journey and that they have inspired you to attempt something more experimental than freeze-drying fruits and vegetables. You can do so much with your freeze-dryer. Enjoy the process, and have some fun!

Conclusion

In this comprehensive guide, we have explored what freeze-drying is and how it can improve your health, save you money, and help you prepare for an emergency situation. We've covered foods you can freeze-dry, recipes you can make at home, food storage, machine updates, cleaning and maintenance, benefits, potential pitfalls, and all parts of the process to take you from a complete beginner to a freeze-drying master.

We've discussed the three different stages of the freeze-drying process and how to rehydrate foods back to their original state, and we've looked at the importance of following food safety guidelines, how to prepare your food appropriately, and additional tips, tricks, and resources to help you stretch your food budget further when times are tough.

Hopefully, this information has given you the confidence to start your own freeze-drying journey, whether that is for your family, helping your local community, or starting your own business. Freeze-drying and preserving foods is a great lifestyle choice that is going to continue saving you money and providing you with delicious, nutritious food all-year-round for many years to come. It will help those in need by eliminating food wastage and ensuring more people have access to easy-to-prepare, nutritional, portable, and tasty food. It will help families to provide healthier, inexpensive snacks for their loved ones, and cut down on processed foods.

Now that you have everything you need, what are you waiting for? All you need to do is choose your machine, grab some tools and accessories, and get started! I'm confident you will be a seasoned pro in no time at all and your freeze-drying journey will open doors you have not even considered. The possibilities are limitless! Use this book as a stepping stone to give you inspiration for meals and snack ideas, and as a resource you can return to for guidance if you find you need further advice along the way.

If you have enjoyed this book and found it to be a valuable resource, I would be incredibly grateful if you could take the time to leave me a quick review so that I can spread the joys of the freeze-drying lifestyle far and wide.

As you turn the final page of "Freeze Drying Mastery for Beginners," we hope that you have found a wealth of knowledge that not only enlightens but also empowers. Your journey into mastering long-term food storage, saving money, reducing waste, and ensuring a well-stocked pantry is one that we have been privileged to accompany you on. We trust that this guide has been a transformative tool, helping you to embrace the art of freeze drying with confidence and ease.

We understand that in a world brimming with endless resources and guides, you chose "Freeze Drying Mastery for Beginners" to be your companion in this new endeavor. As the author of this comprehensive guide, I have poured extensive research, personal experience, and genuine passion into these pages with the singular goal of bringing real value into your kitchen and life.

As you have embarked on this journey with us, we kindly ask you to consider sharing your experience by leaving a 5-star review on Amazon. Your feedback is not just deeply appreciated; it serves a purpose larger than you might imagine. Each review is a testament to the book's impact and a beacon for fellow enthusiasts seeking to embark on a similar path. It helps to foster a community of like-minded individuals who can grow and learn from each other.

For an author, your reviews are much more than just a star rating; they are a source of encouragement and an affirmation that the work has truly resonated with its audience. Your insights give life to the pages and motivate continual growth and sharing of knowledge. It ensures that the message within "Freeze Drying Mastery for Beginners" reaches more people who, just like you, are looking to transform their approach to food preservation.

If this book has equipped you with the tools to save money through efficient food storage, if it has inspired you to reduce waste consciously, or if it has simply given you the peace of mind that comes with a secure and sustainable pantry, then a 5-star review is a powerful way to say thank you. It is the highest compliment you could offer and one that echoes far beyond a simple gesture.

Remember, your words will light the way for newcomers and provide them with the confidence that this book is a valuable and trustworthy guide. Your opinion matters immensely, not just to us, but to the community at large. It's about sharing the gift of knowledge, a gift that you now possess, thanks to your dedication and willingness to learn through "Freeze Drying Mastery for Beginners."

Please take a moment to leave your review on Amazon and share your story. How has this book impacted your approach to food storage? In what ways has it simplified your life? Your journey could be the very sign that someone else needs to take the first step towards mastery in freeze drying.

We are profoundly thankful for your support and for sharing your thoughts. Your review could be the beacon that guides others to make the life-changing decision to embrace freeze drying, ensuring their pantry is always prepared, no matter what the future holds. With gratitude and anticipation.

FREE DOWNLOAD

104 COLOR RECIPES FROM THE BOOK

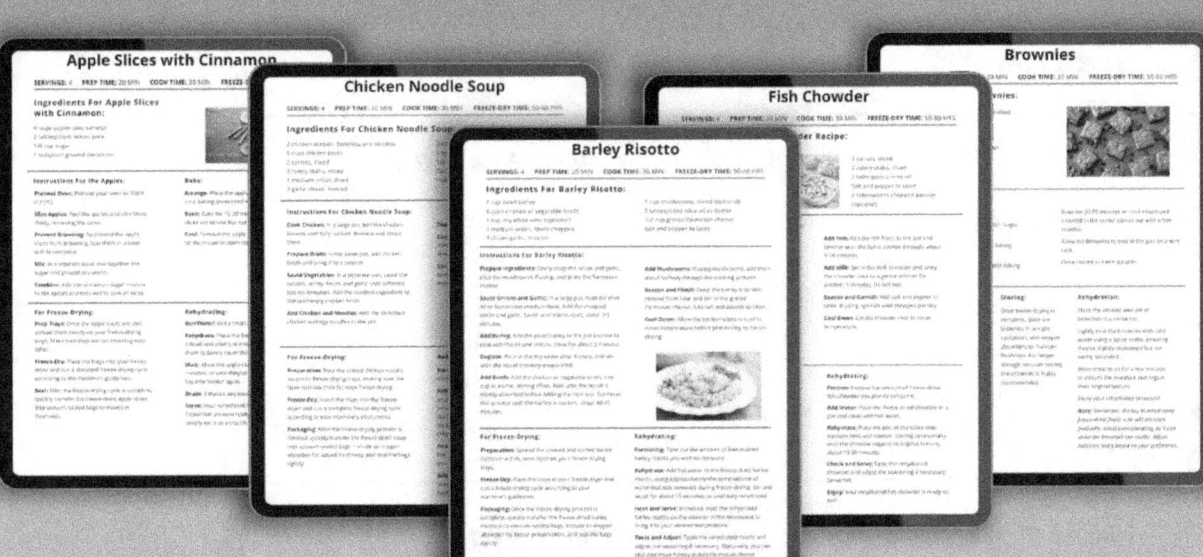

SCAN ME

GREAT FOODS TO FREEZE DRY

Fruit:
- Strawberries
- Apples
- Bananas
- Blueberries
- Raspberries
- Kiwi

Fruit:
- Peaches
- Pears
- Pineapple
- Cherries
- Grapes

Vegetables:
- Bell Peppers
- Tomatoes (may become crumbly)
- Onions
- Green Beans
- Broccoli
- Cauliflower

Vegetables:
- Carrots
- Peas
- Corn
- Zucchini
- Spinach
- Mushrooms

Meats:
- Chicken
- Pork
- Turkey
- Beef
- Fish (Like Salmon)
- Shrimp

Others:
- Coffee
- Tea
- Skim Milk
- Yogurt (in yogurt drops)
- Ice-cream

FOODS TO NEVER FREEZE DRY

High-Fat Foods:

Foods with a high-fat content don't freeze dry well because fat doesn't evaporate like water does. When these foods are freeze-dried, they can become rancid more quickly. This includes:

- Butter
- Cream cheese
- Fatty cuts of meat
- Avocato

High-Sugar Foods:

Foods that are extremely high in sugar can be problematic because the sugar can melt and create a sticky mess in the freeze-dryer. This includes:

- Jams & Jellies
- Syrups

High-Water Foods:

Some foods with a very high water content can become extremely crumbly or lose their original structure when freeze-dried. They include:

- Cucumbers
- Watermelon

Soft Foods With Little Structure:

Some foods lose their structural integrity when freeze-dried, making them unsuitable for the process. This includes:

- Soft Cheeses (Like Brie)

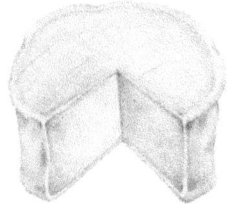

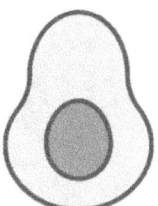

FOODS TO NEVER FREEZE DRY

Food With Strong Odor:
Freeze drying doesn't remove strong odors, and some foods can permeate your freeze dryer and potentially affect future batches. For example:
- Burian
- Fish (Like Cod)

Alcohol:
It doesn't freeze dry and could be dangerous if attempted.

Honey:
Since honey is already naturally preserved, there's no need to freeze-dry it. If attempted, it might become a hard, sugary mass.

Sodas & Carbonated Drinks:
These won't retain their carbonation and might explode in the freeze dryer.

High-Fat Foods:
High-fat foods, such as fatty meat, cream cheese, avocados, etc., will generally go rancid when you store them for long periods of time in mylar bags. They simply don't store well. If you'd like to freeze-dry them, you can totally do it, but eat them within a few days to max few weeks.

*** *It's also worth noting that while many foods can technically be freeze-dried, the result might not always meet your expectations in terms of texture, taste, or appearance. If unsure about a particular food, it might be worth doing a small test batch before freeze-drying large quantities.*

Recipes

The beautiful thing about making meals and freeze-drying them is that they are done! You don't have to cook. All the cooking is done all at the beginning, you can then freeze-dry already made meals. This way, serving them takes minutes. We have 111 recipes ready for you in our book. Flip through the pages, and create your favorite ones.

Recipe Index - 1

Meat-Based Meals:

- Pasta and Meatballs
- Beef Stroganoff
- Chicken Alfredo
- Pork-Fried Rice
- Turkey Chili

Seafood Meals:

- Salmon Patties
- Shrimp Stir-Fry
- Fish Chowder
- Tuna Casserole
- Lemon Garlic Shrimp

Pasta & Rice Meals:

- Spaghetti Bolognese
- Vegetable Lasagna
- Vegetable Risotto
- Sausage & Peppers Pasta
- Vegetable Fried Rice

Vegetarian Meals:

- Stuffed Bell Peppers
- Vegetable Stir-Fry
- Potato & Leek Soup
- Steamed Asparagus
- Roasted Brussels Sprouts

Grain-Based Meals:

- Quinoa Salad
- Barley Risotto
- Couscous with Veggies
- Polenta
- Bulgur Wheat Pilaf

Soups & Stews:

- Chicken Noodle Soup
- Beef & Vegetable Stew
- Minestrone Soup
- Corn Chowder
- Tomato Soup

International Cuisine:

- Paella
- Pad Thai
- Chana Masala
- Chicken Enchiladas
- Garlic Mashed Potatoes

Just Soups:

- Lentil Soup
- Split Pea Soup
- Clam Chowder
- Black Bean Soup
- Potato Soup

   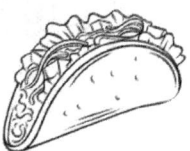

Recipe Index - 2

Breakfast Meals:

- Scrambled Eggs
- Pancakes
- Breakfast Burrito
- Chia Seed Pudding
- Mixed Berry Oatmeal

Comfort Foods:

- Mac & Cheese
- Chicken Pot Pie
- Sloppy Joes
- Creamed Spinach
- Beef & Broccoli Stir-Fry

Desserts:

- Apple Slices with Cinnamon
- Banana Bread
- Chocolate Chip Cookies
- Strawberry Shortcake
- Rice Pudding

Desserts:

- Mango Cubes
- Cheesecake Bites
- Lemon Bars
- Brownies
- Bread Putting

Desserts:

- Coconut Macaroons
- Pumpkin Pie Filling
- Peach Slices
- Maple Syrup Crystals
- Oatmeal Cookies

Snacks:

- Mixed Fruit Slices
- Hummus Pucks
- Granola Bars
- Veggie Chips
- Cheese Crisps

Snacks:

- Trail Mix
- Meat Jerky
- Rice Cakes
- Mini Pancakes
- Licorice Bites

Snacks:

- Salted Caramel Bites
- Marshmallows
- Chocolate Coconut Balls
- Chocolate Covered Bananas
- Chocolate Covered Strawberries

   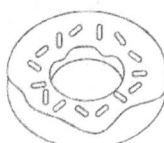

Pasta and Meatballs

SERVINGS: 4   **PREP TIME:** 20 MIN   **COOK TIME:** 30 MIN   **FREEZE-DRY TIME:** 35-45 HRS

Ingredients For Meatballs:

- 1 lb ground beef
- 1/4 cup breadcrumbs
- 1/4 cup grated Parmesan cheese
- 1 egg
- 1 clove garlic, minced
- 1/2 teaspoon salt
- 1/4 teaspoon black pepper
- 1/4 teaspoon dried oregano
- 1/4 teaspoon dried basil

Ingredients For Sauce:

- 1 (28 oz) can crushed tomatoes
- 1 small onion, finely chopped
- 2 cloves garlic, minced
- 1 tablespoon olive oil
- 1 teaspoon dried basil
- 1 teaspoon dried oregano
- Salt and pepper to taste

Additional:
8 oz Spaghetti Noodles

Instructions For Meatballs:

Preheat Oven: Preheat your oven to 400°F (200°C).

Mix Ingredients: In a large bowl, combine the ground beef, breadcrumbs, Parmesan cheese, egg, minced garlic, salt, pepper, oregano, and basil.

Form Meatballs: Using your hands, form small meatballs about 1 inch in diameter.

Bake: Place the meatballs on a baking sheet lined with parchment paper and bake for about 20-25 minutes or until fully cooked.

Instructions For Sauce:

Sauté Onions and Garlic: In a large saucepan, heat the olive oil over medium heat. Add the chopped onion and minced garlic, sautéing until translucent.

Add Tomatoes and Spices: Add the crushed tomatoes, basil, oregano, salt, and pepper to the saucepan.

Simmer: Allow the sauce to simmer on low heat for at least 30 minutes, stirring occasionally. You can let it simmer longer for more flavor if desired.

Instructions For Spaghetti:

Boil Water: In a large pot, bring water to a boil. Add a pinch of salt.

Cook Spaghetti: Add the spaghetti noodles to the boiling water and cook according to package directions until al dente.

Drain: Once cooked, drain the spaghetti and set aside.

Combine:

Mix Meatballs with Sauce: After the meatballs are baked, add them to the sauce and let them simmer together for another 10 minutes.

Combine with Spaghetti: Optionally, you can mix the spaghetti into the sauce and meatballs to combine or leave them separate based on your preference for freeze-drying.

For Freeze-Drying:

Cool Down: Let all components (meatballs, sauce, and spaghetti) cool to room temperature.

Preparation: Remove as much fat as possible from the sauce, as fats don't freeze-dry well.

Place on Trays: Spread the spaghetti, meatballs, and sauce separately on the freeze-dryer trays. Make sure they are in a single layer and not touching for even drying.

Freeze-Dry: Follow your freeze-dryer's instructions for freeze-drying cooked meals.

Rehydrating:

Hot Water: To rehydrate, add hot water to the freeze-dried meatballs, sauce, and spaghetti. Let sit for several minutes, stirring occasionally, until fully rehydrated.

Beef Stroganoff

SERVINGS: 4   **PREP TIME:** 50 MIN   **COOK TIME:** 50 MIN   **FREEZE-DRY TIME:** 25-35 HRS

Ingredients For Beef & Marinade:

1 lb beef sirloin or round steak, thinly sliced into strips
1 tablespoon olive oil
Salt and pepper to taste

Additional:
8 oz Egg Noodles

Ingredients For Sauce:

1 cup mushrooms, sliced
1 medium onion, chopped
1 clove garlic, minced
1 cup beef broth
1 cup sour cream
2 tablespoons all-purpose flour
2 tablespoons butter
Salt and pepper to taste

Instructions For Beef:

Preparation: Marinate the beef strips in olive oil, salt, and pepper for at least 30 minutes.

Cook Beef: In a skillet over medium-high heat, cook the beef strips until browned but not fully cooked. Set aside.

Instructions For Sauce:

Cook Vegetables: In the same skillet, melt the butter and sauté the mushrooms, onion, and garlic until the vegetables are tender.

Make Sauce: Add flour to the skillet, stirring well to combine with the vegetables. Slowly add the beef broth, stirring constantly until the sauce thickens.

Add Sour Cream: Lower the heat and stir in the sour cream. Do not let it boil as the sour cream may curdle. Season with salt and pepper.

Combine with Beef: Add the partially cooked beef back into the sauce and simmer for an additional 5-10 minutes.

Instructions For Egg Noodles:

Boil Water: In a large pot, bring water to a boil. Add a pinch of salt. Cook Noodles: Add the egg noodles and cook according to package directions until al dente.

Drain: Once cooked, drain the noodles and set aside.

Combine:

Mix Together: Optionally, combine the beef stroganoff sauce with the cooked egg noodles or keep them separate based on your preference for freeze-drying.

For Freeze-Drying:

Cool Down: Let all components (beef stroganoff sauce and noodles) cool down to room temperature.

Preparation: Remove as much fat as possible from the sauce, as fats don't freeze-dry well.

Place on Trays: Spread the beef stroganoff sauce and noodles separately on the freeze-dryer trays. Ensure they are in a single layer and not touching for even drying.

Freeze-Dry: Follow your freeze-dryer's instructions for freeze-drying cooked meals.

Rehydrating:

Hot Water: To rehydrate, add hot water to the freeze-dried beef stroganoff and noodles. Let sit for several minutes, stirring occasionally, until fully rehydrated.

Chicken Alfredo

SERVINGS: 4   **PREP TIME:** 20 MIN   **COOK TIME:** 30 MIN   **FREEZE-DRY TIME:** 30-40 HRS

Ingredients For Chicken:

1 lb boneless, skinless chicken breasts, cut into bite-sized pieces
1 tablespoon olive oil
Salt and pepper to taste

Additional:
8 oz Fettuccine Pasta

Ingredients For Sauce:

1 cup milk
1 tablespoon unsalted butter
1 cup grated Parmesan cheese
1 clove garlic, minced
Salt and pepper to taste

Instructions For Chicken:

Season Chicken: Sprinkle the chicken pieces with salt and pepper.

Cook Chicken: In a skillet over medium-high heat, add olive oil and cook the chicken until it's browned but not fully cooked through. Set aside.

Note:
Butter content has been reduced so that the food won't go rancid.

Instructions For Sauce:

Prepare Sauce: In a saucepan over medium heat, melt the butter. Add the minced garlic and sauté until fragrant.

Add Cream: Pour in the heavy cream and bring it to a gentle simmer.

Add Cheese: Lower the heat and whisk in the grated Parmesan cheese until the sauce is smooth. Season with salt and pepper to taste.

Combine with Chicken: Add the partially cooked chicken to the sauce and let it simmer for another 5-10 minutes.

Instructions For Fettuccine:

Boil Water: In a large pot, bring water to a boil. Add a pinch of salt.

Cook Pasta: Add fettuccine and cook according to package directions until al dente.

Drain: Once cooked, drain the pasta and set aside.

Combine:

Mix Together: You can either combine the Alfredo sauce and chicken with the cooked fettuccine or keep them separate, depending on your preference for freeze-drying.

For Freeze-Drying:

Cool Down: Let all components (chicken Alfredo) cool down to room temperature.

Preparation: Remove as much fat as possible from the Alfredo sauce, as fats don't freeze-dry well.

Place on Trays: Spread the chicken Alfredo separately on the freeze-dryer trays. Ensure they are in a single layer and not touching for even drying.

Freeze-Dry: Follow your freeze-dryer's instructions for freeze-drying cooked meals.

Rehydrating:

Hot Water: To rehydrate, add hot water to the freeze-dried chicken Alfredo. Let sit for several minutes, stirring occasionally, until fully rehydrated.

Pork Fried Rice

SERVINGS: 4   **PREP TIME:** 45 MIN   **COOK TIME:** 20 MIN   **FREEZE-DRY TIME:** 25-35 HRS

Ingredients For Pork:

1 lb pork tenderloin, cut into small pieces
1 tablespoon soy sauce
1 tablespoon olive oil
Salt and pepper to taste

Ingredients For Rice:

3 cups cooked jasmine rice (best if left overnight in the fridge)
1 cup frozen peas and carrots mix
1 small onion, finely chopped
2 cloves garlic, minced
2 eggs, beaten
3 tablespoons soy sauce
1 tablespoon sesame oil
2 green onions, chopped (for garnish)
Salt and pepper to taste
1 tablespoon olive oil for stir-frying

Instructions For Pork:

Marinate Pork: In a bowl, mix the pork pieces with soy sauce, olive oil, salt, and pepper. Let it marinate for at least 30 minutes.

Cook Pork: In a large skillet or wok, heat olive oil over medium-high heat. Add the pork and cook until browned but not fully cooked through. Remove and set aside.

Instructions For Rice:

Prepare Skillet: In the same skillet or wok, add a tablespoon of olive oil and heat it over medium-high heat.

Sauté Vegetables: Add the chopped onion and minced garlic to the skillet. Sauté until they are translucent.

Add Peas and Carrots: Stir in the frozen peas and carrots mix, cooking until they are warmed through.

Cook Eggs: Push the vegetables to the side of the skillet and pour in the beaten eggs. Scramble them and mix with the vegetables.

Instructions For Rice:

Combine with Rice: Add the cooked rice to the skillet. Use a spatula to break up any clumps.

Season: Pour in soy sauce and sesame oil, and add salt and pepper to taste. Mix well to combine all the ingredients.

Add Pork: Incorporate the partially cooked pork back into the skillet and stir until well combined.

Combine:

Garnish: Optionally, sprinkle chopped green onions over the top for garnish.

For Freeze-Drying:

Cool Down: Allow the pork fried rice to cool down to room temperature.

Preparation: Spread the pork fried rice in a thin, even layer on your freeze-dryer trays.

Freeze-Dry: Follow your freeze-dryer's guidelines to freeze-dry the meal.

Rehydrating:

Hot Water: To rehydrate, add a small amount of hot water to the freeze-dried pork fried rice. Let sit for several minutes, stirring occasionally, until fully rehydrated.

Turkey Chili

SERVINGS: 4   **PREP TIME:** 20 MIN   **COOK TIME:** 30 MIN   **FREEZE-DRY TIME:** 25-35 HRS

Ingredients For Turkey:

1 lb ground turkey
1 tablespoon olive oil
Salt and pepper to taste

Ingredients For Chili:

1 can (15 oz) kidney beans, drained and rinsed
1 can (15 oz) black beans, drained and rinsed
1 can (15 oz) diced tomatoes
1 small onion, chopped
2 cloves garlic, minced
1 bell pepper, diced
2 cups chicken broth
2 tablespoons chili powder
1 teaspoon ground cumin
1 teaspoon paprika
Salt and pepper to taste

Instructions For Turkey:

Cook Turkey: In a large pot, heat olive oil over medium-high heat. Add the ground turkey, season with salt and pepper, and cook until browned. Break up the meat as it cooks.

Instructions For Chili:

Add Veggies: Add the chopped onion, minced garlic, and diced bell pepper to the pot. Sauté for 3-5 minutes until the vegetables are softened.

Spice It Up: Add the chili powder, ground cumin, and paprika to the pot. Stir to combine.

Add Liquids and Beans: Add the chicken broth and canned diced tomatoes (with their juice) into the pot. Stir in the kidney and black beans.

Instructions For Chili:

Simmer: Bring the mixture to a boil, then reduce heat and let it simmer for about 30-40 minutes. This allows the flavors to meld together. Could you add salt and pepper to taste?

Check Consistency: If the chili is too thick, you can add a little more chicken broth to reach your desired consistency.

Combine:

Garnish: Optionally, sprinkle chopped green onions over the top for garnish.

For Freeze-Drying:

Cool Down: Let the turkey chili cool down to room temperature.

Preparation: Since fats don't freeze-dry well, try to skim off as much surface fat as possible.

Place on Trays: Spread the turkey chili in a thin, even layer on the freeze-dryer trays. Freeze-Dry: Follow the guidelines provided by your freeze-dryer to freeze-dry the meal.

Rehydrating:

Hot Water: To rehydrate, add hot water to the freeze-dried turkey chili. Let sit for several minutes, stirring occasionally, until fully rehydrated.

Shepherd's Pie

SERVINGS: 4   **PREP TIME:** 20 MIN   **COOK TIME:** 30 MIN   **FREEZE-DRY TIME:** 35-45 HRS

Ingredients For Meat Filling:

1 lb ground lamb or beef
1 tablespoon olive oil
1 medium onion, chopped
2 cloves garlic, minced
1 cup frozen mixed vegetables (like peas, carrots, and corn)
2 tablespoons tomato paste

Ingredients For Mashed Potatoes:

1 cup beef or chicken broth
1 teaspoon Worcestershire sauce
Salt and pepper to taste
4 large potatoes, peeled and cut into chunks
1/2 cup milk
2 tablespoons butter
Salt and pepper to taste

Instructions For Meat Filling:

Cook Meat: In a skillet over medium-high heat, add olive oil. Add the ground meat, season with salt and pepper, and cook until browned. Break the meat apart as it cooks.

Add Veggies: Add the chopped onion and minced garlic to the skillet. Sauté until the onion becomes translucent.

Add Frozen Veggies: Stir in the frozen mixed vegetables.

Season: Add the tomato paste, broth, and Worcestershire sauce. Stir to combine.

Simmer: Lower the heat and let the mixture simmer for 10-15 minutes, allowing the flavors to meld together.

Instructions For Mashed Potatoes:

Boil Potatoes: In a large pot, add the potato chunks and enough water to cover them. Bring to a boil and cook until the potatoes are tender.

Mash: Drain the potatoes and place them back into the pot. Add milk, butter, salt, and pepper. Mash until smooth.

Combine:

Assemble: In a baking dish, spread the meat mixture evenly at the bottom. Layer the mashed potatoes on top.

Bake: Preheat your oven to 400°F (200°C) and bake for 20-25 minutes or until the top is golden brown.

For Freeze-Drying:

Cool Down: Let the Shepherd's Pie cool down to room temperature.

Preparation: Cut the Shepherd's Pie into individual portions for easier freeze-drying.

Place on Trays: Arrange the portions on the freeze-dryer trays, ensuring they don't touch for even drying.

Freeze-Dry: Follow your freeze-dryer's guidelines to freeze-dry the meal.

Rehydrating:

Hot Water: To rehydrate, add hot water to the freeze-dried Shepherd's Pie. Let sit for several minutes, stirring occasionally, until fully rehydrated.

Meatloaf

SERVINGS: 4   **PREP TIME:** 20 MIN   **COOK TIME:** 30 MIN   **FREEZE-DRY TIME:** 35-45 HRS

Ingredients For Meatloaf:

- 1.5 lbs ground beef
- 1 cup breadcrumbs
- 1 onion, finely chopped
- 1 egg, beaten
- 3/4 cup milk
- 1/4 cup ketchup
- 2 tablespoons Worcestershire sauce
- 1 teaspoon salt
- 1/2 teaspoon pepper
- 1/2 teaspoon garlic powder

Instructions For Meatloaf:

Preheat Oven: Preheat your oven to 375°F (190°C).

Mix Ingredients: In a large mixing bowl, combine the ground beef, breadcrumbs, chopped onion, beaten egg, milk, ketchup, Worcestershire sauce, salt, pepper, and garlic powder.

Form Loaf: Take the meat mixture and shape it into a loaf. Place it in a baking dish or on a lined baking tray.

Bake: Bake for 45-55 minutes or until the internal temperature reaches 160°F (71°C).

Cool Down: Remove the meatloaf from the oven and let it cool down to room temperature.

For Freeze-Drying:

Slice Meatloaf: Once the meatloaf has cooled down to room temperature, slice it into portions that will fit in your freeze-drying trays.

Place on Trays: Place the meatloaf slices on your freeze-dryer trays. Make sure the pieces are not touching to allow for even freeze-drying.

Freeze-Dry: Follow the guidelines provided by your specific freeze-drying machine. Generally, it will take between 20-40 hours for the meatloaf to be completely freeze-dried, depending on the machine and slice thickness.

Storage: Once the freeze-drying cycle is complete, store the freeze-dried meatloaf in a vacuum-sealed bag with oxygen absorbers. Keep it in a cool, dark place until you're ready to consume it.

Rehydrating:

Portion: Take out the amount of freeze-dried meatloaf you'd like to eat.

Add Water: Place the meatloaf in a bowl and add hot water until it is just covered.

Rehydrate: Allow the meatloaf to sit in the hot water for 20-30 minutes, checking and stirring occasionally to see if it has regained its original texture.

Heat and Serve: For a hotter meal, you can microwave the rehydrated meatloaf for a couple of minutes or place it in a hot oven for about 5-10 minutes.

Enjoy: Your rehydrated meatloaf is ready to be enjoyed!

Chicken Curry

SERVINGS: 4   **PREP TIME:** 20 MIN   **COOK TIME:** 30 MIN   **FREEZE-DRY TIME:** 25-35 HRS

Ingredients For Chicken Curry:

- 1.5 lbs chicken breasts or thighs, cut into cubes
- 2 tablespoons vegetable oil
- 1 large onion, finely chopped
- 3 cloves garlic, minced
- 1-inch piece of ginger, minced
- 2 tablespoons curry powder
- 1 teaspoon ground cumin
- 1 teaspoon ground coriander
- 1/2 teaspoon turmeric
- 1 can (13.5 oz) coconut milk
- 1 cup chicken broth
- Salt and pepper to taste
- Fresh cilantro for garnish (optional)

Instructions For Chicken Curry:

Preparation: Cut the chicken into cubes, chop the onions, and mince the garlic and ginger.

Cook Chicken: Heat vegetable oil in a large skillet over medium heat. Add the chicken cubes and cook until they are no longer pink in the center. Remove the chicken and set it aside.

Sauté Vegetables: In the same skillet, add more oil if needed, then sauté the chopped onion, garlic, and ginger until the onion is translucent.

Add Spices: Add curry powder, ground cumin, ground coriander, and turmeric to the sautéed onion mixture. Stir well to combine.

Combine and Cook: Return the cooked chicken to the skillet. Add the coconut milk and chicken broth. Stir well.

Simmer: Let the curry simmer on low heat for about 20-25 minutes to allow the flavors to meld together. Season with salt and pepper to taste.

Cool Down: Once the curry is done, allow it to cool down to room temperature.

For Freeze-Drying:

Portioning: Once the chicken curry has cooled, portion it into amounts that will fit into your freeze-drying trays.

Place on Trays: Evenly spread the portions on your freeze-drying trays. Make sure the pieces of chicken and sauce are not overlapping for even freeze-drying.

Freeze-Dry: Follow your freeze-drier's instructions to begin the freeze-drying process. This typically takes 20-40 hours, depending on the machine and the quantity of food.

Storage: After freeze-drying is complete, quickly transfer the chicken curry into vacuum-sealed bags with oxygen absorbers. Store in a cool, dark place.

Rehydrating:

Portion: Take out the amount of freeze-dried chicken curry you plan to consume.

Add Water: In a bowl, cover the freeze-dried chicken curry with hot water.

Rehydrate: Let it sit for about 20-30 minutes, stirring occasionally, to allow the food to regain its original texture.

Heat and Serve: If you wish to heat it further, you can microwave or stove-heat the rehydrated curry for a few minutes.

Garnish and Enjoy: Garnish with fresh cilantro if desired and your chicken curry is ready to be served.

Beef Tacos

SERVINGS: 4   **PREP TIME:** 20 MIN   **COOK TIME:** 30 MIN   **FREEZE-DRY TIME:** 25-35 HRS

Ingredients For Beef Tacos:

- 1.5 lbs ground beef
- 1 small onion, finely chopped
- 2 cloves garlic, minced
- 1 packet taco seasoning
- 2/3 cup water
- 8 small corn or flour tortillas
- 1 cup shredded cheddar cheese (optional)
- Toppings: lettuce, tomatoes, sour cream, etc. (for serving)

Instructions For Beef Tacos:

Brown Beef: In a large skillet over medium heat, add the ground beef and cook until no longer pink, breaking it up as you go.

Add Aromatics: Add the chopped onion and minced garlic to the skillet and cook until the onion becomes translucent.

Season: Add the taco seasoning and water to the beef mixture. Stir well and simmer for about 5 minutes, allowing the flavors to blend.

Assemble: Once the meat is cooked and seasoned, you can optionally assemble some tacos by adding a portion of the meat to a tortilla and topping with a bit of shredded cheese.

Cool Down: Allow the meat mixture to cool to room temperature.

For Freeze-Drying:

Portioning: Once the beef taco meat has cooled down, portion it into amounts that will fit into your freeze-drying trays. Do not add any fresh toppings like lettuce, tomatoes, or sour cream at this stage, as they do not freeze-dry well.

Place on Trays: Spread the portions on your freeze-drying trays, ensuring they are not overlapping.

Freeze-Dry: Follow your specific freeze-drying machine's instructions. The process generally takes between 20-40 hours depending on the machine and the quantity of the food.

Storage: Once the freeze-drying cycle is complete, quickly transfer the beef taco meat into vacuum-sealed bags with oxygen absorbers. Store in a cool, dark place.

Rehydrating:

Portion: Remove the amount of freeze-dried beef taco meat you plan to consume.

Add Water: Place the freeze-dried meat in a bowl and cover it with hot water.

Rehydrate: Allow the meat to sit for 15-20 minutes, stirring occasionally, to rehydrate.

Heat and Serve: Optionally, heat the rehydrated meat in a skillet over medium heat for a couple of minutes or microwave it.

Assemble Tacos: Place the rehydrated meat in tortillas and add fresh toppings like lettuce, tomatoes, and sour cream as desired.

Enjoy: Your rehydrated beef tacos are ready to eat!

Salmon Patties

SERVINGS: 4   **PREP TIME:** 20 MIN   **COOK TIME:** 30 MIN   **FREEZE-DRY TIME:** 20-30 HRS

Ingredients For Salmon Patties:

- 1 can (14-16 oz) of salmon, drained and flaked
- 1 small onion, finely chopped
- 1 egg, beaten
- 1 cup breadcrumbs
- 1/2 teaspoon salt
- 1/4 teaspoon black pepper
- 1/4 teaspoon garlic powder
- 2 tablespoons chopped parsley (optional)
- 2 tablespoons olive oil for frying

Instructions For Salmon Patties:

Preparation: Drain the can of salmon and remove any bones and skin. Flake the salmon into a mixing bowl.

Mix Ingredients: Add the finely chopped onion, beaten egg, breadcrumbs, salt, pepper, garlic powder, and optional parsley to the flaked salmon. Mix until well combined.

Form Patties: Using your hands, shape the mixture into small patties, about 2-3 inches in diameter.

Cook Patties: Heat olive oil in a large skillet over medium heat. Cook the salmon patties for about 3-4 minutes per side or until they are golden brown.

Cool Down: Remove the patties from the skillet and let them cool to room temperature.

For Freeze-Drying:

Prepare for Freeze-Drying: Once the salmon patties have cooled to room temperature, arrange them in a single layer on your freeze-drying trays.

Freeze-Dry: Place the trays in the freeze-dryer and follow the machine's instructions for freeze-drying. The time required will vary depending on your machine, but expect it to take between 20-40 hours.

Storage: After freeze-drying is complete, remove the salmon patties and place them in vacuum-sealed bags with oxygen absorbers. Store these in a cool, dark place.

Rehydrating:

Portion: Take out the number of freeze-dried salmon patties you plan to eat.

Add Water: Place the freeze-dried salmon patties in a bowl and add enough hot water to cover them.

Rehydrate: Allow the salmon patties to sit in the hot water for 15-20 minutes, checking occasionally to see if they have regained their original texture.

Heat and Serve: For a hotter meal, you can heat the rehydrated salmon patties in a skillet for a couple of minutes on each side or microwave them for 1-2 minutes.

Enjoy: Your rehydrated salmon patties are ready to eat!

Shrimp Stir-Fry

SERVINGS: 4   **PREP TIME:** 20 MIN   **COOK TIME:** 30 MIN   **FREEZE-DRY TIME:** 25-35 HRS

Ingredients For Shrimp Stir-Fry:

1 lb shrimp, peeled and deveined
4 cups mixed vegetables (e.g., bell peppers, broccoli, carrots)
3 tablespoons olive oil
2 cloves garlic, minced
1 teaspoon ginger, grated
1/4 cup soy sauce
1 tablespoon oyster sauce (optional)
1 tablespoon cornstarch
1/4 cup water

Instructions For Shrimp Stir-Fry:

Prepare Ingredients: Peel and devein the shrimp. Cut the vegetables into bite-sized pieces.

Make Sauce: In a small bowl, mix the soy sauce, oyster sauce (if using), cornstarch, and water. Set aside.

Cook Shrimp: Heat 1 tablespoon of olive oil in a wok or large skillet over medium-high heat. Add the shrimp and cook until pink, about 2-3 minutes per side. Remove from the pan and set aside.

Sauté Vegetables: In the same wok, add the remaining olive oil. Sauté the garlic and ginger until fragrant. Add the mixed vegetables and stir-fry until tender but still crisp, around 5-7 minutes.

Combine and Cook: Return the cooked shrimp to the wok. Pour in the sauce mixture. Stir well to combine and cook for another 2-3 minutes.

Cool Down: Let the stir-fry cool to room temperature.

For Freeze-Drying:

Prepare for Freeze-Drying: Once the shrimp stir-fry has cooled down, spread it evenly on your freeze-drying trays. Make sure the shrimp and vegetables are in a single layer and not overlapping.

Freeze-Dry: Place the trays in the freeze-dryer and follow your machine's instructions. The process generally takes between 20-40 hours.

Storage: Once the freeze-drying cycle is complete, quickly transfer the shrimp stir-fry into vacuum-sealed bags with oxygen absorbers. Store in a cool, dark place.

Rehydrating:

Portion: Remove the amount of freeze-dried shrimp stir-fry you plan to consume.

Add Water: Place the freeze-dried food in a bowl and cover it with hot water.

Rehydrate: Allow it to sit for about 15-20 minutes, stirring occasionally, until it regains its original texture.

Heat and Serve: Optionally, heat the rehydrated shrimp stir-fry in a skillet over medium heat for a couple of minutes, or microwave it for 1-2 minutes.

Enjoy: Your rehydrated shrimp stir-fry is ready to eat!

Fish Chowder

SERVINGS: 4   **PREP TIME:** 20 MIN   **COOK TIME:** 30 MIN   **FREEZE-DRY TIME:** 20-30 HRS

Ingredients For Fish Chowder Recipe:

- 1 lb white fish fillets (e.g., cod, halibut)
- 4 cups vegetable or fish broth
- 2 cups whole milk or cream
- 3 medium potatoes, diced
- 1 onion, finely chopped
- 2 cloves garlic, minced
- 2 carrots, diced
- 2 celery stalks, diced
- 2 tablespoons olive oil
- Salt and pepper to taste
- 2 tablespoons chopped parsley (optional)

Instructions For Fish Chowder Recipe:

Prepare Ingredients: Chop the vegetables and fish fillets into bite-sized pieces.

Sauté Vegetables: Heat olive oil in a large pot over medium heat. Add the onions and garlic, and sauté until translucent.

Add Vegetables: Add the diced carrots and celery to the pot and cook for another 5 minutes.

Add Broth and Potatoes: Pour in the vegetable or fish broth and add the diced potatoes. Bring to a simmer and cook until the potatoes are tender, about 15-20 minutes.

Add Fish: Add the fish fillets to the pot and simmer until the fish is cooked through, about 5-10 minutes.

Add Milk: Stir in the milk or cream and bring the chowder back to a gentle simmer for another 5 minutes. Do not boil.

Season and Garnish: Add salt and pepper to taste. If using, sprinkle with chopped parsley.

Cool Down: Let the chowder cool to room temperature.

For Freeze-Drying:

Preparation: Once the chowder has cooled down, portion it into amounts that will fit into your freeze-drying trays.

Spread on Trays: Pour the portions onto your freeze-drying trays. Make sure to spread it evenly.

Freeze-Dry: Place the trays in the freeze-dryer and follow the machine's instructions. The process usually takes between 20-40 hours, depending on your machine.

Storage: After freeze-drying is complete, transfer the chowder into vacuum-sealed bags with oxygen absorbers. Store in a cool, dark place.

Rehydrating:

Portion: Remove the amount of freeze-dried fish chowder you plan to consume.

Add Water: Place the freeze-dried chowder in a pot and cover with hot water.

Rehydrate: Place the pot on the stove over medium heat and simmer, stirring occasionally, until the chowder regains its original texture, about 15-20 minutes.

Check and Serve: Taste the rehydrated chowder and adjust the seasoning if necessary. Serve hot.

Enjoy: Your rehydrated fish chowder is ready to eat!

Tuna Casserole

SERVINGS: 4   **PREP TIME:** 20 MIN   **COOK TIME:** 30 MIN   **FREEZE-DRY TIME:** 25-35 HRS

Ingredients For Tuna Casserole:

- 1 can (10-12 oz) of tuna, drained and flaked
- 2 cups cooked pasta (e.g., macaroni or fusilli)
- 1 can (10.5 oz) condensed cream of mushroom soup
- 1 cup shredded cheddar cheese
- 1 cup frozen peas
- 1/2 cup milk
- 1 small onion, finely chopped
- 1/2 teaspoon salt
- 1/4 teaspoon black pepper
- 1 cup breadcrumbs (optional, for topping)

Instructions For Tuna Casserole:

Preheat Oven: Preheat your oven to 375°F (190°C).

Prepare Ingredients: Cook the pasta according to package directions and drain. Chop the onion and drain the tuna.

Mix Ingredients: In a large mixing bowl, combine the drained tuna, cooked pasta, condensed cream of mushroom soup, shredded cheddar cheese, frozen peas, milk, chopped onion, salt, and pepper.

Assemble Casserole: Pour the mixture into a greased 9x13-inch baking dish.

Optional Topping: If you like, sprinkle breadcrumbs over the top for added crunch.

Bake: Place the dish in the preheated oven and bake for 25-30 minutes, or until the top is golden and the casserole is bubbling.

Cool Down: Remove the casserole from the oven and allow it to cool to room temperature

For Freeze-Drying:

Prepare for Freeze-Drying: Once the casserole has cooled to room temperature, cut it into serving-sized portions that will fit on your freeze-drying trays.

Freeze-Dry: Arrange the portions on your freeze-drying trays in a single layer. Place the trays in the freeze-dryer and follow your machine's instructions. The process generally takes between 20-40 hours.

Storage: After the freeze-drying cycle is complete, quickly transfer the casserole portions to vacuum-sealed bags with oxygen absorbers. Store these bags in a cool, dark place.

Rehydrating:

Portion: Remove the amount of freeze-dried tuna casserole you plan to consume.

Add Water: Place the freeze-dried casserole in a bowl and cover it with hot water.

Rehydrate: Allow the casserole to sit in the hot water for 15-20 minutes, stirring occasionally, until it regains its original texture.

Heat and Serve: For a hot meal, you can heat the rehydrated casserole in a microwave for 1-2 minutes or in an oven at 350°F (175°C) for 5-10 minutes.

Enjoy: Your rehydrated tuna casserole is ready to eat!

Spaghetti Bolognese

SERVINGS: 4   **PREP TIME:** 20 MIN   **COOK TIME:** 30 MIN   **FREEZE-DRY TIME:** 25-35 HRS

Ingredients For Spaghetti Bolognese:

- 8 oz spaghetti
- 1 lb ground beef
- 1 large onion, finely chopped
- 3 cloves garlic, minced
- 1 can (14 oz) crushed tomatoes
- 1 can (6 oz) tomato paste
- 1 teaspoon dried basil
- 1 teaspoon dried oregano
- Salt and pepper to taste
- 2 tablespoons olive oil
- Grated Parmesan cheese (optional, for serving)

Instructions For Spaghetti Bolognese:

Prepare Pasta: Cook the spaghetti according to package instructions until al dente. Drain and set aside.

Sauté Onion and Garlic: In a large skillet, heat the olive oil over medium heat. Add the chopped onion and minced garlic, and sauté until translucent.

Cook Ground Beef: Add the ground beef to the skillet. Cook, breaking it up into small pieces, until it is no longer pink.

Add Tomatoes and Seasonings: Pour in the crushed tomatoes and tomato paste. Stir well to combine. Add the basil, oregano, salt, and pepper.

Simmer: Reduce the heat to low, cover the skillet, and let it simmer for 20-30 minutes to allow the flavors to meld.

Combine with Pasta: Once the sauce is ready, you can either mix it with the spaghetti or keep them separate for freeze-drying.

Cool Down: Allow the spaghetti and meat sauce to cool to room temperature.

For Freeze-Drying:

Prepare for Freeze-Drying: Spread the cooked spaghetti and meat sauce separately on freeze-drying trays. Make sure they are in a single layer to facilitate the freeze-drying process.

Freeze-Dry: Place the trays into your freeze-dryer and follow the manufacturer's guidelines. This process may take between 20-40 hours.

Storage: Once the freeze-drying cycle is complete, quickly transfer the spaghetti and meat sauce into separate vacuum-sealed bags, add an oxygen absorber to each, and seal.

Rehydrating:

Portion: Take out the amount of freeze-dried spaghetti and meat sauce you plan to eat.

Add Water: For the spaghetti, cover it with hot water in a bowl and allow it to sit for about 10-15 minutes to rehydrate. For the meat sauce, add hot water gradually while stirring, until it reaches your desired consistency.

Heat and Serve: After rehydration, you can heat both the spaghetti and meat sauce together in a pot over medium heat or in a microwave for 1-2 minutes.

Optional: Sprinkle-grated Parmesan cheese on top before serving.

Enjoy: Your rehydrated Spaghetti Bolognese is ready to eat!

Vegetable Lasagna

SERVINGS: 4 **PREP TIME:** 20 MIN **COOK TIME:** 30 MIN **FREEZE-DRY TIME:** 20-30 HRS

Ingredients For Vegetable Lasagna:

- 9 lasagna noodles
- 1 tablespoon olive oil
- 1 small onion, chopped
- 3 cloves garlic, minced
- 1 zucchini, diced
- 1 red bell pepper, diced
- 1 cup mushrooms, sliced
- 1 (15-ounce) container ricotta cheese
- 2 cups shredded mozzarella cheese
- 1 cup grated Parmesan cheese
- 1 (24-ounce) jar marinara sauce
- 1 teaspoon dried oregano
- Salt and pepper to taste

Instructions For Vegetable Lasagna:

Preheat Oven: Preheat your oven to 375°F (190°C).

Cook Noodles: Boil lasagna noodles according to package instructions until al dente. Drain and set aside.

Prepare Vegetables: Heat olive oil in a skillet over medium heat. Add onions and garlic and sauté until translucent. Add zucchini, red bell pepper, and mushrooms; cook until soft. Season with salt and pepper.

Make Cheese Layer: In a separate bowl, mix ricotta cheese with 1 cup of mozzarella cheese, half of the grated Parmesan cheese, and dried oregano.

Assemble Lasagna: In a 9x13-inch baking dish, spread a layer of marinara sauce. Place a layer of noodles on top, followed by half of the vegetable mixture, and half of the cheese mixture. Repeat layers.

Top and Bake: Finish with a layer of noodles, the remaining marinara sauce, and sprinkle with the remaining mozzarella and Parmesan cheese. Cover with foil and bake for 25-30 minutes. Uncover and bake for an additional 10 minutes or until cheese is melted and bubbly.

Cool Down: Once out of the oven, allow the lasagna to cool to room temperature.

For Freeze-Drying:

Portion for Freeze-Drying: Cut the cooled lasagna into serving-sized pieces that fit onto your freeze-drying trays.

Place on Trays: Arrange the lasagna pieces on the freeze-drying trays in a single layer.

Freeze-Dry: Load the trays into your freeze-dryer and run the freeze-drying cycle according to the manufacturer's guidelines. This usually takes between 20-40 hours.

Storage: Once the freeze-drying is complete, quickly transfer the lasagna pieces into vacuum-sealed bags with oxygen absorbers. Seal and store in a cool, dark place.

Rehydrating:

Portion: Take out a serving of freeze-dried vegetable lasagna.

Rehydrate with Water: Place the lasagna in a dish and cover it with hot water. Allow it to sit for 15-20 minutes.

Heat and Serve: Drain off any excess water. You can heat the rehydrated lasagna in a microwave for 1-2 minutes or in an oven at 350°F (175°C) for 5-10 minutes.

Enjoy: Your rehydrated vegetable lasagna is now ready to eat!

Risotto

SERVINGS: 4   **PREP TIME:** 20 MIN   **COOK TIME:** 30 MIN   **FREEZE-DRY TIME:** 25-35 HRS

Ingredients For Risotto:

1 1/2 cups Arborio rice
4 cups chicken or vegetable broth
1 cup dry white wine (optional)
1 small onion, finely chopped
2 cloves garlic, minced
2 tablespoons olive oil

1/2 cup grated Parmesan cheese
Salt and pepper to taste

Optional:
1 cup of your choice of vegetables (like mushrooms, peas, or asparagus)

Instructions For Risotto:

Prepare Broth: Keep the broth warm over low heat in a separate pot.

Sauté Onion and Garlic: Heat olive oil in a large skillet over medium heat. Add the chopped onion and garlic, and sauté until translucent.

Cook Rice: Add the Arborio rice to the skillet, stirring to coat it with oil. Sauté for 2-3 minutes.

Add Wine: If using wine, add it now and let it evaporate fully before proceeding.

Cook with Broth: Begin adding the warm broth, one ladle at a time, stirring frequently. Wait until the liquid is almost fully absorbed before adding the next ladle. Continue until the rice is cooked to al dente and has a creamy texture. This takes about 18-20 minutes.

Add Vegetables: If you're using additional vegetables, fold them in during the last 5 minutes of cooking.

Finish with Cheese: Remove from heat, stir in the grated Parmesan cheese, and season with salt and pepper.

Cool Down: Allow the risotto to cool to room temperature.

For Freeze-Drying:

Prepare for Freeze-Drying: Spread the cooled risotto on freeze-drying trays in a single, even layer.

Freeze-Dry: Place the trays in your freeze-dryer and follow your machine's instructions for freeze-drying. This process will take between 20-40 hours depending on your machine and the quantity of food.

Storage: Once the freeze-drying process is complete, transfer the risotto into vacuum-sealed bags, add an oxygen absorber, and seal tightly.

Rehydrating:

Portion: Measure out the amount of freeze-dried risotto you want to rehydrate.

Add Water: Cover the freeze-dried risotto with hot water in a bowl. Allow it to sit for about 15-20 minutes, stirring occasionally to help it rehydrate evenly.

Heat and Serve: Once rehydrated, you can heat the risotto in a pot over medium heat for a few minutes, or in a microwave for 1-2 minutes.

Optional: You can garnish with additional grated Parmesan cheese before serving.

Enjoy: Your rehydrated risotto is ready to eat!

Sausage and Peppers Pasta

SERVINGS: 4   **PREP TIME:** 20 MIN   **COOK TIME:** 30 MIN   **FREEZE-DRY TIME:** 35-45 HRS

Ingredients For Sausage and Peppers Pasta:

- 12 oz pasta (penne, rigatoni, or your choice)
- 1 lb sausage (Italian, spicy, or your preference), sliced into rounds
- 2 bell peppers (any color), sliced
- 1 onion, sliced
- 3 cloves garlic, minced
- 1 (24-ounce) jar of marinara sauce
- 2 tablespoons olive oil
- Salt and pepper to taste
- 1 cup shredded mozzarella cheese (optional)
- Fresh basil or parsley for garnish (optional)

Instructions For Sausage and Peppers Pasta:

Cook Pasta: Cook the pasta according to package instructions until al dente. Drain and set aside.

Prepare Sausage and Vegetables: Heat olive oil in a large skillet over medium heat. Add the sausage slices and cook until browned. Remove from the skillet and set aside.

Cook Peppers and Onions: In the same skillet, add sliced bell peppers, onions, and minced garlic. Cook until the vegetables are soft. Season with salt and pepper.

Combine Ingredients: Return the cooked sausage to the skillet. Add the marinara sauce and stir to combine.

Mix with Pasta: Add the cooked pasta to the skillet and mix well. If using cheese, sprinkle it on top and let it melt slightly.

Cool Down: Allow the dish to cool down to room temperature before proceeding to freeze-dry.

For Freeze-Drying:

Prepare for Freeze-Drying: Once cooled, spread the pasta dish in a single layer on your freeze-drying trays. The thinner the layer, the more efficiently it will freeze-dry.

Freeze-Dry: Place the trays into your freeze-dryer and start the freeze-drying cycle according to your machine's manual. This process usually takes 20-40 hours.

Packaging: After the freeze-drying cycle is complete, quickly transfer the pasta into vacuum-sealed bags, add an oxygen absorber, and seal the bags tightly.

Rehydrating:

Portion Out: Take the amount of freeze-dried Sausage and Peppers Pasta that you'd like to rehydrate.

Rehydrate: Place the freeze-dried food in a bowl and cover it with hot water. Allow it to sit for 15-20 minutes, stirring occasionally to make sure it rehydrates evenly.

Heat and Serve: Drain any excess water. You can reheat the pasta in a pot on the stovetop over medium heat for a few minutes or in the microwave for 1-2 minutes.

Garnish and Enjoy: Add fresh basil or parsley if desired, and your rehydrated Sausage and Peppers Pasta is ready to eat!

Stuffed Bell Peppers

SERVINGS: 4   **PREP TIME:** 20 MIN   **COOK TIME:** 30 MIN   **FREEZE-DRY TIME:** 25-35 HRS

Ingredients For Stuffed Bell Peppers:

- 6 large bell peppers (any color)
- 1 lb ground beef or turkey
- 1 cup cooked rice
- 1 (14.5 oz) can of diced tomatoes, drained
- 1 onion, finely chopped
- 3 cloves garlic, minced
- 1 tsp ground cumin
- 1 tsp paprika
- Salt and pepper to taste
- 1 1/2 cups shredded cheese (cheddar, mozzarella, or your choice)
- 2 tbsp olive oil
- Fresh parsley or cilantro for garnish (optional)

Instructions For Stuffed Bell Peppers:

Preheat Oven: Preheat your oven to 375°F (190°C).

Prepare Bell Peppers: Cut the tops off the bell peppers and remove the seeds and membranes. Set aside.

Cook the Filling: Heat olive oil in a skillet over medium heat. Add chopped onions and garlic and sauté until translucent. Add ground meat and cook until browned. Drain any excess fat.

Add Spices and Tomatoes: Stir in the cumin, paprika, salt, and pepper. Add the drained diced tomatoes and let the mixture simmer for a few minutes.

Combine with Rice: Remove from heat and stir in the cooked rice.

Stuff the Peppers: Evenly fill the prepared bell peppers with the meat and rice mixture. Place them in a baking dish.

Bake: Cover the baking dish with aluminum foil and bake for 35 minutes. Remove the foil, top each pepper with shredded cheese, and bake for an additional 10 minutes.

Cool Down: Allow the stuffed peppers to cool to room temperature before freeze-drying.

For Freeze-Drying:

Prepare for Freeze-Drying: Cut the cooked stuffed peppers in half to expose more surface area for freeze-drying. Place them on your freeze-drying trays.

Freeze-Dry: Place the trays into your freeze-dryer and start the freeze-drying cycle according to your machine's manual.

Packaging: Once the cycle is complete, promptly transfer the stuffed peppers into vacuum-sealed bags, add an oxygen absorber, and seal tightly.

Rehydrating:

Portion Out: Take the amount of freeze-dried stuffed peppers you'd like to eat.

Rehydrate: Put the freeze-dried stuffed peppers in a bowl and cover them with hot water. Let them sit for about 20-30 minutes, checking occasionally to see if they have rehydrated fully.

Heat and Serve: Drain any excess water and heat the stuffed peppers either in a microwave for 2-3 minutes or in a covered pan over medium heat.

Garnish and Enjoy: Top with fresh parsley or cilantro if desired.

Vegetable Stir-Fry

SERVINGS: 4   **PREP TIME:** 20 MIN   **COOK TIME:** 30 MIN   **FREEZE-DRY TIME:** 25-35 HRS

Ingredients For Vegetable Stir-Fry:

- 4 cups mixed vegetables (broccoli, bell peppers, carrots, snap peas, etc.)
- 1 onion, sliced
- 3 cloves garlic, minced
- 1 thumb-sized piece of ginger, minced
- 2 tablespoons soy sauce
- 1 tablespoon oyster sauce (optional)
- 1 tablespoon cornstarch
- 2 tablespoons vegetable oil
- Salt and pepper to taste
- Cooked rice for serving (optional)

Instructions For Vegetable Stir-Fry:

Preparation: Wash and chop all vegetables into bite-sized pieces.

Make Sauce: In a small bowl, combine soy sauce, oyster sauce, and cornstarch. Stir until smooth and set aside.

Cook Vegetables: Heat vegetable oil in a large wok or skillet over medium-high heat. Add the minced garlic and ginger, sauté for about 30 seconds.

Add Vegetables: Add the onion first and sauté until translucent. Then add the rest of the vegetables, cooking until they are tender but still crisp.

Add Sauce: Pour the sauce mixture into the wok and stir well to coat the vegetables.

Season: Add salt and pepper to taste.

Cool Down: Allow the stir-fry to cool down to room temperature before moving on to freeze-drying.

For Freeze-Drying:

Preparation: Spread the cooled vegetable stir-fry evenly on your freeze-drying trays.

Freeze-Dry: Place the trays into your freeze-dryer and run the freeze-drying cycle according to the manufacturer's instructions.

Packaging: Once the freeze-drying cycle is complete, quickly transfer the vegetable stir-fry into vacuum-sealed bags, add an oxygen absorber, and seal the bags tightly.

Rehydrating:

Portioning: Take the amount of freeze-dried vegetable stir-fry you wish to eat.

Rehydrate: Place the freeze-dried food in a bowl and add hot water until the vegetables are submerged. Allow them to sit for 10-15 minutes or until fully rehydrated.

Drain and Heat: Drain off any excess water, then heat the stir-fry on a skillet for a few minutes to bring it back to your desired temperature. Alternatively, you can microwave it for 1-2 minutes.

Serve and Enjoy: Serve the rehydrated vegetable stir-fry over rice if desired.

Potato and Leek Soup

SERVINGS: 4   **PREP TIME:** 20 MIN   **COOK TIME:** 30 MIN   **FREEZE-DRY TIME:** 35-45 HRS

Ingredients For Potato and Leek Soup:

4 large potatoes, peeled and diced
3 leeks, white and light green parts only, sliced and washed
1 medium onion, diced
3 cloves garlic, minced

4 cups chicken or vegetable broth
2 cups water
1 cup heavy cream (optional)
2 tablespoons olive oil or butter
Salt and pepper to taste

Instructions For Potato and Leek Soup:

Preparation: Prepare the leeks by cutting off the dark green parts and discarding them. Cut the white and light green parts into thin slices.

Sauté Vegetables: In a large pot, heat the olive oil or butter over medium heat. Add the leeks, onion, and garlic. Sauté until they become translucent.

Add Potatoes: Add the diced potatoes to the pot and stir to combine.

Add Liquid: Pour in the chicken or vegetable broth and water. Bring the mixture to a boil, then reduce heat to low and simmer until the potatoes are tender, about 20-25 minutes.

Season: Add salt and pepper to taste. Optionally, you can add the heavy cream for a richer texture.

Blend: Use an immersion blender to purée the soup to your desired consistency. If you don't have an immersion blender, you can use a regular blender, blending the soup in batches and returning it to the pot.

Cool Down: Allow the soup to cool to room temperature.

For Freeze-Drying:

Preparation: Pour the cooled soup into shallow trays. Make sure not to fill the trays to the brim to allow for expansion.

Freeze-Dry: Place the trays in your freeze-dryer and run the freeze-drying cycle according to your machine's guidelines.

Packaging: Once the freeze-drying process is complete, quickly transfer the freeze-dried soup into vacuum-sealed bags, include an oxygen absorber, and seal tightly.

Rehydrating:

Portioning: Take the amount of freeze-dried potato and leek soup you wish to eat.

Rehydrate: Add hot water to the freeze-dried soup, using about the same volume of water that was removed during freeze-drying. Stir and let it sit for approximately 15 minutes, or until fully rehydrated.

Heat and Serve: Once rehydrated, you may need to heat the soup over the stove or in a microwave to bring it to your desired temperature.

Taste and Adjust: Taste the rehydrated soup and adjust the seasoning if needed.

Quinoa Salad

SERVINGS: 4 **PREP TIME:** 20 MIN **COOK TIME:** 30 MIN **FREEZE-DRY TIME:** 20-30 HRS

Ingredients For Quinoa Salad:

1 cup quinoa
2 cups water for cooking quinoa
1 cup cherry tomatoes, halved
1 cucumber, diced
1 red bell pepper, diced

1/2 cup red onion, finely chopped
1/2 cup parsley, chopped
1/4 cup olive oil
2 tablespoons lemon juice
Salt and pepper to taste

Instructions For Quinoa Salad:

Cook Quinoa: In a medium-sized pot, bring 2 cups of water to a boil. Add a pinch of salt and the quinoa. Reduce heat to low, cover, and simmer for about 15 minutes, or until quinoa is cooked and water is absorbed. Fluff with a fork and let it cool to room temperature.

Prepare Vegetables: While the quinoa is cooking, wash and chop all the vegetables and parsley.

Mix Salad: In a large mixing bowl, combine the cooked quinoa, cherry tomatoes, cucumber, red bell pepper, and red onion.

Make Dressing: In a small bowl, whisk together olive oil, lemon juice, salt, and pepper.

Combine: Pour the dressing over the quinoa and vegetable mixture. Add the chopped parsley and mix well.

Cool Down: Allow the quinoa salad to cool down to room temperature.

For Freeze-Drying:

Preparation: Spread the quinoa salad in a thin, even layer on your freeze-drying trays. Try to avoid clumps for even freeze-drying.

Freeze-Dry: Insert the trays into your freeze-dryer and initiate the freeze-drying process according to the manufacturer's instructions.

Packaging: Once freeze-drying is complete, promptly transfer the quinoa salad into vacuum-sealed bags, add an oxygen absorber, and seal tightly.

Rehydrating:

Portioning: Take out the amount of freeze-dried quinoa salad you wish to consume.

Rehydrate: Add cold or room-temperature water to the freeze-dried quinoa salad, using approximately the same volume of water as was originally removed during freeze-drying. Allow the salad to sit for about 10-15 minutes or until fully rehydrated.

Drain: If there's any excess water, drain it off.

Serve and Enjoy: Taste and adjust seasoning if necessary. Your rehydrated quinoa salad is now ready to be enjoyed!

Barley Risotto

SERVINGS: 4   **PREP TIME:** 20 MIN   **COOK TIME:** 30 MIN   **FREEZE-DRY TIME:** 35-45 HRS

Ingredients For Barley Risotto:

- 1 cup pearl barley
- 4 cups chicken or vegetable broth
- 1 cup dry white wine (optional)
- 1 medium onion, finely chopped
- 3 cloves garlic, minced
- 1 cup mushrooms, sliced (optional)
- 2 tablespoons olive oil or butter
- 1/2 cup grated Parmesan cheese
- Salt and pepper to taste

Instructions For Barley Risotto:

Prepare Ingredients: Finely chop the onion and garlic, slice the mushrooms if using, and grate the Parmesan cheese.

Sauté Onions and Garlic: In a large pot, heat the olive oil or butter over medium heat. Add the chopped onion and garlic. Sauté until translucent, about 3-5 minutes.

Add Barley: Add the pearl barley to the pot and stir to coat with the oil and onions. Cook for about 2 minutes.

Deglaze: Pour in the dry white wine if using, and stir until the liquid is mostly evaporated.

Add Broth: Add the chicken or vegetable broth, one cup at a time, stirring often. Wait until the liquid is mostly absorbed before adding the next cup. Continue this process until the barley is cooked, about 40-45 minutes.

Add Mushrooms: If using mushrooms, add them about halfway through the cooking process.

Season and Finish: Once the barley is tender, remove from heat and stir in the grated Parmesan cheese. Add salt and pepper to taste.

Cool Down: Allow the barley risotto to cool to room temperature before proceeding to freeze-drying.

For Freeze-Drying:

Preparation: Spread the cooked and cooled barley risotto in a thin, even layer on your freeze-drying trays.

Freeze-Dry: Place the trays in your freeze-dryer and run a freeze-drying cycle according to your machine's guidelines.

Packaging: Once the freeze-drying process is complete, quickly transfer the freeze-dried barley risotto into vacuum-sealed bags. Include an oxygen absorber for better preservation, and seal the bags tightly.

Rehydrating:

Portioning: Take out the amount of freeze-dried barley risotto you wish to consume.

Rehydrate: Add hot water to the freeze-dried barley risotto, using approximately the same volume of water that was removed during freeze-drying. Stir and let sit for about 15 minutes, or until fully rehydrated.

Heat and Serve: If needed, heat the rehydrated barley risotto on the stove or in the microwave to bring it to your desired temperature.

Taste and Adjust: Taste the rehydrated risotto and adjust the seasoning if necessary. Optionally, you can also add more freshly grated Parmesan cheese before serving.

Couscous with Veggies

SERVINGS: 4   **PREP TIME:** 20 MIN   **COOK TIME:** 30 MIN   **FREEZE-DRY TIME:** 25-35 HRS

Ingredients For Couscous with Veggies:

- 1 cup couscous
- 1 1/4 cup water for cooking couscous
- 2 tablespoons olive oil
- 1 medium onion, diced
- 1 bell pepper, diced
- 1 zucchini, diced
- 1 carrot, diced
- 2 cloves garlic, minced
- 1 teaspoon salt (or to taste)
- 1/2 teaspoon black pepper (or to taste)
- Optional: Fresh herbs like parsley or cilantro for garnish

Instructions For Couscous with Veggies:

Cook Couscous: Bring 1 1/4 cup of water to a boil. Add a pinch of salt and the couscous. Remove from heat, cover, and let sit for 5 minutes. Fluff with a fork and set aside.

Prepare Veggies: While the couscous is cooking, dice the onion, bell pepper, zucchini, and carrot. Mince the garlic.

Sauté Veggies: Heat olive oil in a pan over medium heat. Add the onions and garlic and sauté until translucent. Add the bell pepper, zucchini, and carrot. Sauté until the veggies are tender.

Combine and Season: Add the cooked couscous to the pan with the veggies. Stir well to combine. Add salt and pepper to taste. If using, chop and add fresh herbs for garnish.

Cool Down: Allow the mixture to cool down to room temperature before proceeding to the freeze-drying step.

For Freeze-Drying:

Preparation: Spread the couscous and veggie mixture in a thin, even layer on your freeze-drying trays. The thinner the layer, the more effectively it will freeze-dry.

Freeze-Dry: Place the trays into your freeze-dryer and run a freeze-drying cycle according to your machine's instructions.

Packaging: Once the freeze-drying process is complete, promptly transfer the freeze-dried mixture into vacuum-sealed bags. Add an oxygen absorber for better preservation and seal the bags tightly.

Rehydrating:

Portioning: Take out the amount of freeze-dried couscous and veggies you wish to consume.

Rehydrate: Add hot water to the freeze-dried mixture, using approximately the same volume of water as the food. Allow it to sit for about 10-15 minutes or until fully rehydrated.

Drain and Heat: If there's any excess water, drain it off. Heat the rehydrated food in a microwave or on a stovetop until it reaches your desired temperature.

Serve and Enjoy: Your rehydrated couscous with veggies is now ready to be enjoyed!

Italian Polenta

SERVINGS: 4   **PREP TIME:** 20 MIN   **COOK TIME:** 30 MIN   **FREEZE-DRY TIME:** 30-40 HRS

Ingredients For Polenta:

1 cup cornmeal (coarse or fine, as you prefer)
4 cups water
2 tablespoons olive oil or butter
Salt to taste
Optional: grated Parmesan cheese, herbs for garnish

Instructions For Polenta:

Boil Water: In a large pot, bring 4 cups of water to a boil.

Season Water: Add a generous pinch of salt to the boiling water.

Add Cornmeal: While continuously whisking, gradually add the cornmeal into the boiling water to prevent lumps from forming.

Reduce Heat and Cook: Reduce the heat to low, and cook the cornmeal, stirring frequently to prevent sticking or burning. This will take about 20-30 minutes depending on the coarseness of the cornmeal.

Add Oil or Butter: Once the polenta is cooked and smooth, stir in the olive oil or butter for extra richness.

Season and Garnish: Season with additional salt to taste. Add grated Parmesan cheese and herbs if desired.

Cool Down: Allow the cooked polenta to cool down to room temperature.

For Freeze-Drying:

Preparation: Spread the cooked and cooled polenta in a thin, even layer on the freeze-drying trays.

Freeze-Dry: Load the trays into your freeze-dryer and operate it according to your machine's instructions.

Packaging: After the freeze-drying process is complete, quickly transfer the freeze-dried polenta into vacuum-sealed bags. Add an oxygen absorber for better preservation, and seal the bags tightly.

Rehydrating:

Portioning: Take out the amount of freeze-dried polenta you wish to consume.

Rehydrate: Add hot water to the freeze-dried polenta, using roughly the same volume of water that was removed during freeze-drying. Allow it to sit for about 15-20 minutes, or until fully rehydrated.

Heat and Serve: If necessary, heat the rehydrated polenta on the stove or in the microwave until it reaches your desired temperature.

Adjust Seasoning: Taste the rehydrated polenta and adjust the seasoning if necessary. You can also add more freshly grated Parmesan cheese or herbs before serving.

Chicken Noodle Soup

SERVINGS: 4　　**PREP TIME:** 20 MIN　　**COOK TIME:** 30 MIN　　**FREEZE-DRY TIME:** 35-45 HRS

Ingredients For Chicken Noodle Soup:

- 2 chicken breasts, boneless and skinless
- 8 cups chicken broth
- 2 carrots, sliced
- 2 celery stalks, sliced
- 1 medium onion, diced
- 3 garlic cloves, minced
- 2 cups egg noodles
- 1 teaspoon salt (or to taste)
- 1/2 teaspoon black pepper (or to taste)
- Optional: herbs like parsley, thyme, or rosemary for garnish

Instructions For Chicken Noodle Soup:

Cook Chicken: In a large pot, boil the chicken breasts until fully cooked. Remove and shred them.

Prepare Broth: In the same pot, add chicken broth and bring it to a simmer.

Sauté Vegetables: In a separate pan, sauté the carrots, celery, onion, and garlic until softened but not browned. Add the sautéed vegetables to the simmering chicken broth.

Add Chicken and Noodles: Add the shredded chicken and egg noodles to the pot.

Season: Add salt and pepper to taste.

Cook: Allow the soup to simmer for about 10-15 minutes, or until the noodles and vegetables are tender.

Cool Down: Let the soup cool down to room temperature before moving on to the freeze-drying step.

For Freeze-Drying:

Preparation: Pour the cooled chicken noodle soup into freeze-drying trays, making sure the layer isn't too thick for even freeze-drying.

Freeze-Dry: Insert the trays into the freeze-dryer and run a complete freeze-drying cycle according to your machine's instructions.

Packaging: After the freeze-drying process is finished, quickly transfer the freeze-dried soup into vacuum-sealed bags. Include an oxygen absorber for added freshness, and seal the bags tightly.

Rehydrating:

Portioning: Take out the amount of freeze-dried chicken noodle soup you wish to consume.

Rehydrate: Add hot water to the freeze-dried soup. Generally, you'll need to add the same volume of water that was initially removed during the freeze-drying process. Allow it to sit for about 15-20 minutes, or until fully rehydrated.

Heat and Serve: Heat the rehydrated soup on the stove or in the microwave until it reaches your desired temperature.

Adjust Seasoning and Garnish: Check for seasoning and adjust as needed. Garnish with herbs like parsley, if desired.

Minestrone Soup

SERVINGS: 4   **PREP TIME:** 20 MIN   **COOK TIME:** 30 MIN   **FREEZE-DRY TIME:** 35-45 HRS

Ingredients For Minestrone Soup:

- 1 tablespoon olive oil
- 1 medium onion, chopped
- 2 cloves garlic, minced
- 3 carrots, sliced
- 3 celery stalks, sliced
- 1 zucchini, chopped
- 1 can (15 oz) kidney beans, drained and rinsed
- 1 can (14.5 oz) diced tomatoes, undrained
- 4 cups vegetable broth
- 1 teaspoon dried basil
- 1 teaspoon dried oregano
- Salt and pepper to taste
- Optional: 1 cup small pasta like elbow macaroni or ditalini (cook separately)

Instructions For Minestrone Soup:

Sauté the Base: Heat the olive oil in a large pot over medium heat. Add the chopped onions and minced garlic. Sauté until the onions are translucent.

Add Vegetables: Add the carrots and celery to the pot and sauté for about 5 minutes, or until they begin to soften.

More Vegetables: Add the zucchini and sauté for an additional 2 minutes.

Beans and Tomatoes: Add the kidney beans and diced tomatoes (with their juice) to the pot.

Add Broth and Season: Pour in the vegetable broth and add the basil, oregano, salt, and pepper.

Simmer: Bring the soup to a simmer and let it cook for about 20 minutes, allowing the flavors to meld together. If you're using pasta, cook it separately according to package instructions and add it just before serving or freeze-drying.

Cool Down: Let the soup cool to room temperature before moving on to the freeze-drying step.

For Freeze-Drying:

Preparation: Distribute the cooled soup evenly among the freeze-drying trays, taking care not to overfill.

Freeze-Dry: Place the trays in your freeze-dryer and run a complete freeze-drying cycle based on your machine's instructions.

Packaging: Once the freeze-drying process is complete, transfer the freeze-dried Minestrone into vacuum-sealed bags. Include an oxygen absorber for a longer shelf life and seal the bags.

Rehydrating:

Portioning: Remove the amount of freeze-dried Minestrone soup you plan to consume.

Rehydrate: Add hot water to the freeze-dried soup, roughly using the same volume of water that was initially removed during freeze-drying. Let it sit for about 15-20 minutes or until fully rehydrated.

Heat and Serve: Transfer the rehydrated soup to a pot and heat it on the stove until it reaches your desired temperature. If it seems too thick, you can add a little extra water.

Adjust Seasoning: Taste the soup and adjust salt and other seasonings as necessary.

Corn Chowder

SERVINGS: 4　　**PREP TIME:** 20 MIN　　**COOK TIME:** 30 MIN　　**FREEZE-DRY TIME:** 35-45 HRS

Ingredients For Corn Chowder:

2 tablespoons butter
1 medium onion, diced
2 cloves garlic, minced
1 red bell pepper, diced
4 cups chicken or vegetable broth
4 cups frozen or fresh corn kernels
2 large potatoes, peeled and diced
1 cup heavy cream (or milk for a lighter version)
Salt and pepper to taste
Optional: Chopped chives for garnish

Instructions For Corn Chowder:

Sauté the Base: Melt the butter in a large pot over medium heat. Add the onions and garlic, sautéing until translucent, about 5 minutes.

Add Vegetables: Add the diced red bell pepper, corn, and potatoes to the pot.

Add Broth: Pour in the chicken or vegetable broth.

Season: Add salt and pepper to taste.

Simmer: Bring the mixture to a boil, then reduce the heat and let it simmer for about 20-25 minutes, until the potatoes are tender.

Add Cream: Stir in the heavy cream and cook for an additional 5 minutes.

Cool Down: Allow the soup to cool to room temperature.

For Freeze-Drying:

Preparation: Once the soup is cool, distribute it evenly across your freeze-drying trays.

Freeze-Dry: Place the trays in your freeze-dryer and run a complete freeze-drying cycle based on your machine's instructions.

Packaging: After freeze-drying is complete, quickly transfer the freeze-dried Corn Chowder into vacuum-sealed bags. Include an oxygen absorber for extended shelf life and seal the bags.

Rehydrating:

Portioning: Remove the amount of freeze-dried Corn Chowder you intend to consume.

Rehydrate: Add hot water to the freeze-dried Corn Chowder, approximately using the same volume of water that was initially removed during freeze-drying. Let it sit for about 15-20 minutes or until fully rehydrated.

Heat and Serve: Transfer the rehydrated chowder to a pot and warm it on the stove until it reaches your desired temperature. If the chowder seems too thick, add a bit of extra water.

Adjust Seasoning: Taste the chowder and adjust the seasoning, adding more salt or pepper as necessary.

Garnish: Optionally, garnish with chopped chives before serving.

Paella

SERVINGS: 4   **PREP TIME:** 20 MIN   **COOK TIME:** 30 MIN   **FREEZE-DRY TIME:** 30-40 HRS

Ingredients For Paella:

- 1.5 cups Arborio rice or short-grain rice
- 2 tablespoons olive oil
- 1 medium onion, finely chopped
- 3 cloves garlic, minced
- 1 red bell pepper, sliced
- 1 green bell pepper, sliced
- 1 teaspoon paprika
- 1 teaspoon saffron threads (or saffron powder)
- 1 teaspoon salt
- 1/2 teaspoon black pepper
- 4 cups chicken broth
- 2 chicken breasts, cut into bite-sized pieces
- 1 cup frozen peas
- 1 lemon, cut into wedges for garnish

Instructions For Paella:

Preheat the Oven: Preheat your oven to 375°F (190°C).

Prepare the Pan: In a large, oven-safe pan, heat olive oil over medium heat.

Sauté Vegetables: Add the chopped onions, garlic, and bell peppers to the pan. Sauté until the onions are translucent.

Add Chicken: Add the chicken pieces to the pan and cook until they are browned on all sides.

Add Rice: Stir in the rice, making sure it's well-coated with the oil and veggies.

Add Spices: Sprinkle the paprika, saffron, salt, and black pepper over the rice and stir well.

Add Broth: Pour the chicken broth into the pan and stir once to combine everything.

Oven Time: Carefully transfer the pan to the preheated oven. Bake for 30-35 minutes or until the rice is cooked and the liquid is mostly absorbed.

Add Peas: Remove the pan from the oven, stir in the frozen peas, and return it to the oven for another 5 minutes.

Cool and Check: Remove the pan from the oven and let it cool to room temperature.

For Freeze-Drying:

Portion: Divide the paella into portion-sized amounts. This will make it easier to freeze-dry and rehydrate later.

Pre-Freeze: Before freeze-drying, freeze the portions in a standard freezer for at least 4 hours to speed up the freeze-drying process.

Load the Freeze Dryer: Place the frozen paella portions in the trays of your freeze dryer.

Freeze-Drying: Run the freeze dryer according to the manufacturer's guidelines.

Packaging: Once the cycle is complete, remove the paella and immediately seal it in vacuum-sealed bags with oxygen absorbers to ensure long-term storage.

Rehydrating:

Water Prep: Boil enough water to cover the freeze-dried paella.

Rehydrate: Place the freeze-dried paella in a bowl and pour the boiling water over it. Cover and let it sit for 20-30 minutes, stirring occasionally.

Check and Serve: Ensure that the food has fully rehydrated. Adjust salt and pepper to taste and serve with lemon wedges.

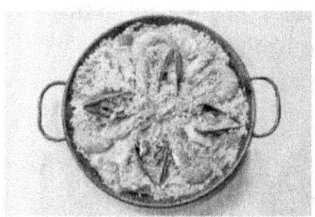

Pad Thai

SERVINGS: 4   **PREP TIME:** 20 MIN   **COOK TIME:** 30 MIN   **FREEZE-DRY TIME:** 30-40 HRS

Ingredients For Pad Thai:

8 oz rice noodles
2 tablespoons vegetable oil
1 small onion, thinly sliced
2 cloves garlic, minced
1 cup bean sprouts
1 cup diced tofu or cooked chicken
2 eggs, lightly beaten
1/4 cup crushed peanuts
Lime wedges, for garnish

Ingredients For Sauce:

3 tablespoons fish sauce
1 tablespoon tamarind paste
1 tablespoon sugar

Instructions For Pad Thai:

Prepare the Sauce: In a small bowl, mix together fish sauce, tamarind paste, and sugar. Set aside.

Cook the Noodles: Follow package instructions to cook the rice noodles until al dente. Drain and set aside.

Prepare the Pan: Heat vegetable oil in a large skillet or wok over medium heat.

Sauté Aromatics: Add the onions and garlic to the pan and sauté until the onions are translucent.

Add Protein: Incorporate your choice of tofu or chicken to the pan, cooking until browned.

Add Eggs: Push the contents of the pan to one side and pour the lightly beaten eggs into the empty half of the pan. Allow the eggs to set for a few seconds before scrambling them. Mix the scrambled eggs with the rest of the ingredients in the pan.

Combine: Add the cooked noodles and prepared sauce to the pan. Toss everything together to combine well.

Final Touches: Add bean sprouts and give the mixture another toss. Turn off the heat.

Garnish and Serve: Sprinkle crushed peanuts over the top, and serve with lime wedges on the side

For Freeze-Drying:

Cool Down: Allow the Pad Thai to cool down to room temperature.

Portion: Divide the Pad Thai into portions suitable for your freeze-dryer trays.

Freeze: Pre-freeze the Pad Thai in your freezer for about 1-2 hours.

Freeze-Drying: Place the pre-frozen Pad Thai into your freeze-dryer and run it through a standard freeze-drying cycle.

Packaging: Once the cycle is complete, quickly remove the Pad Thai and place it in airtight, vacuum-sealed bags to maintain freshness.

Rehydrating:

Add Water: To rehydrate, add warm water to the freeze-dried Pad Thai. The amount of water will vary, so add gradually and stir until the Pad Thai reaches your desired consistency.

Let Sit: Allow the mixture to sit for 10-15 minutes, stirring occasionally.

Heat and Serve: Optionally, you can heat the rehydrated Pad Thai in a skillet over low heat for a few minutes before serving.

Garnish: Add fresh lime wedges and extra crushed peanuts if desired.

Chana Masala

SERVINGS: 4   **PREP TIME:** 20 MIN   **COOK TIME:** 30 MIN   **FREEZE-DRY TIME:** 35-45 HRS

Ingredients For Chana Masala:

- 2 cans (15.5 oz each) chickpeas, drained and rinsed
- 1 large onion, chopped
- 2 cloves garlic, minced
- 1-inch ginger, minced
- 1 can (14 oz) diced tomatoes
- 2 tablespoons vegetable oil
- 1 teaspoon cumin seeds
- 1 teaspoon mustard seeds
- 2 teaspoons garam masala
- 1 teaspoon turmeric powder
- 1 teaspoon chili powder
- Salt to taste
- Fresh cilantro leaves for garnish
- Lemon wedges for serving

Instructions For Chana Masala:

Heat Oil: Heat vegetable oil in a large pan over medium heat.

Sauté Seeds: Add cumin seeds and mustard seeds to the hot oil. Wait for them to sizzle and pop.

Add Aromatics: Add chopped onions, garlic, and ginger to the pan. Sauté until the onions turn translucent.

Add Spices: Stir in garam masala, turmeric powder, and chili powder.

Tomatoes: Add the diced tomatoes to the pan, including their juice. Cook for 5-7 minutes until tomatoes are softened.

Chickpeas: Add the drained and rinsed chickpeas to the pan.

Simmer: Mix well and let the mixture simmer for 10-15 minutes so that the flavors meld together. Add salt to taste.

Garnish: Sprinkle fresh cilantro leaves over the Chana Masala before removing it from heat.

For Freeze-Drying:

Cool Down: Allow the Chana Masala to cool to room temperature.

Portion: Portion out the Chana Masala onto freeze-dryer trays in a single layer for even drying.

Pre-Freeze: Pre-freeze the trays in your freezer for about 1-2 hours.

Freeze-Drying: Place the pre-frozen trays in your freeze-dryer and run them through a standard freeze-drying cycle.

Packaging: Once the freeze-drying cycle is complete, quickly transfer the freeze-dried Chana Masala into vacuum-sealed, airtight bags.

Rehydrating:

Add Water: To rehydrate, add hot water to the freeze-dried Chana Masala. Use about the same amount of water as the volume of the food you're rehydrating.

Stir and Wait: Stir the mixture well and let it sit for 15-20 minutes to absorb the water.

Heat: Optionally, heat the rehydrated Chana Masala on the stove over low heat for 3-5 minutes.

Garnish and Serve: Add fresh cilantro and a squeeze of lemon before serving.

Chicken Enchiladas

SERVINGS: 4   **PREP TIME:** 20 MIN   **COOK TIME:** 30 MIN   **FREEZE-DRY TIME:** 35-45 HRS

Ingredients For Chicken Enchiladas:

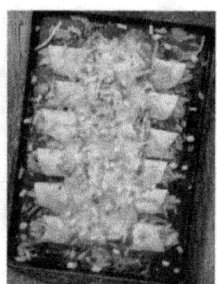

2 cups cooked and shredded chicken
2 cups shredded cheese (Cheddar or Mexican blend)
1 can (10 oz) enchilada sauce
8 small flour tortillas
1 small onion, diced
1 clove garlic, minced
1 tablespoon vegetable oil
Salt to taste
Optional: Sour cream, avocado slices, and cilantro for serving

Instructions For Chicken Enchiladas:

Preheat Oven: Preheat your oven to 350°F (175°C).

Prepare Filling: In a skillet, heat the vegetable oil over medium heat. Add the diced onion and minced garlic and sauté until translucent. Add the shredded chicken, mix well, and set aside.

Assemble Enchiladas: Place a generous spoonful of the chicken mixture in the center of each flour tortilla. Sprinkle some cheese over it. Roll up the tortilla around the filling and place it seam-side down in a baking dish.

Add Sauce and Cheese: Pour the enchilada sauce over the rolled tortillas in the baking dish. Sprinkle the remaining cheese on top.

Bake: Cover the baking dish with aluminum foil and bake for 20 minutes. Remove the foil and bake for an additional 5 minutes, or until the cheese is melted and bubbly.

Cool: Allow the enchiladas to cool to room temperature.

For Freeze-Drying:

Portion: Cut the enchiladas into serving-size pieces and place them on freeze-dryer trays in a single layer.

Pre-Freeze: Pre-freeze the trays in your freezer for 1-2 hours.

Freeze-Drying: Place the pre-frozen trays in your freeze-dryer and run them through a standard freeze-drying cycle.

Packaging: Once the freeze-drying cycle is complete, quickly transfer the freeze-dried enchiladas into vacuum-sealed, airtight bags.

Rehydrating:

Add Water: To rehydrate, add hot water to the freeze-dried enchiladas. Use about the same amount of water as the volume of the food you're rehydrating.

Stir and Wait: Stir the mixture well and let it sit for 15-20 minutes to absorb the water.

Heat: Optionally, heat the rehydrated enchiladas in a microwave or on a stovetop skillet for a few minutes.

Garnish and Serve: Add sour cream, avocado slices, and cilantro, if desired, before serving.

Garlic Mashed Potatoes

SERVINGS: 4   **PREP TIME:** 20 MIN   **COOK TIME:** 30 MIN   **FREEZE-DRY TIME:** 30-40 HRS

Ingredients For Garlic Mashed Potatoes:

4 large russet potatoes, peeled and cut into chunks

1 head of garlic, separated into cloves and peeled

1 cup whole milk or cream

⅓ cup sour cream or Greek yogurt

4 tablespoons unsalted butter

Salt and pepper to taste

Optional: chives or parsley for garnish

Instructions For Garlic Mashed Potatoes:

Boil Potatoes and Garlic: Place the potato chunks and peeled garlic cloves in a large pot filled with water. Bring the water to a boil and cook until the potatoes are tender (about 15-20 minutes).

Drain: Drain the potatoes and garlic and return them to the pot.

Mash: Use a potato masher or hand mixer to mash the potatoes and garlic until smooth.

Add Dairy: Heat the milk or cream and butter together in a small saucepan or in the microwave. Gradually add the warm milk mixture to the mashed potatoes, stirring until well combined.

Season: Add salt and pepper to taste. If you're using herbs like chives or parsley, you can fold them in at this stage.

Cool Down: Let the mashed potatoes cool down to room temperature.

For Freeze-Drying:

Prep Trays: Spread the mashed potatoes in a thin, even layer on the freeze-drying trays.

Pre-Freeze: Place the trays in your freezer for about 1-2 hours.

Freeze-Drying: Transfer the trays to your freeze dryer and run a standard freeze-drying cycle.

Packaging: Once the freeze-drying process is complete, promptly transfer the freeze-dried garlic mashed potatoes into vacuum-sealed bags to maintain freshness.

Rehydrating:

Boil Water: Boil an equal amount of water to the volume of freeze-dried garlic mashed potatoes you wish to rehydrate.

Add Water to Potatoes: Slowly add the boiling water to the freeze-dried mashed potatoes, stirring continuously to prevent lumps.

Let Sit: Allow the mixture to sit for a few minutes so that the potatoes can absorb the water.

Additional Heat: If needed, you can further heat the rehydrated mashed potatoes in a microwave or on a stovetop.

Season and Serve: Taste and adjust seasoning, if needed. Serve hot, garnished with chives or parsley if desired.

Steamed Asparagus

SERVINGS: 4   **PREP TIME:** 20 MIN   **COOK TIME:** 30 MIN   **FREEZE-DRY TIME:** 25-35 HRS

Ingredients For Steamed Asparagus:

1 bunch of fresh asparagus (about 1 pound)
Salt to taste
Optional: 1-2 tablespoons olive oil
Optional: Lemon wedges for serving

Instructions For Steamed Asparagus:

Prepare the Asparagus: Wash the asparagus and snap off the woody ends. You can also peel the lower third of the asparagus for a more tender texture.

Steam Asparagus: Fill a pot with a couple of inches of water and bring it to a boil. Place a steamer basket inside, and lay the asparagus in the basket. Cover and steam for 3-5 minutes, depending on the thickness of the stalks. You want them to be tender but still crisp.

Season: Remove the asparagus from the steamer and immediately season with salt. If using olive oil, you can drizzle it over the asparagus at this stage.

Cool Down: Let the asparagus cool to room temperature.

For Freeze-Drying:

Prep Trays: Lay the steamed and cooled asparagus in a single layer on the freeze-drying trays. Make sure they are not overlapping.

Freeze-Drying: Place the trays in the freeze dryer and run a standard freeze-drying cycle.

Packaging: Once freeze-drying is complete, quickly transfer the asparagus into vacuum-sealed bags to maintain freshness and prevent moisture from getting in.

Rehydrating:

Boil Water: Boil water in a pot or kettle.

Rehydrate Asparagus: Place the freeze-dried asparagus in a bowl and pour the boiling water over them. Cover the bowl to keep the heat in.

Wait: Allow the asparagus to sit in the hot water for about 5 minutes to rehydrate.

Drain and Serve: Carefully drain the asparagus and pat them dry with a paper towel. Season again with salt if needed, and serve with lemon wedges if desired.

Roasted Brussels Sprouts

SERVINGS: 4   **PREP TIME:** 20 MIN   **COOK TIME:** 30 MIN   **FREEZE-DRY TIME:** 25-35 HRS

Ingredients For Roasted Brussels Sprouts:

1 pound Brussels sprouts
2 tablespoons olive oil
Salt and pepper to taste
Optional: 1-2 cloves of garlic, minced
Optional: Balsamic vinegar for drizzling

Instructions For Roasted Brussels Sprouts:

Preheat Oven: Preheat your oven to 400°F (200°C).

Prep Brussels Sprouts: Wash the Brussels sprouts, remove any loose or yellow leaves, and cut off the stem ends. Cut each sprout in half lengthwise.

Season: Place the halved Brussels sprouts in a bowl, and toss with olive oil, salt, and pepper. Add minced garlic if you're using it.

Arrange on Tray: Spread the seasoned Brussels sprouts in a single layer on a baking sheet lined with parchment paper or a silicone baking mat.

Roast: Roast the Brussels sprouts in the preheated oven for 20-25 minutes, turning them halfway through, until they are golden brown and crisp on the edges.

Cool Down: Let the Brussels sprouts cool down to room temperature.

For Freeze-Drying:

Prep Trays: Lay the roasted and cooled Brussels sprouts in a single layer on the freeze-drying trays. Make sure they are not overlapping.

Freeze-Drying: Place the trays in the freeze dryer and run a standard freeze-drying cycle according to the manufacturer's instructions.

Packaging: Once freeze-drying is complete, quickly transfer the Brussels sprouts into vacuum-sealed bags to maintain their freshness and prevent moisture from getting in.

Rehydrating:

Boil Water: Boil a pot of water.

Rehydrate Brussels Sprouts: Place the freeze-dried Brussels sprouts in a bowl and pour boiling water over them. Cover the bowl to keep the heat in.

Wait: Let the Brussels sprouts sit in the hot water for about 5 minutes to rehydrate.

Drain and Serve: Drain the rehydrated Brussels sprouts carefully and pat them dry with a paper towel. Drizzle with a little olive oil or balsamic vinegar if desired, and adjust seasoning as needed.

Glazed Carrots

SERVINGS: 4   **PREP TIME:** 20 MIN   **COOK TIME:** 30 MIN   **FREEZE-DRY TIME:** 30-40 HRS

Ingredients For Glazed Carrots:

1 pound of baby carrots or carrot sticks
2 tablespoons of unsalted butter
2 tablespoons of honey or maple syrup
Salt to taste
Optional: A pinch of cinnamon or nutmeg for flavor

Instructions For Glazed Carrots:

Prepare Carrots: If you're using whole carrots, peel them and cut them into sticks. If using baby carrots, make sure they're clean and dry.

Boil Carrots: Place the carrots in a saucepan with enough water to cover them. Bring to a boil and simmer for about 5-7 minutes until the carrots are fork-tender but not mushy.

Drain Carrots: Drain the carrots in a colander and set aside.

Prepare Glaze: In the same saucepan, melt the butter over low heat. Add the honey (or maple syrup) and stir until combined. If using optional spices, add them now.

Add Carrots: Add the drained carrots back into the saucepan with the glaze.

Glaze Carrots: Toss the carrots to coat them evenly in the glaze. Cook for another 2-3 minutes to allow the flavors to meld.

Cool Down: Let the glazed carrots cool to room temperature.

For Freeze-Drying:

Prep Trays: Lay the cooled, glazed carrots in a single layer on the freeze-drying trays. Make sure they are not overlapping.

Freeze-Dry: Place the trays into your freeze dryer and run a standard freeze-drying cycle according to your machine's guidelines.

Packaging: Once the freeze-drying process is complete, immediately transfer the carrots into vacuum-sealed bags or airtight containers to keep moisture out.

Rehydrating:

Boil Water: Boil a small amount of water in a saucepan or kettle.

Rehydrate Carrots: Place the freeze-dried glazed carrots in a bowl and pour the boiling water over them.

Cover: Cover the bowl with a lid or plastic wrap to retain heat and moisture.

Wait: Let the carrots sit for about 5 minutes to rehydrate.

Drain and Serve: Drain any excess water from the bowl. Optionally, you can heat the rehydrated carrots in a saucepan for a minute or two to restore their original texture.

Taste and Adjust: If needed, you can add a little more honey or butter for flavor before serving.

Scrambled Eggs

SERVINGS: 4   **PREP TIME:** 20 MIN   **COOK TIME:** 30 MIN   **FREEZE-DRY TIME:** 25-35 HRS

Ingredients For Scrambled Eggs:

4 large eggs
1/4 cup milk (optional for creaminess)
Salt and pepper to taste
2 tablespoons butter or oil
Optional: cheese, herbs, or diced vegetables for added flavor

Instructions For Scrambled Eggs:

Whisk Eggs: Crack the eggs into a bowl, add milk if you're using it, and whisk together until well combined. Season with salt and pepper.

Preheat Pan: Place a non-stick skillet over medium heat and add the butter or oil.

Pour Eggs: Once the butter is melted and the pan is hot, pour the whisked eggs into the skillet.

Cook: Gently stir the eggs with a spatula. If you're adding cheese, herbs, or vegetables, add them now.

Monitor Consistency: Continue stirring occasionally to make sure the eggs are evenly cooked. Remove the pan from heat when the eggs are mostly set but still a bit runny. They will continue to cook from the residual heat.

Cool Down: Let the scrambled eggs cool down to room temperature.

For Freeze-Drying:

Prep Trays: Spread the cooled scrambled eggs evenly on the freeze-drying trays, breaking them into smaller pieces for more effective freeze-drying.

Freeze-Dry: Load the trays into the freeze dryer and start a standard freeze-drying cycle as per your machine's instructions.

Packaging: Once the freeze-drying process is done, quickly transfer the scrambled eggs to vacuum-sealed bags or airtight containers.

Rehydrating:

Boil Water: Bring a small amount of water to boil in a kettle or pot.

Rehydrate: Place the freeze-dried scrambled eggs in a bowl and pour the boiling water over them.

Cover: Cover the bowl with a lid or plastic wrap to keep in the heat and moisture.

Wait: Allow the eggs to sit for about 5-10 minutes to absorb the water and rehydrate.

Taste and Adjust: After rehydration, taste the scrambled eggs. Add additional seasoning if necessary, and feel free to mix in fresh herbs or cheese before serving.

Pancakes

SERVINGS: 4   **PREP TIME:** 20 MIN   **COOK TIME:** 30 MIN   **FREEZE-DRY TIME:** 20-30 HRS

Ingredients For Pancakes:

- 1 cup all-purpose flour
- 2 tablespoons sugar
- 2 teaspoons baking powder
- 1/2 teaspoon salt
- 1 cup milk
- 1 egg
- 2 tablespoons melted butter, plus more for greasing the pan

Instructions For Pancakes:

Combine Dry Ingredients: In a mixing bowl, whisk together the flour, sugar, baking powder, and salt.

Add Wet Ingredients: In another bowl, combine the milk, egg, and melted butter. Whisk until well combined.

Mix Together: Pour the wet ingredients into the dry ingredients and stir until just combined. The batter will be a bit lumpy; that's okay.

Preheat Pan: Heat a non-stick skillet or griddle over medium heat and lightly coat with butter.

Cook Pancakes: Using a ladle or measuring cup, pour the batter onto the skillet to form pancakes of your desired size. Cook until bubbles form on the surface, then flip and cook until the other side is golden brown.

Cool Down: Allow the pancakes to cool down to room temperature on a wire rack.

For Freeze-Drying:

Prep Trays: Place the cooled pancakes in a single layer on the freeze-drying trays.

Freeze-Dry: Insert the trays into your freeze dryer and run a standard freeze-drying cycle according to your machine's guidelines.

Packaging: Once the freeze-drying is complete, quickly transfer the pancakes into vacuum-sealed bags or airtight containers.

Rehydrating:

Boil Water: Bring water to a boil.

Rehydrate: Place the freeze-dried pancakes in a shallow dish and pour the boiling water over them until they are covered.

Cover and Wait: Cover the dish with a lid or plastic wrap. Let it sit for about 5-10 minutes to absorb the water and rehydrate.

Check and Serve: After rehydration, check the texture. If they're still too dry, you can add a bit more hot water. Serve with your favorite toppings like syrup, butter, or fresh fruit.

Breakfast Burrito

SERVINGS: 4   **PREP TIME:** 20 MIN   **COOK TIME:** 30 MIN   **FREEZE-DRY TIME:** 35-45 HRS

Ingredients For Breakfast Burrito:

4 large eggs
1/2 cup shredded cheddar cheese
1/2 pound breakfast sausage
1/2 onion, diced
1 bell pepper, diced
Salt and pepper to taste
4 medium-sized flour tortillas
Optional: salsa, sour cream, or guacamole for serving

Instructions For Breakfast Burrito:

Cook Sausage and Veggies: In a skillet over medium heat, cook the breakfast sausage until it's no longer pink. Add the diced onion and bell pepper, cooking until the vegetables are tender. Remove the mixture from the skillet and set aside.

Scramble Eggs: In a separate bowl, whisk the eggs and season them with salt and pepper. Pour them into the skillet and scramble until cooked but still moist.

Assemble Burritos: Warm the flour tortillas for about 10-15 seconds in the microwave to make them more pliable. Lay out each tortilla and evenly distribute the sausage and vegetable mixture, scrambled eggs, and shredded cheese among them.

Roll Burritos: Fold in the sides of each tortilla and then roll them up to create a burrito.

Optional Grilling: For an extra touch, you can grill the burritos on a hot skillet for about 2 minutes per side to crisp up the tortilla and ensure that the cheese is melted.

Cool Down: Let the burritos cool to room temperature.

For Freeze-Drying:

Prep Trays: Slice each burrito into halves or thirds to allow for more even freeze-drying. Place the pieces on your freeze-drying trays.

Freeze-Dry: Load the trays into your freeze-dryer and run a standard cycle per your machine's instructions.

Packaging: Once freeze-drying is complete, quickly place the burrito pieces into vacuum-sealed bags to maintain freshness.

Rehydrating:

Boil Water: Bring water to a boil.

Rehydrate: Place the freeze-dried burrito pieces in a shallow dish. Pour hot water over them just until covered.

Cover and Wait: Cover the dish with a lid or plastic wrap and allow it to sit for 10-15 minutes to rehydrate.

Check and Serve: After rehydration, test a small piece to ensure it has returned to its original texture. If it's still too dry, let it sit in the hot water a bit longer. Once rehydrated, heat in a microwave or on a skillet, and serve with optional salsa, sour cream, or guacamole.

Chia Seed Pudding

SERVINGS: 4   **PREP TIME:** 20 MIN   **COOK TIME:** 30 MIN   **FREEZE-DRY TIME:** 25-35 HRS

Ingredients For Chia Seed Pudding:

3 cups almond milk (or any milk of your choice)
1/2 cup chia seeds
2-3 tablespoons honey or maple syrup
1 teaspoon vanilla extract
Optional: Fresh fruits, nuts, or spices like cinnamon for flavor

Instructions For Chia Seed Pudding:

Mix Ingredients: In a mixing bowl, combine the almond milk, chia seeds, honey, and vanilla extract. Whisk until well mixed.

Let Sit: Cover the bowl and let it sit in the refrigerator for at least 4 hours or overnight. The chia seeds will absorb the liquid and create a pudding-like texture.

Stir and Check: After 4 hours or the next day, stir the mixture well. If it looks too thick, you can add a little more milk; if it's too thin, add a few more chia seeds.

Optional Flavoring: This is the time to add any optional fresh fruits, nuts, or spices. Stir them into the pudding for extra flavor.

Final Refrigeration: After any final adjustments, put the pudding back in the refrigerator for another 30 minutes to let it set.

For Freeze-Drying:

Prep Trays: Spread the prepared chia seed pudding evenly on your freeze-drying trays. Try to make the layer as uniform as possible for even freeze-drying.

Freeze-Dry: Load the trays into your freeze-dryer and run a standard cycle per your machine's instructions.

Packaging: Once freeze-drying is complete, quickly transfer the chia seed pudding into vacuum-sealed bags to maintain freshness.

Rehydrating:

Boil Water: Bring water to a near-boil. It doesn't have to be boiling, just hot.

Rehydrate: Transfer the freeze-dried chia seed pudding to a bowl. Slowly add hot water, stirring as you go, until it reaches your desired consistency.

Stir and Wait: Allow the mixture to sit for about 5 minutes to fully rehydrate. Stir again to check the consistency and make any adjustments as needed.

Optional Flavoring: You can add additional fresh fruits, nuts, or spices at this point if you like.

Serve: Once it reaches the desired texture, your rehydrated chia seed pudding is ready to be enjoyed!

Mac and Cheese

SERVINGS: 4 **PREP TIME:** 20 MIN **COOK TIME:** 30 MIN **FREEZE-DRY TIME:** 35-45 HRS

Ingredients For Mac and Cheese:

8 ounces elbow macaroni or other pasta of choice
2 cups shredded cheddar cheese
1 cup milk
2 tablespoons butter
Salt and pepper to taste
Optional: 1/2 teaspoon paprika or cayenne pepper for some spice

Instructions For Mac and Cheese:

Boil Pasta: Bring a pot of salted water to a boil and cook the pasta according to the package instructions until al dente. Drain and set aside.

Make Cheese Sauce: In a separate pot, melt the butter over medium heat. Add the milk and heat until it's warm but not boiling. Gradually add the shredded cheddar cheese, stirring continuously until the cheese is completely melted and the sauce is smooth.

Combine: Add the drained pasta to the cheese sauce, and mix until the pasta is well coated.

Season: Add salt and pepper to taste. If you're using paprika or cayenne, add it now.

Cool Down: Allow the Mac and Cheese to cool to room temperature.

For Freeze-Drying:

Prep Trays: Spread the prepared Mac and Cheese evenly on your freeze-drying trays. Try to keep the layer even for consistent freeze-drying.

Freeze-Dry: Place the trays into your freeze-dryer and run a standard cycle as per your machine's guidelines.

Packaging: Once the freeze-drying is complete, promptly transfer the freeze-dried Mac and Cheese into vacuum-sealed bags to maintain its freshness.

Rehydrating:

Boil Water: Bring water to a near-boil.

Rehydrate: Place the freeze-dried Mac and Cheese in a bowl and slowly add the hot water while stirring, until you reach your desired consistency.

Wait and Stir: Let the Mac and Cheese sit for about 5-10 minutes to fully rehydrate. Stir once more to check for consistency and make any needed adjustments.

Heat: If the Mac and Cheese is not warm enough after rehydration, you can heat it in a microwave or stovetop until it reaches your desired temperature.

Serve: Your rehydrated Mac and Cheese is now ready to eat!

Chicken Pot Pie

SERVINGS: 4   **PREP TIME:** 20 MIN   **COOK TIME:** 30 MIN   **FREEZE-DRY TIME:** 30-40 HRS

Ingredients For the Filling:

- 2 cups cooked, diced chicken
- 1 cup frozen mixed vegetables (e.g., carrots, peas, corn)
- 1 small onion, diced
- 1/3 cup butter
- 1/3 cup all-purpose flour
- 1/2 teaspoon salt
- 1/4 teaspoon pepper
- 1/4 teaspoon celery seed (optional)
- 1 3/4 cups chicken broth
- 2/3 cup milk

For the Pie Crust:
- 1 store-bought pie crust

Instructions For the Filling:

Sauté Veggies: In a large skillet, melt the butter over medium heat. Add the onion and sauté until translucent. Add the frozen mixed vegetables and cook until soft.

Make Roux: Add the flour, salt, and pepper to the vegetable mixture. Stir well to combine and cook for a minute or two.

Add Liquids: Gradually add in the chicken broth and milk while stirring constantly. Continue to cook until the mixture thickens.

Add Chicken: Stir in the cooked, diced chicken. Remove from heat.

Assemble and Bake:

Preheat Oven: Preheat your oven to 425°F (220°C).

Prepare Pie Crust: Place one pie crust into a 9-inch pie dish.

Fill Pie: Pour the chicken and vegetable mixture into the pie crust.

Top Pie: Place the second pie crust over the filling. Seal and flute the edges. Cut a few small slits in the top crust to allow steam to escape.

Bake: Bake for 30-35 minutes or until the crust is golden brown. Let it cool before proceeding to the next steps.

For Freeze-Drying:

Slice and Cool: Once the Chicken Pot Pie has cooled to room temperature, slice it into portions.

Freeze-Dry Prep: Place the sliced portions on your freeze-drying trays, ensuring enough space between each piece for adequate air circulation.

Freeze-Dry: Insert the trays into the freeze-dryer and run a standard freeze-drying cycle according to your machine's guidelines.

Packaging: After the cycle is complete, promptly place the freeze-dried Chicken Pot Pie slices into vacuum-sealed bags to maintain freshness.

Rehydrating:

Boil Water: Bring water to a near-boil.

Rehydrate: Place a slice of freeze-dried Chicken Pot Pie in a bowl. Slowly pour hot water over it, being cautious not to add too much.

Wait: Cover the bowl and let it sit for 5-10 minutes to allow for full rehydration.

Heat: If it's not warm enough, you can further heat it in a microwave or on a stovetop.

Serve: Your Chicken Pot Pie is now ready to be enjoyed!

Sloppy Joes

SERVINGS: 4   **PREP TIME:** 20 MIN   **COOK TIME:** 30 MIN   **FREEZE-DRY TIME:** 35-45 HRS

Ingredients For Sloppy Joes:

1 lb ground beef
1 small onion, finely chopped
1/2 green bell pepper, finely chopped
1 cup ketchup
2 tablespoons mustard
1 tablespoon brown sugar
1 teaspoon garlic powder
Salt and pepper to taste
4 hamburger buns

Instructions For the Filling:

Brown Meat: In a large skillet over medium heat, brown the ground beef, breaking it apart as it cooks.

Add Veggies: Add the chopped onion and green bell pepper to the skillet. Cook until the vegetables are soft and the meat is no longer pink.

Drain Fat: Drain off excess fat from the meat and veggies.

Add Sauce: Add ketchup, mustard, brown sugar, garlic powder, salt, and pepper to the meat mixture. Stir well to combine.

Simmer: Reduce heat and simmer for about 10 minutes, stirring occasionally.

Taste Test: Adjust seasoning if necessary.

Serve:

Assemble: Spoon the meat mixture onto hamburger buns.

For Freeze-Drying:

Cool Down: Allow the Sloppy Joe filling to cool to room temperature.

Prep Trays: Spread the Sloppy Joe mixture evenly on your freeze-drying trays. The thinner you spread it, the faster and more evenly it will dry.

Freeze-Dry: Insert the trays into the freeze-dryer and run a standard freeze-drying cycle according to your machine's guidelines.

Seal: Once the cycle is complete, quickly transfer the freeze-dried Sloppy Joe mixture into vacuum-sealed bags for long-term storage.

Rehydrating:

Boil Water: Bring water to a near-boil.

Rehydrate: Place the freeze-dried Sloppy Joe mixture in a bowl. Slowly add hot water, stirring as you go, until the mixture reaches your desired consistency.

Heat: If the mixture is not warm enough, you can microwave it for 30-60 seconds or heat it in a pan on the stove.

Assemble: Once the Sloppy Joe mixture is rehydrated and heated, spoon it onto hamburger buns.

Serve: Your rehydrated Sloppy Joes are now ready to be enjoyed!

Apple Slices with Cinnamon

SERVINGS: 4   **PREP TIME:** 20 MIN   **COOK TIME:** 30 MIN   **FREEZE-DRY TIME:** 25-35 HRS

Ingredients For Apple Slices with Cinnamon:

4 large apples (any variety)
2 tablespoons lemon juice
1/4 cup sugar
1 teaspoon ground cinnamon

Instructions For the Apples:

Preheat Oven: Preheat your oven to 350°F (175°C).

Slice Apples: Peel the apples and slice them thinly, removing the cores.

Prevent Browning: To prevent the apple slices from browning, toss them in a bowl with lemon juice.

Mix: In a separate bowl, mix together the sugar and ground cinnamon.

Combine: Add the cinnamon-sugar mixture to the apples and toss well to coat all slices.

Bake:

Arrange: Place the apple slices in a single layer on a baking sheet lined with parchment paper.

Bake: Bake for 15-20 minutes, or until the apple slices are tender but not mushy.

Cool: Remove the apple slices from the oven and let them cool to room temperature.

For Freeze-Drying:

Prep Trays: Once the apple slices are cool, spread them evenly on your freeze-drying trays. Make sure they are not touching each other.

Freeze-Dry: Place the trays into your freeze-dryer and run a standard freeze-drying cycle according to the machine's guidelines.

Seal: After the freeze-drying cycle is complete, quickly transfer the freeze-dried apple slices into vacuum-sealed bags to maintain freshness.

Rehydrating:

Boil Water: Boil a small amount of water.

Rehydrate: Place the freeze-dried apple slices in a bowl and pour just enough hot water over them to barely cover the slices

Wait: Allow the apple slices to sit for 5-10 minutes, or until they've absorbed the water and become tender again.

Drain: If there's any excess water, drain it off.

Serve: Your rehydrated Apple Slices with Cinnamon are now ready to enjoy or you can simply eat it as a crunch snack!

Banana Bread

SERVINGS: 4   **PREP TIME:** 20 MIN   **COOK TIME:** 30 MIN   **FREEZE-DRY TIME:** 35-45 HRS

Ingredients For Banana Bread:

3 ripe bananas, mashed
75g melted butter
200g sugar
1 beaten egg
1 teaspoon vanilla extract

1 teaspoon baking soda
Pinch of salt
190g of all-purpose flour

Instructions For Banana Bread:

Preheat Oven: Preheat your oven to 350°F (175°C).

Prepare Pan: Grease a 4x8-inch loaf pan.

Mix Wet Ingredients: In a mixing bowl, combine the mashed bananas, melted butter, sugar, beaten egg, and vanilla extract.

Add Dry Ingredients: Sprinkle baking soda and salt over the wet mixture. Then add the flour and mix well until combined.

Pour and Smooth: Pour the mixture into the prepared loaf pan, smoothing the top.

Bake: Place the pan in the oven and bake for 50-60 minutes or until a toothpick inserted into the center comes out clean.

Cool: Remove the bread from the oven, and allow it to cool completely in the pan.

For Freeze-Drying:

Slice Bread: Once the banana bread has cooled, slice it into portions suitable for freeze-drying.

Prep Trays: Place the slices on the freeze-dryer trays, making sure they do not touch each other.

Freeze-Dry: Put the trays in the freeze-dryer and start the freeze-drying cycle as per your machine's guidelines.

Package: Once the cycle is complete, quickly transfer the freeze-dried slices into vacuum-sealed bags to maintain freshness.

Rehydrating:

Boil Water: Boil a small amount of water.

Soak: Place the freeze-dried banana bread slices in a shallow dish and pour the hot water over them.

Rehydrate: Let the slices sit for about 5-10 minutes to absorb the water and regain their original texture.

Check: Test the texture; if it's still too dry, you can sprinkle a bit more water and let it sit for an additional few minutes.

Eat: Your rehydrated Banana Bread is now ready to be enjoyed!

Chocolate Chip Cookies

SERVINGS: 10   **PREP TIME:** 20 MIN   **COOK TIME:** 40 MIN   **FREEZE-DRY TIME:** 35-45 HRS

Ingredients For Chocolate Chip Cookies:

1 cup (2 sticks or 226g) unsalted butter, melted and cooled
3/4 cup granulated sugar
1 cup packed brown sugar
2 large eggs

1 teaspoon vanilla extract
3 cups all-purpose flour
1/2 teaspoon salt
1/2 teaspoon baking soda
2 cups chocolate chips

Instructions For Chocolate Chip Cookies:

Preheat Oven: Preheat your oven to 375°F (190°C).

Line Baking Sheet: Line a baking sheet with parchment paper or a silicone baking mat.

Mix Wet Ingredients: In a large bowl, mix together the melted butter, granulated sugar, and brown sugar until well combined.

Add Eggs and Vanilla: Stir in the eggs and vanilla extract.

Mix Dry Ingredients: In a separate bowl, whisk together the flour, salt, and baking soda.

Combine Mixtures: Gradually add the dry mixture to the wet mixture and mix until just combined.

Add Chocolate Chips: Fold in the chocolate chips.

Drop Cookies: Using a cookie scoop or a spoon, drop balls of dough onto the lined baking sheet, spacing them about 2 inches apart.

Bake: Bake for 9-11 minutes, or until edges are golden but centers are still soft.

Cool: Allow cookies to cool on the baking sheet for 5 minutes before transferring to a wire rack to cool completely.

For Freeze-Drying:

Prep Trays: Place the fully cooled cookies on freeze-drying trays, ensuring they do not touch.

Freeze-Dry: Load the trays into the freeze-dryer and run the freeze-drying cycle according to your machine's guidelines.

Seal: Once the freeze-drying cycle is complete, quickly seal the cookies in vacuum-sealed bags to maintain freshness.

Rehydrating:

Prepare Water: Boil a small amount of water and let it cool slightly.

Mist: Lightly mist the freeze-dried cookies with the warm water using a spray bottle.

Rehydrate: Let the cookies sit for about 5-10 minutes to absorb the water.

Check: Test the texture. If it's too dry, mist a bit more water and let it sit for another few minutes.

Enjoy: Your rehydrated Chocolate Chip Cookies are ready to eat!

Strawberry Shortcake

SERVINGS: 4   **PREP TIME:** 20 MIN   **COOK TIME:** 30 MIN   **FREEZE-DRY TIME:** 30-40 HRS

Ingredients For the Shortcake:

2 cups all-purpose flour
1/4 cup granulated sugar
1 tablespoon baking powder
1/2 teaspoon salt
1/2 cup unsalted butter, cold and cut into small pieces
2/3 cup whole milk
1 teaspoon vanilla extract

Ingredients For the Strawberry Filling:

1 lb fresh strawberries, hulled and sliced
1/4 cup granulated sugar (adjust based on the sweetness of the strawberries)
1 teaspoon lemon juice

Ingredients For the Whipped Cream:

(Prepare after rehydration, not for freeze-drying)

1 cup heavy cream
2 tablespoons powdered sugar
1 teaspoon vanilla extract

Instructions For Shortcake:

Prepare the Strawberries: In a mixing bowl, combine the strawberries, sugar, and lemon juice. Stir well and let them sit for at least 30 minutes, stirring occasionally.

Make the Shortcakes: Preheat your oven to 400°F (200°C). In a large mixing bowl, combine flour, sugar, baking powder, and salt. Cut in the cold butter using a pastry blender or two knives until the mixture resembles coarse crumbs.

Pour in the milk and vanilla extract: Stir just until the dough comes together; don't overmix.

Turn the dough out onto a lightly floured surface and knead it a few times to bring it together. Pat the dough into a 3/4-inch thick rectangle. Using a round cutter, cut out shortcakes.

Place the shortcakes on a baking sheet and bake for 15-20 minutes, or until golden brown. Let them cool.

For Freeze-Drying:

Shortcakes: Place the cooled shortcakes on the freeze dryer trays. Make sure they don't touch.

Strawberries: Spread the strawberry filling on another tray in a single layer.

Follow your freeze dryer's instructions for freeze-drying fruits and baked goods. Depending on the model, this process can take between 20-40 hours.

Rehydrating and Assembly:

Shortcakes: To rehydrate, place the shortcakes in an airtight container with a damp paper towel on the bottom (don't let them touch the towel). Seal and let them sit for several hours.

Strawberries: Place the freeze-dried strawberries in a bowl and sprinkle a few tablespoons of water over them. Stir occasionally, allowing them to absorb moisture and regain their original texture.

Whipped Cream: In a mixing bowl, beat the heavy cream until soft peaks form. Add powdered sugar and vanilla extract. Beat until stiff peaks form.

To assemble, slice the rehydrated shortcakes in half horizontally. Place a generous amount of strawberries on the bottom half, followed by a dollop of whipped cream. Top with the other half of the shortcake.

Rice Pudding

SERVINGS: 10 **PREP TIME:** 20 MIN **COOK TIME:** 20 MIN **FREEZE-DRY TIME:** 35-45 HRS

Ingredients For Rice Pudding:

1 cup uncooked white rice (short or long grain, as you prefer)
2 cups water
4 cups whole milk
1/2 cup granulated sugar
1/4 teaspoon salt}

1 teaspoon vanilla extract
1/2 teaspoon ground cinnamon (optional)
1/4 cup raisins (optional)
Zest of 1 lemon or orange (optional)

Instructions For Rice Pudding:

In a saucepan, bring the 2 cups of water to a boil. Add the rice and a pinch of salt, then reduce the heat to low, cover, and let it simmer until the rice is tender and the water is absorbed, about 15-20 minutes.

Once the rice is cooked, add the milk, sugar, and salt to the saucepan. Increase the heat to medium and cook, stirring frequently, until the mixture starts to boil.

Reduce the heat to low and let the mixture simmer gently until it thickens and looks creamy, about 20-30 minutes. Make sure to stir it frequently to prevent sticking and burning.

Remove from heat and stir in the vanilla extract, ground cinnamon, raisins, and citrus zest if using.

Let the rice pudding cool for a bit, then transfer it to a bowl and cover with plastic wrap, pressing the wrap directly onto the surface of the pudding to prevent a skin from forming. Chill in the refrigerator until it's fully cold.

For Freeze-Drying:

Spread the cooled rice pudding in an even layer on your freeze dryer trays.

Follow your freeze dryer's instructions for freeze-drying dairy and grain products. The drying time will typically range from 20-40 hours, depending on the model and settings

Rehydrating:

To rehydrate, place the desired amount of freeze-dried rice pudding in a bowl. Slowly add cold or room temperature water while stirring, a tablespoon at a time, until the rice pudding regains its original creamy consistency. It's better to add water gradually to avoid making it too runny.

Allow the rice pudding to sit for a few minutes, so the rice kernels can fully rehydrate and become tender.

If desired, you can also heat the rehydrated rice pudding in a microwave or stovetop for a warm treat. Serve and enjoy!

Note: *Rice pudding tends to be quite forgiving, so if you accidentally add too much water during rehydration, you can simply heat it on the stovetop to evaporate some of the excess liquid. Adjust the texture as needed to your preference.*

Mango Cubes

SERVINGS: 10   **PREP TIME:** 20 MIN   **COOK TIME:** 30 MIN   **FREEZE-DRY TIME:** 30-40 HRS

Ingredients For Mango Cubes Recipe:

Fresh ripe mangoes (as many as you'd like to freeze-dry)

Instructions For Mango Cubes Recipe:

Start by washing the mangoes thoroughly under running water.

Using a sharp knife, cut around the mango's pit to separate the flesh from the seed. You should end up with two large pieces or "cheeks."

Make vertical and horizontal cuts on each mango cheek, creating a grid pattern. Be sure not to cut through the skin.

Push the mango skin upwards, turning it inside out. This will push the mango cubes outwards, making them easier to cut off from the skin.

Using your knife, cut the mango cubes away from the skin.

Repeat with all the mangoes.

For Freeze-Drying:

Spread the mango cubes in a single layer on your freeze dryer trays, ensuring they aren't touching so they can freeze-dry properly.

Place the trays in the freeze dryer and run a standard fruit cycle. Follow your freeze dryer's manufacturer's guidelines. Depending on the model and settings, the freeze-drying process for fruits typically takes between 20-36 hours.

Storing:

Once the freeze-drying process is complete, store the mango cubes in an airtight container with an oxygen absorber or vacuum-seal the cubes to ensure they remain crisp and to extend their shelf life.

Rehydration:

While freeze-dried mango cubes are delicious to eat as a crunchy snack without rehydration, if you do wish to rehydrate them:

Place the desired amount of freeze-dried mango cubes in a bowl.

Cover the mango cubes with cold or room temperature water. Allow them to soak for approximately 5-10 minutes, or until they regain their original texture.

Drain any excess water, and the mango cubes are ready to be enjoyed in their original, juicy state!

Note: *The rehydration time might vary based on the size of the mango cubes and how ripe they were before freeze-drying. Adjust soaking time as needed.*

Cheesecake Bites

SERVINGS: 10   **PREP TIME:** 20 MIN   **COOK TIME:** 50 MIN   **FREEZE-DRY TIME:** 35-45 HRS

Ingredients For Cheesecake Bites:

2 cups of graham cracker crumbs
8 tablespoons unsalted butter, melted
3 cups cream cheese, softened
1 cup granulated sugar
1 teaspoon pure vanilla extract
3 large eggs
1/2 cup sour cream
Zest of 1 lemon (optional)

Instructions For the Crust:

Mix graham cracker crumbs and melted butter until the crumbs are evenly moistened. Press the mixture into the bottom of a baking pan to form a crust.

Instructions For the Filling:

Beat the cream cheese, sugar, and vanilla together until smooth and creamy. Add the eggs one at a time, beating well after each addition. Stir in the sour cream and lemon zest.

Pour the filling over the crust.

Preheat the oven to 325°F (165°C). Bake the cheesecake for 40-45 minutes, or until it's set and the top is slightly golden.

Allow the cheesecake to cool in the oven with the door slightly open for an hour. Then, refrigerate for at least 4 hours, or overnight for best results.

Once set, cut the cheesecake into bite-sized squares.

For Freeze-Drying:

Spread the cheesecake bites in a single layer on your freeze dryer trays, ensuring they aren't touching to allow for proper freeze-drying.

Place the trays in the freeze dryer. Run a standard cycle appropriate for dairy/creamy foods. Refer to your freeze dryer's manufacturer guidelines. Typically, this can take between 24-48 hours.

Storing:

Once freeze-drying is complete, store the cheesecake bites in an airtight container with an oxygen absorber or vacuum-seal the bites. This will help maintain their crisp texture and extend shelf life.

Rehydration:

Place the desired number of cheesecake bites in a container.

Using a spray bottle, lightly mist the bites with cold water until they're coated but not saturated. The cheesecake will absorb the moisture and soften.

Allow them to sit for about 10-15 minutes to regain their original texture.

Enjoy!

Remember: Over-spraying can make them soggy, so go slow. The rehydration process for cheesecake bites is quite rapid due to their creamy nature, so they might not need as much time or moisture as other freeze-dried foods. Adjust accordingly.

Lemon Bars

SERVINGS: 4   **PREP TIME:** 20 MIN   **COOK TIME:** 30 MIN   **FREEZE-DRY TIME:** 30-40 HRS

Ingredients For the Crust:

1 cup (2 sticks) unsalted butter, softened
1/2 cup granulated sugar
2 cups all-purpose flour
1/4 teaspoon salt

Ingredients For the Lemon Filling:

4 large eggs
1 1/2 cups granulated sugar
1/4 cup all-purpose flour
2/3 cup fresh lemon juice (about 3-4 lemons)
1 tablespoon lemon zest

Instructions For the Crust:

Preheat your oven to 350°F (175°C).

In a medium bowl, mix the softened butter, sugar, flour, and salt until combined.

Press into the bottom of a greased 9x13 inch baking pan.

Bake for 20 minutes or until firm and golden.

Instructions For the Filling:

While the crust is baking, whisk together eggs, sugar, flour, lemon juice, and lemon zest in a bowl until smooth.

Pour the filling over the baked crust
Return to the oven and bake for an additional 20-25 minutes, or until the lemon filling is set and the top has a slight crust.

Let the lemon bars cool completely, then refrigerate for a couple of hours.

After cooling, cut into squares.

For Freeze-Drying:

Lay the lemon bar squares in a single layer on the freeze dryer trays, ensuring space between each to allow for proper freeze-drying.

Load the trays into your freeze dryer.

Start a cycle for "fruits" or similar (depending on your machine's settings) since the lemon bars have a high moisture content. The cycle may take between 24-36 hours depending on the model and settings.

Storing:

Once the freeze-drying cycle is complete, promptly store the lemon bars in an airtight container with an oxygen absorber to maintain freshness or vacuum-seal them.

Rehydration:

Place the desired amount of lemon bars in a container.

Using a spray bottle, lightly mist the lemon bars with cold water until they're slightly moist but not saturated.

Allow them to sit for 5-10 minutes to absorb the moisture and regain their original texture.

Serve and enjoy!

Note: As with most freeze-dried foods, it's essential not to oversaturate during rehydration. Adjust the moisture level based on your preference.

Brownies

SERVINGS: 4   **PREP TIME:** 20 MIN   **COOK TIME:** 30 MIN   **FREEZE-DRY TIME:** 35-45 HRS

Ingredients For Brownies:

1/2 cup (1 stick) unsalted butter, melted
1 cup granulated sugar
2 large eggs
1 teaspoon vanilla extract
1/3 cup unsweetened cocoa powder
1/2 cup all-purpose flour
1/4 teaspoon salt
1/4 teaspoon baking powder

Instructions For Brownies:

Preheat your oven to 350°F (175°C).

In a large bowl, combine melted butter, sugar, eggs, and vanilla extract.

Stir in cocoa powder, flour, salt, and baking powder until well combined.

Pour the batter into a greased 8x8-inch baking pan and spread evenly.

Bake for 20-25 minutes or until a toothpick inserted in the center comes out with a few crumbs.

Allow the brownies to cool in the pan on a wire rack.

Once cooled, cut into squares.

For Freeze-Drying:

Place the brownie squares in a single layer on the freeze dryer trays, ensuring space between each for effective freeze-drying.

Load the trays into your freeze dryer.

Start the freeze dryer cycle, typically using a "fruit" or similar setting (the exact setting may vary based on your machine).

The freeze-drying process may take between 24-36 hours, depending on your freeze dryer model and its settings.

Storing:

Once freeze-drying is complete, store the brownies in airtight containers with oxygen absorbers to maintain freshness. For longer storage, vacuum-sealing the brownies is highly recommended.

Rehydration:

Place the desired amount of brownies in a container.

Lightly mist the brownies with cold water using a spray bottle, ensuring they're slightly moistened but not overly saturated.

Allow them to sit for a few minutes to absorb the moisture and regain their original texture.

Enjoy your rehydrated brownies!

Note: Remember, the key to rehydrating freeze-dried foods is to add moisture gradually. Avoid oversaturating, as it can make the brownies too mushy. Adjust moisture levels based on your preference.

Bread Pudding

SERVINGS: 4   **PREP TIME:** 20 MIN   **COOK TIME:** 30 MIN   **FREEZE-DRY TIME:** 35-45 HRS

Ingredients For Bread Pudding:

4 cups stale bread, cubed (about 6-8 slices)
2 cups whole milk
2 large eggs, lightly beaten
3/4 cup granulated sugar
1 teaspoon vanilla extract

1/2 teaspoon ground cinnamon
1/4 teaspoon ground nutmeg
1/2 cup raisins or other dried fruit (optional)
4 tablespoons unsalted butter, melted

Instructions For Bread Pudding:

Preheat your oven to 350°F (175°C).

In a large bowl, soak bread cubes in milk for about 10 minutes, pressing down occasionally to ensure all bread is soaked.

In a separate bowl, whisk together eggs, sugar, vanilla, cinnamon, and nutmeg.

Add the egg mixture to the soaked bread and mix well. Stir in raisins or other dried fruits if using.

Pour the melted butter into a baking dish (around 8x8 inches or similar size).

Pour the bread mixture over the butter.

Bake for 35-45 minutes, or until the top is golden brown and the center is set.

Remove from the oven and allow to cool.

For Freeze-Drying:

Once cooled, cut the bread pudding into squares or portions.

Place these portions in a single layer on the freeze dryer trays.

Load the trays into your freeze dryer.

Start the freeze dryer cycle. For most freeze dryers, using a "fruit" or similar setting should work (the exact setting may vary based on your machine).

The freeze-drying process will likely take between 24-36 hours, depending on the specific model of your freeze dryer and its settings.

Storing:

Once the freeze-drying process is complete, store the bread pudding pieces in airtight containers with oxygen absorbers to maintain freshness. Vacuum-sealing is recommended for longer storage.

Rehydration:

Place the desired amount of bread pudding pieces in a container.

Gradually add warm milk or water to the bread pudding, ensuring it's moistened but not overly soggy. Depending on your preference, you might use between 1/4 to 1/2 cup of liquid for every serving.

Let the bread pudding sit for a few minutes to absorb the liquid and regain its original texture.

Warm the rehydrated bread pudding in a microwave or oven if desired, and enjoy!

Note: *The key to rehydrating freeze-dried foods is to introduce moisture gradually. Adjust the amount of liquid based on your preferred consistency for the bread pudding.*

Coconut Macaroons

SERVINGS: 4   **PREP TIME:** 20 MIN   **COOK TIME:** 30 MIN   **FREEZE-DRY TIME:** 35-45 HRS

Ingredients For Coconut Macaroons:

3 cups unsweetened shredded coconut
4 large egg whites
1/2 cup granulated sugar
1 teaspoon vanilla extract

1/4 teaspoon salt
Optional: 4 ounces of dark chocolate (for dipping)

Instructions For Coconut Macaroons:

Preheat your oven to 325°F (160°C) and line a baking sheet with parchment paper.

In a mixing bowl, whisk together the egg whites, sugar, vanilla extract, and salt until the mixture is frothy.

Fold in the shredded coconut, ensuring it's well coated with the egg white mixture.

Using a spoon or a small ice cream scoop, drop dollops of the coconut mixture onto the prepared baking sheet, spacing them about an inch apart.

Bake in the preheated oven for 20-25 minutes or until the macaroons are golden brown on the edges.

Remove from the oven and let them cool on the baking sheet for several minutes, then transfer to a wire rack to cool completely.

Optional: Once cooled, you can melt the dark chocolate in a microwave or over a double boiler. Dip the bottom of each macaroon into the melted chocolate, then place back on the parchment paper or wire rack to let the chocolate set.

For Freeze-Drying:

Once the macaroons (and optional chocolate) are completely cooled, place them in a single layer on the freeze dryer trays.

Load the trays into your freeze dryer.

Begin the freeze dryer cycle. A standard "fruit" setting or similar should suffice, though the exact setting might differ based on your freeze dryer model.

The process may take between 20-30 hours, depending on the size of the macaroons and the model of your freeze dryer.

Storing:

After freeze drying, store the macaroons in airtight containers with oxygen absorbers to maintain freshness. Vacuum-sealing is an excellent option for long-term storage.

Rehydration:

To rehydrate, simply place the macaroons on a plate or dish.

Lightly spritz them with water using a spray bottle. The coconut will naturally absorb the moisture.

Allow them to sit for about 10 minutes to regain their original texture.

If needed, you can slightly warm them in an oven or microwave. Be careful not to overheat, especially if they have chocolate.

Note: Coconut macaroons rehydrate relatively quickly due to their porous structure. Always be cautious not to add too much moisture, as it can make the macaroons soggy. Adjust based on preference.

Pumpkin Pie Filling

SERVINGS: 4   **PREP TIME:** 20 MIN   **COOK TIME:** 30 MIN   **FREEZE-DRY TIME:** 25-35 HRS

Ingredients For Pumpkin Pie Filling:

- 2 cups pureed pumpkin (canned or fresh)
- 3/4 cup granulated sugar
- 1/2 teaspoon salt
- 1 teaspoon ground cinnamon
- 1/2 teaspoon ground ginger
- 1/4 teaspoon ground cloves
- 1/4 teaspoon ground nutmeg
- 2 large eggs
- 1 cup evaporated milk

Instructions For Pumpkin Pie Filling:

If using fresh pumpkin: Cut the pumpkin in half, scoop out the seeds, and roast in the oven at 400°F (200°C) until soft. Once cooled, scoop out the flesh and puree in a blender or food processor until smooth.

In a large bowl, whisk together the pumpkin puree, sugar, salt, cinnamon, ginger, cloves, and nutmeg.

Beat the eggs separately, then add them to the pumpkin mixture.

Gradually stir in the evaporated milk until everything is combined and smooth.

Pour the filling into a pie crust and bake at 425°F (220°C) for 15 minutes. Then reduce the temperature to 350°F (175°C) and continue baking for another 35-40 minutes, or until a knife inserted into the center comes out clean.

Let the pie cool on a wire rack for 2 hours to allow the filling to set.

For Freeze-Drying:

Once the pumpkin pie has completely cooled, slice it into preferred serving sizes.

Place the slices on the freeze dryer trays in a single layer, ensuring that the pieces aren't touching.

Load the trays into your freeze dryer.

Begin the freeze dryer cycle. A standard "fruit" or "cake" setting should work, but the exact setting might differ based on your freeze dryer model.

The process may take between 20-30 hours, depending on the thickness of your slices and your freeze dryer model.

Storing:

After freeze drying, store the slices in airtight containers with oxygen absorbers to maintain freshness. Vacuum-sealing is an excellent option for long-term storage.

Rehydration:

To rehydrate the pumpkin pie slices, place them on a plate.

Lightly mist them with water using a spray bottle, ensuring even coverage.

Allow them to sit for about 15-20 minutes to regain their original texture.

If needed, you can slightly warm them in an oven or microwave to replicate that fresh-out-of-the-oven taste.

Note: Rehydration times may vary based on the thickness of the slices and the conditions under which they're rehydrated. Adjust based on preference.

Peach Slices

SERVINGS: 4   **PREP TIME:** 20 MIN   **COOK TIME:** 30 MIN   **FREEZE-DRY TIME:** 25-35 HRS

Ingredients For Peach Slices:

Freeze-drying peach slices is simple since the preparation is minimal, and the natural sweetness and flavor of the peach are preserved beautifully through the freeze-drying process

Fresh peaches (as many as you'd like)

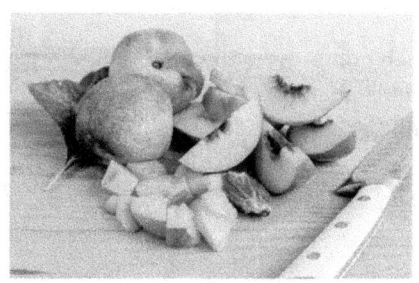

Instructions For Peach Slices:

Start by washing the peaches thoroughly under cold running water.

Using a sharp knife, cut around the peach to split it in half. Remove the stone and then slice the halves into even slices (about 1/4 to 1/2 inch thick). The thinner the slices, the faster they will freeze-dry.

Optional: To prevent browning and to preserve color, you can dip the slices in a solution made from 1/4 cup lemon juice and 1 quart of water. Ensure each slice gets thoroughly soaked, then drain and pat dry.

For Freeze-Drying:

Place the peach slices in a single layer on the freeze dryer trays. Ensure they aren't touching so they don't stick together.

Load the trays into your freeze dryer.

Start the freeze dryer cycle. A standard "fruit" setting should work. The process may take between 20-30 hours, depending on the thickness of your slices and your freeze dryer model.

Storing:

Once freeze-dried, store the peach slices in airtight containers with oxygen absorbers to maintain freshness. Vacuum-sealing is ideal for long-term storage, preventing moisture and air from getting in.

Rehydration:

Place the desired amount of freeze-dried peach slices in a bowl.

Pour just enough cold or room temperature water over the slices to cover them.

Allow them to sit for 5-10 minutes to absorb the water and regain their original texture.

Drain any excess water, and the peach slices are ready to eat!

Note: Rehydration times may vary depending on the thickness of the slices and the conditions under which they're rehydrated. Adjust based on preference. Freeze-dried peaches can also be enjoyed without rehydrating, as they'll be crispy and flavorful!

Maple Sugar Crystals

SERVINGS: 4   **PREP TIME:** 20 MIN   **COOK TIME:** 30 MIN   **FREEZE-DRY TIME:** 25-35 HRS

Ingredients For Maple Sugar Crystals:

Instead of freeze-drying maple syrup directly, you can convert it into maple sugar crystals, which is essentially what you'd get if you were to remove all the water from the syrup.

Use pure maple syrup

Instructions For Maple Sugar Crystals:

Reduce the Maple Syrup: Pour the maple syrup into a large pot. On low heat, allow the maple syrup to simmer until it has reduced by about half. This will concentrate the sugars.

Once reduced, remove from heat and allow it to cool. You should have a thicker consistency but still liquid.

For Freeze-Drying:

Spread the reduced maple syrup thinly on the freeze dryer trays, ensuring an even layer. A silicone mat might be helpful here.

Load the trays into your freeze dryer.

Start the freeze dryer cycle. Due to the high sugar content, it might take longer than other products. Keep a close watch to ensure it doesn't turn into a hard, glass-like texture.

Once the cycle is complete, you should have maple sugar crystals.

Storing:

Store the maple sugar in an airtight container. Since it's sugar, it should have a long shelf life if kept dry.

Rehydration:

To rehydrate or revert back to a syrup-like consistency:

Measure the amount of maple sugar you'd like to rehydrate.

Add a small amount of warm water, starting with just a few drops.

Stir continuously. The maple sugar will dissolve in the water, creating a syrup. Adjust the amount of water based on your preferred consistency.

Keep in mind that the rehydrated version might not have the exact same texture or consistency as original maple syrup. However, the flavor should be concentrated and sweet. If you're looking for a syrup texture without the freeze-drying step, simply reducing the syrup on the stove (as in the preparation step) might be your best bet.

Oatmeal Cookies

SERVINGS: 4 **PREP TIME:** 20 MIN **COOK TIME:** 30 MIN **FREEZE-DRY TIME:** 30-40 HRS

Ingredients For Oatmeal Cookies:

1 cup (2 sticks) unsalted butter, softened
1 cup brown sugar, packed
1/2 cup granulated sugar
2 large eggs
1 teaspoon vanilla extract
1 1/2 cups all-purpose flour
1 teaspoon baking soda

1/2 teaspoon salt
3 cups rolled oats
1 cup raisins or other dried fruits (optional)
1/2 cup chopped nuts (optional)

Instructions For Oatmeal Cookies:

Preheat the Oven: Preheat your oven to 350°F (175°C).

Mix Wet Ingredients: In a large mixing bowl, cream together the softened butter, brown sugar, and granulated sugar until smooth. Beat in the eggs one at a time, then stir in the vanilla.

Dry Ingredients: In a separate bowl, whisk together the flour, baking soda, and salt. Gradually beat this into the butter mixture.

Oats and Add-ins: Stir in the oats, raisins, and nuts (if using).

Shape and Bake: Drop by rounded spoonfuls onto ungreased baking sheets. Bake for 10 to 12 minutes in the preheated oven, or until golden brown. Allow cookies to cool on baking sheet for 5 minutes before transferring to a wire rack to cool completely.

For Freeze-Drying:

Cool Completely: Ensure the oatmeal cookies have cooled completely to room temperature after baking.

Place on Trays: Arrange the cookies in a single layer on the freeze dryer trays. Ensure they are not touching.

Freeze-Dry: Start the freeze dryer and run it through its cycle (usually 20-40 hours depending on the machine and size of cookies).

Packaging: Once the freeze-drying cycle is complete, remove the cookies and immediately place them in airtight storage bags or containers. For best shelf-life, use vacuum-sealed bags.

Rehydration:

Spritz Method: To bring back some of the original texture, lightly spritz the freeze-dried oatmeal cookies with clean water using a spray bottle. Allow them to sit for a few minutes, and they will regain some of their original texture. They won't be exactly as before freeze-drying but will be soft enough to enjoy.

Enjoy As-Is: Alternatively, freeze-dried oatmeal cookies can be enjoyed as they are. They'll be crunchy, light, and will still carry the delightful flavors of the cookie.

Remember, the beauty of freeze-dried food is that it retains nearly all its original flavor. Whether you choose to rehydrate or enjoy them crunchy, these oatmeal cookies will be a treat!

Mixed Fruit Slices

SERVINGS: 4   **PREP TIME:** 20 MIN   **COOK TIME:** 30 MIN   **FREEZE-DRY TIME:** 25-35 HRS

Ingredients For Mixed Fruit Slices:

Apples - 2, thinly sliced
Pears - 2, thinly sliced
Strawberries - 1 cup, hulled and sliced
Kiwi - 2, peeled and sliced
Pineapple - 5 slices
Mango - 1, peeled and thinly sliced
Banana - 1, sliced
Any other fruit of your choice!

Instructions For Mixed Fruit Slices:

Begin by washing all the fruits thoroughly.

Slicing: For fruits like apples, pears, and mangoes, remove the core or pit and slice them thinly. For strawberries, hull them and slice. Peel the kiwi and slice. Continue this process with any other fruits you're using.

Optional (To Prevent Browning): For fruits that brown quickly like apples and bananas, you can dip the slices in a solution of 1 cup water mixed with 1 tablespoon lemon juice for about 2 minutes, then drain.

Drying (If Using a Regular Dehydrator): If you have a food dehydrator, you can pre-dry your fruit slices. Spread the fruit slices on the dehydrator trays, ensuring they don't overlap. Dry at 135°F (57°C) for 6-12 hours or until pliable.

For Freeze-Drying:

Place on Trays: Arrange the fruit slices in a single layer on your freeze dryer trays. Make sure they don't overlap.

Freeze-Dry: Turn on your freeze dryer and run it through its cycle. The duration will typically be between 20-40 hours, depending on the freeze dryer and the thickness and water content of the fruit slices.

Packaging: Once the freeze-drying cycle is done, promptly remove the fruit slices and place them in airtight storage bags or containers. Vacuum-sealed bags will give the best shelf-life.

Rehydration:

Soaking: To rehydrate freeze-dried fruit slices, place them in a bowl and cover them with cold water. Let them sit for 5-10 minutes. Drain off the excess water, and they should be ready to eat. They might have a slightly different texture than fresh, but the flavor will be concentrated and delightful.

Direct Eating: Freeze-dried fruit slices can also be eaten as they are without rehydration. They will be crunchy and will have a concentrated flavor.

Whether you opt to rehydrate them or munch on them directly, these freeze-dried fruit slices will offer a burst of flavors and are perfect for snacking, adding to cereals, or including in baked goods.

Hummus Pucks

SERVINGS: 4 **PREP TIME:** 20 MIN **COOK TIME:** 30 MIN **FREEZE-DRY TIME:** 35-45 HRS

Ingredients For Hummus Pucks:

- Cooked chickpeas (canned or freshly boiled) - 2 cups
- Tahini (sesame paste) - 1/4 cup
- Fresh lemon juice - 3 tbsp
- Garlic cloves - 2, minced
- Extra-virgin olive oil - 2 tbsp (plus extra for serving)
- Ground cumin - 1/2 tsp
- Salt - 1/2 tsp
- Water or chickpea liquid (from the can or boiling) - 2 to 3 tbsp
- Paprika or parsley (for garnish, optional)

Instructions For Hummus Pucks:

Blending: In a food processor, combine the tahini and lemon juice and process for 1 minute. Add additional ingredients: garlic, olive oil, cumin, and salt. Process until smooth. Add chickpeas and process until thoroughly blended and smooth. If the consistency is too thick, slowly add water or chickpea liquid, 1 tablespoon at a time, until you reach the desired consistency.

Forming Pucks: Once your hummus is ready, line a muffin tin with plastic wrap or parchment paper. Scoop hummus into each muffin cup, filling them about halfway. Flatten the top using a spatula. Place the muffin tin in the freezer for a couple of hours or until the hummus becomes solid.

Removing Pucks: Once solid, take out the hummus pucks from the muffin tin by lifting the plastic wrap or parchment paper. You can then place them together in a freezer-friendly container or bag until ready to freeze-dry.

For Freeze-Drying:

Place on Trays: Arrange the frozen hummus pucks in a single layer on your freeze dryer trays.

Freeze-Dry: Start your freeze dryer and let it run through its complete cycle. Depending on your machine and the size of your pucks, this could take between 20-30 hours.

Packaging: Once the cycle is complete, promptly store the hummus pucks in airtight bags or containers. Vacuum sealing is ideal for longer shelf life.

Rehydration:

Water Bath: To rehydrate your freeze-dried hummus pucks, place them in a bowl and cover with cold water. Allow them to sit for about 20 minutes or until they've reached their original consistency. Drain any excess water.

Serving: Once rehydrated, you can drizzle with a bit of olive oil and sprinkle with paprika or parsley for garnish. Serve with bread, crackers, or veggies.

Remember, the texture might be slightly different from fresh hummus, but the taste will be just as delightful. Enjoy your homemade hummus pucks!

Granola Bars

SERVINGS: 4   **PREP TIME:** 20 MIN   **COOK TIME:** 30 MIN   **FREEZE-DRY TIME:** 30-40 HRS

Ingredients For Granola Bars:

Rolled oats - 2 cups
Honey or maple syrup - 1/2 cup
Nut butter (like peanut or almond butter) - 1/2 cup
Vanilla extract - 1 tsp
Chopped nuts (such as almonds, walnuts, or pecans) - 1/2 cup
Dried fruits (raisins, cranberries, apricots, etc.) - 1/2 cup
Seeds (like sunflower or pumpkin seeds) - 1/4 cup
Dark chocolate chips or chunks (optional) - 1/4 cup
Salt - 1/4 tsp

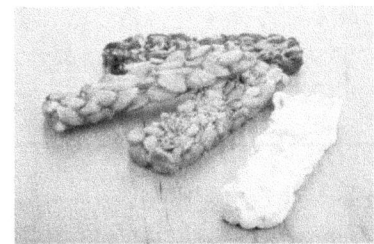

Instructions For Granola Bars:

Preparation: Preheat your oven to 350°F (175°C). Line an 8-inch square baking dish with parchment paper, leaving some overhang for easy removal.

Combine Wet Ingredients: In a small saucepan, combine the honey (or maple syrup) and nut butter. Warm over low heat until melted and well combined. Remove from heat and stir in the vanilla extract.

Mix Dry Ingredients: In a large mixing bowl, combine the oats, chopped nuts, dried fruits, seeds, chocolate chips (if using), and salt.

Combine: Pour the wet mixture over the dry ingredients and mix thoroughly until everything is well coated.

Press and Bake: Transfer the mixture to the prepared baking dish and press down firmly to ensure the mixture is compacted. Bake for 15-20 minutes or until the edges turn golden brown. Remove from the oven and allow to cool completely in the dish before removing and cutting into bars.

For Freeze-Drying:

Preparation: Once your granola bars have cooled and are cut into the desired size, place them in a single layer on your freeze dryer trays. Make sure the bars aren't touching to allow for even drying.

Freeze-Dry: Start your freeze dryer and run through its complete cycle. The drying time can vary based on the machine and moisture content, but it generally takes between 20-30 hours.

Packaging: After the freeze-drying process is complete, quickly store the granola bars in airtight bags or containers. Vacuum sealing can be ideal for maximizing shelf life.

Rehydration:

Quick Rehydrate: Place the freeze-dried granola bar in a container and mist it lightly with water using a spray bottle. Allow it to sit for 5-10 minutes. This method will restore some of its original chewy texture.

Eat As-Is: The freeze-dried granola bars can also be enjoyed as a crunchy snack without rehydration.

Please note that the texture after freeze-drying will be different — it'll be more crispy than the original chewy granola bar. But the taste will still be delightful!

Veggie Chips

SERVINGS: 4   **PREP TIME:** 20 MIN   **COOK TIME:** 30 MIN   **FREEZE-DRY TIME:** 25-35 HRS

Ingredients For Veggie Chips:

Root vegetables: Choose a combination of sweet potatoes, beets, carrots, parsnips, or zucchinis.
Olive oil or avocado oil - 2 to 3 tablespoons
Sea salt - to taste
Optional seasonings: black pepper, paprika, garlic powder, or rosemary.

Instructions For Veggie Chips:

Preparation: Preheat your oven to 275°F (135°C). If you have a mandoline slicer, it's ideal for this; otherwise, use a sharp knife to slice your vegetables thinly.

Wash & Slice: Clean the chosen vegetables and slice them thinly. If you're using zucchini, make sure to slice them a tad thicker since they have more water content.

Season: In a large mixing bowl, toss the sliced vegetables with oil, salt, and any other seasonings you're using. Ensure every slice is lightly coated.

Bake: Place the seasoned veggie slices in a single layer on a baking sheet lined with parchment paper. Bake for about 1 to 1.5 hours, flipping the slices halfway through. Cooking times will vary based on the vegetable and thickness of the slices. They should be crisp and slightly golden when done.

Cool: Remove from the oven and let them cool completely. They will continue to crisp up as they cool.

For Freeze-Drying:

Preparation: Spread the cooled veggie chips in a single layer on the freeze-drying trays. Make sure they aren't overlapping or touching, which ensures even drying.

Freeze-Dry: Start the freeze dryer and run through its complete cycle. Drying time can vary based on the machine and the moisture content of the veggies, but it generally takes between 20-30 hours.

Packaging: Once the freeze-drying process is finished, quickly store the veggie chips in airtight bags or containers. Vacuum sealing is a great way to maximize their shelf life.

Rehydration:

Quick Rehydrate: Place the freeze-dried veggie chips in a container and mist lightly with water using a spray bottle. Let them sit for a few minutes. This will give them a slightly chewier texture.

Eat As-Is: Veggie chips are fantastic as they are after freeze-drying, offering a light and crunchy texture.

Keep in mind, rehydration isn't always necessary for freeze-dried foods, especially snacks like veggie chips. They can be a delightful, crunchy treat straight from the freeze dryer.

Cheese Crisps

SERVINGS: 4   **PREP TIME:** 20 MIN   **COOK TIME:** 30 MIN   **FREEZE-DRY TIME:** 35-45 HRS

Ingredients For Cheese Crisps:

2 cups of shredded hard cheese (like Parmesan, Cheddar, or Asiago)
Optional: Seasonings like black pepper, garlic powder, or red pepper flakes for added flavor

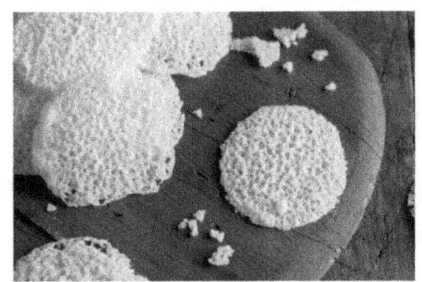

Instructions For Cheese Crisps:

Preparation: Preheat your oven to 400°F (200°C). Line a baking sheet with parchment paper or a silicone baking mat.

Form the Crisps: Place tablespoon-sized piles of shredded cheese on the lined baking sheet, ensuring there's enough space between each one. If you're using additional seasonings, sprinkle them over the top now.

Bake: Put the baking sheet in the oven and bake for 5-7 minutes or until the edges of the crisps are golden.

Cool: Once out of the oven, allow them to cool and harden for about 5 minutes on the baking sheet. After that, move them to a cooling rack to cool completely.

For Freeze-Drying:

Preparation: Lay the cooled cheese crisps in a single layer on your freeze-drying trays, ensuring they aren't overlapping.

Freeze-Dry: Start your freeze dryer and run it through its complete cycle. Cheese is generally quicker to dry than many other foods, often taking only 12-18 hours, but this can vary based on the specific freeze dryer and the thickness of the cheese crisps.

Packaging: Once freeze-drying is complete, quickly transfer the cheese crisps to airtight bags or containers. For the best shelf life, consider using vacuum-sealed bags.

Rehydration:

For cheese crisps, rehydration isn't typically necessary or recommended. When freeze-dried, they become even crisper and can be enjoyed straight from the bag as a crunchy snack. If you wanted them to have a chewier texture (which is not their typical form), you could mist them lightly with water and let sit, but it's not common to rehydrate cheese crisps. They're most enjoyed for their crunchy, freeze-dried texture.

Trail Mix

SERVINGS: 4   **PREP TIME:** 20 MIN   **COOK TIME:** 30 MIN   **FREEZE-DRY TIME:** 25-35 HRS

Ingredients For Trail Mix:

1 cup roasted almonds
1 cup roasted cashews
1/2 cup dried cranberries
1/2 cup raisins
1/2 cup chocolate chips or chocolate-covered nuts (you can also use dark chocolate for a healthier version)
1/2 cup pumpkin seeds (pepitas)
1/2 cup sunflower seeds

Instructions For Trail Mix:

Mixing: In a large mixing bowl, combine all the ingredients and toss well to combine.

Storing: Store in an airtight container or bag until ready to freeze-dry.

For Freeze-Drying:

Preparation: Spread the trail mix in a single, even layer on your freeze-drying trays.

Freeze-Dry: Start your freeze dryer and run it through its complete cycle. Depending on your specific freeze dryer and the volume of trail mix, the drying time can range from 12-24 hours.

Packaging: Once freeze-drying is complete, quickly transfer the trail mix to airtight bags or containers. Using vacuum-sealed bags will offer a longer shelf life.

Rehydration:

Trail mix doesn't require rehydration. The freeze-drying process is used here primarily for preservation, ensuring the fruits, nuts, and seeds retain their natural flavors and crunch without the need for additives or preservatives. When you're ready to eat, simply open the package and enjoy. If freeze-drying chocolate or chocolate-covered items, be aware that they can change in texture, becoming more crumbly but retaining their flavor.

Meat Jerky

SERVINGS: 4   **PREP TIME:** 20 MIN   **COOK TIME:** 30 MIN   **FREEZE-DRY TIME:** 40-50 HRS

Ingredients For Meat Jerky:

2 pounds of lean beef (flank steak or top round are good choices)
1/4 cup soy sauce
1/4 cup Worcestershire sauce
2 tablespoons honey or brown sugar
2 teaspoons black pepper

1 teaspoon onion powder
1 teaspoon garlic powder
1/2 teaspoon smoked paprika (optional)
1/2 teaspoon chili flakes (for a spicy kick, adjust according to preference)

Instructions For Meat Jerky:

Preparation: Freeze the beef for about 1-2 hours; this makes it easier to slice.

Slice the Meat: Remove the beef from the freezer and slice it against the grain into thin strips, about 1/4 inch thick.

Marinate: In a bowl, combine soy sauce, Worcestershire sauce, honey, black pepper, onion powder, garlic powder, smoked paprika, and chili flakes. Place the beef strips into the marinade, ensuring all pieces are well-coated. Refrigerate for at least 6 hours, ideally overnight.

Drying: Preheat your oven to its lowest setting (around 150-170°F or 65-77°C). Place a wire rack on a large baking tray. Arrange the marinated beef strips on the rack, ensuring they don't overlap. Place the tray in the oven and let it dry for 3-5 hours, or until the jerky bends and cracks but doesn't break.

Cool: Once dried, remove the jerky from the oven and let it cool completely.

For Freeze-Drying:

Preparation: Lay the cooled jerky pieces on freeze-drying trays in a single layer, ensuring they don't overlap.

Freeze-Dry: Run your freeze dryer through its complete cycle. Depending on the thickness of your jerky and your specific freeze dryer, this can take between 12-24 hours.

Packaging: Once freeze-drying is complete, quickly transfer the jerky to vacuum-sealed bags or airtight containers.

Rehydration:

Typically, meat jerky is enjoyed in its dried form for its chewy texture and concentrated flavor. If you ever do want to rehydrate it (which is less common for jerky):

Place the jerky in a bowl and cover it with cold water.

Allow it to sit for 30 minutes to an hour. The jerky will soften and expand slightly.

Drain any excess water and enjoy.

Note: *The texture after rehydration will be different than both the fresh and dehydrated versions. It's best enjoyed as a dried snack. Freeze-drying jerky can help in extending its shelf life and preserving its flavor and nutrition.*

Rice Cakes

SERVINGS: 4   **PREP TIME:** 20 MIN   **COOK TIME:** 30 MIN   **FREEZE-DRY TIME:** 25-35 HRS

Ingredients For Rice Cakes:

2 cups of glutinous rice (also known as sticky rice or sweet rice)
Water for soaking
1/2 teaspoon of salt

Instructions For Rice Cakes:

Preparation: Rinse the glutinous rice a few times in cold water until the water runs clear. This removes excess starch.

Soak: Soak the rice in water for at least 4 hours or overnight.

Drain: After soaking, drain the rice thoroughly using a fine-mesh sieve or colander.

Steam: Prepare a steamer with water and bring it to a boil. Spread the soaked rice on a steamer cloth or steamer basket in an even layer. Steam the rice for about 30-40 minutes or until translucent and tender.

Shape: Once cooked, while it's still hot, transfer the rice to a wooden or plastic surface and add salt. Quickly spread and flatten the rice into a thin, even layer (about 1/2 inch thick) using a rice paddle or spatula.

Cool: Allow the rice sheet to cool completely. Once cooled, use a round cookie cutter or a glass to cut out rice cakes.

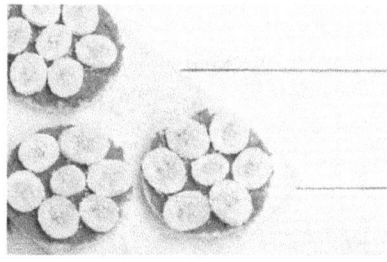

For Freeze-Drying:

Preparation: Once the rice cakes are completely cooled, place them in a single layer on the freeze-drying trays, ensuring they don't overlap.

Freeze-Dry: Run your freeze dryer through its standard cycle. Depending on the size and thickness of your rice cakes and your specific freeze dryer, this can take between 18-30 hours.

Packaging: Once the freeze-drying cycle is complete, immediately transfer the rice cakes to vacuum-sealed bags or airtight containers to maintain freshness.

Rehydration:

Submersion: To rehydrate the rice cakes, simply immerse them in cold water for about 2-4 hours. They should regain much of their original texture.

Steam: If you want them to be softer or if they are not fully rehydrated, steam the rehydrated rice cakes for an additional 5-10 minutes.

Enjoy: Serve the rehydrated rice cakes as desired. They can be incorporated into various dishes or eaten with dipping sauces.

Note: Freeze-drying rice cakes can extend their shelf life and preserve their texture and flavor. The rehydration process should bring them close to their original texture, though there might be slight differences.

Mini Pancakes

SERVINGS: 4   **PREP TIME:** 20 MIN   **COOK TIME:** 30 MIN   **FREEZE-DRY TIME:** 25-35 HRS

Ingredients For Mini Pancakes:

1 cup all-purpose flour
1 tablespoon granulated sugar
1 teaspoon baking powder
1/2 teaspoon baking soda
1/4 teaspoon salt
3/4 cup buttermilk (or regular milk with a splash of lemon juice/vinegar)
1 large egg
2 tablespoons unsalted butter, melted
Optional: Chocolate chips, blueberries, or other mix-ins

Instructions For Mini Pancakes:

Mix Dry Ingredients: In a large bowl, whisk together the flour, sugar, baking powder, baking soda, and salt.

Add Wet Ingredients: In another bowl, mix together the buttermilk, egg, and melted butter. Pour this mixture into the dry ingredients and stir until just combined. If you're using any mix-ins, fold them into the batter now.

Cook: Heat a non-stick skillet or griddle over medium heat. For each pancake, drop a tablespoon of batter onto the skillet. Cook until bubbles appear on the surface, then flip and cook for another 1-2 minutes, or until browned on the other side.

Cool: Allow the mini pancakes to cool completely on a wire rack.

For Freeze-Drying:

Preparation: Place the cooled mini pancakes in a single layer on the freeze-drying trays. Ensure they don't overlap to allow for even freeze-drying.

Freeze-Dry: Start your freeze dryer and run it through its standard cycle. Depending on your specific machine, this can take between 20-36 hours.

Packaging: Once the freeze-drying process is completed, immediately transfer the mini pancakes to vacuum-sealed bags or airtight containers to ensure freshness and avoid moisture reentry.

Rehydration:

Steam or Microwave: To rehydrate your mini pancakes, you can either steam them for a few minutes until they become soft, or you can microwave them in 10-second intervals until they're warm and soft. They can also be warmed in an oven or toaster oven at a low temperature.

Serve: Once rehydrated, serve the mini pancakes with your favorite toppings like maple syrup, butter, fresh fruits, or whipped cream.

Note: Freeze-drying the mini pancakes is a fantastic way to preserve them for extended periods. The rehydration process should get them close to their original fluffy texture, but there might be slight variations. Enjoy your ready-to-eat breakfast treat!

Licorice Bites

SERVINGS: 4   **PREP TIME:** 20 MIN   **COOK TIME:** 30 MIN   **FREEZE-DRY TIME:** 15-25 HRS

Ingredients For Licorice Bites:

1 cup all-purpose flour
1/2 cup molasses or dark corn syrup
1/2 cup granulated sugar
1/4 cup unsalted butter
2 tablespoons water
1 1/2 teaspoons anise extract (or licorice flavoring)
1/4 teaspoon salt
1/4 teaspoon baking soda

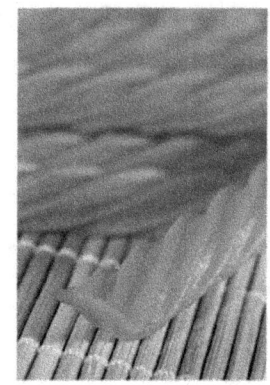

Instructions For Licorice Bites:

Preparation: Line an 8x8-inch baking pan with parchment paper.

Cook: In a saucepan, combine molasses, sugar, butter, and water. Heat over medium heat until the sugar has dissolved and the mixture comes to a boil. Remove from heat.

Mix: Stir in the anise extract, followed by the flour, salt, and baking soda. Mix well until the dough forms.

Shape: Transfer the dough to the prepared baking pan and press it evenly into the pan.

Cool: Allow the mixture to cool completely. Once cooled, cut it into bite-sized pieces using a sharp knife.

For Freeze-Drying:

Preparation: Place the licorice bites in a single layer on the freeze-drying trays, ensuring they do not touch to prevent them from sticking together.

Freeze-Dry: Start your freeze dryer and run it through its standard cycle. Depending on your specific machine, this can take between 20-36 hours.

Packaging: Once the freeze-drying process is completed, immediately transfer the licorice bites to vacuum-sealed bags or airtight containers to ensure freshness and avoid moisture reentry.

Rehydration:

For licorice bites, rehydration isn't the typical goal since the freeze-drying process will primarily be used to extend their shelf life while preserving their flavor. However, if you find them too hard:

Mist with Water: Lightly mist the licorice bites with water using a spray bottle. Allow them to sit for a few minutes.

Enjoy: After a short waiting period, the licorice bites should have a softer texture, closer to their original form.

Note: *Always ensure that your freeze-dried foods are stored in a cool, dark place in airtight containers to maximize their shelf life.*

Salted Caramel Bites

SERVINGS: 4   **PREP TIME:** 20 MIN   **COOK TIME:** 30 MIN   **FREEZE-DRY TIME:** 25-35 HRS

Ingredients For Salted Caramel Bites:

1 cup granulated sugar
6 tablespoons unsalted butter, room temperature, cut into pieces
1/2 cup heavy cream
1 teaspoon vanilla extract
1 teaspoon sea salt or kosher salt, plus extra for sprinkling

Instructions For Salted Caramel Bites:

Caramelization: In a medium saucepan, heat sugar over medium heat, stirring constantly using a rubber spatula. The sugar will form lumps and eventually melt into a thick amber-colored liquid as you continue to stir.

Butter Addition: Once sugar is completely melted, immediately add the butter. Be careful, as the caramel will bubble rapidly when the butter is added. Stir until butter is completely melted, about 2 minutes.

Cream Addition: Slowly drizzle in the heavy cream while stirring continuously. Allow the mixture to boil for 1 minute. It will rise in the pan as it boils.

Final Touches: Remove from heat and stir in the vanilla and salt. Allow to cool slightly in the pan before transferring to a dish lined with parchment paper. Spread evenly and sprinkle with a bit more salt if desired. Allow to fully cool and set.

Cutting: Once the caramel is set, use a sharp knife to cut it into bite-sized pieces.

For Freeze-Drying:

Preparation: Place the salted caramel bites in a single layer on freeze-drying trays, ensuring there's space between them to prevent sticking.

Freeze-Dry: Start the freeze dryer and run through its standard cycle. This typically takes between 20-36 hours, depending on the machine.

Packaging: Once freeze-drying is complete, promptly transfer the caramel bites to vacuum-sealed bags or airtight containers to ensure freshness and prevent moisture reentry.

Rehydration:

Salted caramel bites are best enjoyed in their freeze-dried state for an extended shelf life and a unique texture. However, if you wish to return them to their original soft and chewy state:

Atmospheric Rehydration: Simply leave the caramel bites exposed to room atmosphere for a few hours. The natural humidity will soften them slightly.

For Faster Rehydration: Wrap them in a damp (not wet) paper towel and microwave them on low for a few seconds.

Enjoy your salted caramel bites either freeze-dried or rehydrated!

Marshmallows

SERVINGS: 4 **PREP TIME:** 20 MIN **COOK TIME:** 30 MIN **FREEZE-DRY TIME:** 15-25 HRS

Ingredients For Marshmallows:

3 packages unflavored gelatin
1 1/2 cups granulated sugar
1 cup light corn syrup
1/4 teaspoon kosher salt
1 tablespoon pure vanilla extract
Confectioners' sugar, for dusting

Instructions For Marshmallows:

Gelatin Preparation: In the bowl of an electric mixer fitted with the whisk attachment, combine the gelatin and 1/2 cup of cold water. Allow to sit while you make the syrup.

Syrup: In a small saucepan, combine the sugar, corn syrup, salt, and 1/2 cup water. Cook over medium heat until the sugar dissolves. Then, raise the heat to high and cook until the syrup reaches 240°F on a candy thermometer. Remove from heat.

Mixing: Turn the mixer on low speed and slowly pour the sugar syrup into the dissolved gelatin. Increase the speed to high and whip until very thick, about 15 minutes. Add the vanilla and mix thoroughly.

Setting: Dust a non-metal, 9x13-inch baking dish with confectioners' sugar. Pour the marshmallow mixture into the pan and smooth the top. Dust with more confectioners' sugar. Let stand uncovered overnight until it dries out.

Cutting: Turn the marshmallow slab out onto a cutting board and cut it into squares using a pizza cutter dusted with confectioners' sugar.

For Freeze-Drying:

Preparation: Place the marshmallow squares in a single layer on freeze-drying trays, making sure they're not touching.

Freeze-Dry: Start the freeze dryer and run through its standard cycle. This typically takes between 20-36 hours, depending on the machine and the size of the marshmallows.

Packaging: Once freeze-drying is complete, quickly transfer the marshmallows to vacuum-sealed bags or airtight containers to maintain their freshness and prevent moisture reentry.

Rehydration:

Marshmallows are usually consumed in their freeze-dried state for a crunchy texture. They don't typically require rehydration. However, if you desire to return them to their softer state:

Atmospheric Rehydration: Leave the marshmallows exposed to room atmosphere for several hours. The natural humidity will soften them slightly.

Steam Method: Using a steamer or a pot with a small amount of boiling water (and a strainer to keep the marshmallows above the water), steam the marshmallows for a few seconds until they start to soften.

Enjoy your marshmallows either freeze-dried for a unique crunchy texture or rehydrated for their traditional soft and squishy feel!

Chocolate Coconut Balls

SERVINGS: 4   **PREP TIME:** 20 MIN   **COOK TIME:** 30 MIN   **FREEZE-DRY TIME:** 35-45 HRS

Ingredients For Chocolate Coconut Balls:

1 cup unsweetened shredded coconut
1/2 cup condensed milk
1/2 cup semisweet chocolate chips
1/2 tsp vanilla extract
1/4 cup unsweetened cocoa powder (for coating, optional)
A pinch of salt

Instructions For Chocolate Coconut Balls:

Mix Ingredients: In a mixing bowl, combine shredded coconut, condensed milk, chocolate chips, vanilla extract, and a pinch of salt. Mix until everything is well combined.

Shape: Using your hands, shape the mixture into small balls, about 1 inch in diameter.

Coating (Optional): Roll each ball in cocoa powder until it's fully coated. This adds an extra layer of chocolate flavor and keeps the balls from being too sticky.

Set: Place the balls on a parchment-lined tray or plate and refrigerate for at least 2 hours, or until they harden.

For Freeze-Drying:

Preparation: Place the hardened chocolate coconut balls in a single layer on freeze-drying trays, ensuring they are not touching.

Freeze-Dry: Place the trays in the freeze dryer and run through its standard cycle. The duration will generally be between 20-36 hours, but this can vary based on machine and the size of the chocolate coconut balls.

Packaging: Once the freeze-drying process is finished, swiftly transfer the chocolate coconut balls to vacuum-sealed bags or airtight containers. This step ensures they remain fresh and prevents moisture from seeping in.

Rehydration:

Chocolate Coconut Balls, when freeze-dried, offer a delightful crunch and are usually consumed in this state. However, if you wish to rehydrate:

Misting: Lightly mist the chocolate coconut balls with water using a spray bottle. Be sure not to soak them.

Rest: Place them in a sealed container for a few hours, allowing the moisture to evenly distribute and soften the balls.

While rehydrated Chocolate Coconut Balls won't exactly match their original consistency, they'll still be delicious. For the best experience, many prefer to consume them directly in their freeze-dried, crunchy state. Enjoy!

Chocolate Covered Bananas

SERVINGS: 4   **PREP TIME:** 20 MIN   **COOK TIME:** 30 MIN   **FREEZE-DRY TIME:** 25-35 HRS

Ingredients For Chocolate Covered Bananas:

14 ripe bananas
1 cup dark or semi-sweet chocolate chips
2 tablespoons coconut oil (optional, for smoother chocolate consistency)
Toppings of your choice (chopped nuts, sprinkles, shredded coconut, etc.)
Popsicle sticks or skewers

Instructions For Chocolate Covered Bananas:

Peel the bananas and cut them in half crosswise. Insert a popsicle stick or skewer into the cut end of each banana half.

Place them on a baking sheet lined with parchment paper and freeze for about 1 hour or until firm.

Chocolate Coating: In a microwave-safe bowl, combine the chocolate chips and coconut oil. Microwave in 30-second intervals, stirring after each interval, until the chocolate is completely melted and smooth.

Coating the Bananas: Dip each frozen banana half into the melted chocolate, turning to coat all sides. If desired, roll the coated banana in your chosen toppings. Place the chocolate-covered bananas back on the parchment paper and return to the freezer until the chocolate is set, about 15-20 minutes.

For Freeze-Drying:

Once the chocolate-covered bananas are set, arrange them in a single layer on the trays of your freeze dryer.

Place the trays in your freeze dryer and run a standard freeze-drying cycle (typically this lasts 24-36 hours, depending on the machine and its settings).

Storing:

Once the freeze-drying cycle is complete, promptly remove the bananas from the freeze dryer.

Store the freeze-dried chocolate-covered bananas in airtight bags or containers with oxygen absorbers to prevent moisture and air from getting in. Store in a cool, dark place.

Rehydration:

To eat, simply remove a chocolate-covered banana from its storage bag or container. They can be enjoyed as is without the need for rehydration. The texture will be crispy with the intense flavor of the banana and chocolate.

Note: While the freeze-drying process will make the bananas crunchy, the chocolate will remain relatively the same in texture, albeit a bit more crumbly. Enjoy your treat!

Chocolate Covered Strawberries

SERVINGS: 4   **PREP TIME:** 20 MIN   **COOK TIME:** 30 MIN   **FREEZE-DRY TIME:** 25-35 HRS

Ingredients For Chocolate Covered Strawberries:

1 pound fresh strawberries (about 20), washed and dried thoroughly
8 ounces semi-sweet chocolate or dark chocolate
1 tablespoon coconut oil (optional, for smoother chocolate consistency)
White chocolate or sprinkles for decoration (optional)

Instructions For Chocolate Covered Strawberries:

Preparation: Line a baking sheet with parchment paper or a silicone baking mat. Ensure strawberries are completely dry. Any moisture can prevent the chocolate from sticking properly.

Chocolate Melt: In a microwave-safe bowl, combine the chocolate chips and coconut oil. Heat in the microwave in 30-second intervals, stirring in between until the chocolate is completely melted and smooth. Ensure not to overheat, as chocolate can seize.

Dipping Strawberries: Holding a strawberry by the stem, dip it into the melted chocolate, ensuring it's generously coated. Let any excess chocolate drip back into the bowl.
Place the coated strawberry on the prepared baking sheet.
Repeat with the remaining strawberries.
If desired, drizzle with melted white chocolate or add sprinkles for decoration before the chocolate sets.

Setting: Allow the chocolate to set for about 30 minutes, or you can speed up the process by placing them in the refrigerator.

For Freeze-Drying:

Once the chocolate on the strawberries is fully set, arrange the strawberries in a single layer on the trays of your freeze dryer.

Place the trays in the freeze dryer and run a standard freeze-drying cycle (typically 24-36 hours, depending on the machine and settings).

Storing:

After freeze-drying, promptly remove the strawberries and store in airtight bags or containers with oxygen absorbers to ensure they stay crisp.

Store the containers in a cool, dark place.

Rehydration:

For freeze-dried chocolate-covered strawberries, rehydration isn't typically necessary. They can be enjoyed as a crispy snack with intense flavors straight from the storage bag or container.

However, if you wish to rehydrate them, lightly mist the strawberries with cold water and allow them to sit for a few minutes. They won't return to the exact original texture, but they will soften slightly.

Candy Recipe Index

Candy:
- Mint Patties
- Peanutbutter Cups
- Candied Ginger
- Lemon Drops
- Chocolate Mint Wafers

Candy:
- Jelly Beans
- Caramel Popcorn
- Almond Joyfuls
- Fruit Leather Pieces
- Candy Apple Slices

Candy:
- Yogurt Drops
- Nut Clusters
- Fudge Cubes
- Candy Cane Bites
- Orange Peels

Candy:
- Gummy Bears
- Raspberry Jellies
- Peanut butter Morsels
- Cherry Cordials
- Dulce de Leche Bites

Candy:
- Berry Bites
- Raspberry Chocolates
- Tutti Frutti Candy
- Toffee Crunch
- Mocha Bites

Candy:
- Honey Almond Candy
- Maple Pecan Treats
- Vanilla Bean White Chocolate Truffles
- Pistacchio Brittle

*** Freeze Drying times for candy will vary depending on the freeze-dryer model you own and the size of your trays. Recipes are based on a 4-tray Harvest Right freeze-dryer. Adjust as needed.

 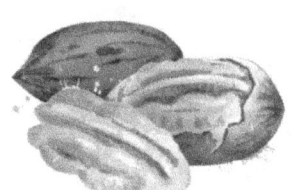 

Mint Patties

SERVINGS: 4   **PREP TIME:** 20 MIN   **COOK TIME:** 30 MIN   **FREEZE-DRY TIME:** 25-35 HRS

Ingredients For Mint Patties:

4 cups powdered sugar
1/4 cup unsalted butter, melted
1/3 cup light corn syrup
1-2 tsp peppermint extract (to taste)
Dark chocolate or semisweet chocolate for coating

Instructions For Mint Patties:

In a large mixing bowl, combine the powdered sugar, melted butter, corn syrup, and peppermint extract. Mix until you have a smooth and pliable dough. If it's too dry, add a tad more corn syrup.

Dust a flat surface with a bit of powdered sugar and roll out the dough to about a 1/4-inch thickness.

Use a round cookie cutter (or any desired shape) to cut out patties. Place them on a parchment-lined baking sheet.

Allow the patties to dry for about 1 hour, turning them once to ensure both sides dry out slightly.

Melt the chocolate in a double boiler or microwave. Using a fork, dip each patty into the chocolate, ensuring it's fully coated. Place them back on the parchment paper.

Allow the chocolate to set completely, which may take a couple of hours. You can speed up the process by placing them in the refrigerator for about 30 minutes.

For Freeze-Drying:

Once the mint patties are set, arrange them in a single layer on the trays of your freeze dryer.

Run a standard freeze-drying cycle, which usually lasts between 24-36 hours, depending on the machine and specific settings.

After the cycle completes, ensure the mint patties are completely dried and have a crunchy texture.

Rehydration (If desired):

While you can enjoy freeze-dried mint patties as a crunchy treat, if you wish to rehydrate:

Place the freeze-dried mint patties in an airtight container.

Add a few moisture-absorbing packets (found in food storage sections or with certain food products). Do NOT add water.

Seal the container and let the patties sit for several hours. The moisture from the packets will help soften the mint patties slightly, bringing them closer to their original texture.

Note: *They will not return to their exact original state, but this method can help soften them if the crunchy texture isn't desired.*

Peanut Butter Cups

SERVINGS: 4   **PREP TIME:** 20 MIN   **COOK TIME:** 30 MIN   **FREEZE-DRY TIME:** 35-45 HRS

Ingredients For Peanut Butter Cups:

2 cups milk chocolate or dark chocolate, melted
1/2 cup creamy peanut butter
1/4 cup powdered sugar
2 tablespoons unsalted butter, softened
Mini cupcake liners

Instructions For Peanut Butter Cups:

Line a mini muffin tin with cupcake liners.

Melt the chocolate in a microwave in 20-second intervals or use a double boiler. Stir until smooth. Drop a teaspoon of melted chocolate into the bottom of each cupcake liner.

In a mixing bowl, combine the peanut butter, powdered sugar, and butter. Mix until smooth and creamy.

Drop a teaspoon of the peanut butter mixture onto the chocolate in each liner.

Top each peanut butter dollop with another teaspoon of melted chocolate.

Chill the peanut butter cups in the refrigerator for at least an hour, or until they're set.

For Freeze-Drying:

Once the peanut butter cups are set, remove them from the cupcake liners and place them in a single layer on the trays of your freeze dryer.

Run a standard freeze-drying cycle, which generally lasts between 24-36 hours depending on your machine and its settings.

After the cycle completes, ensure the peanut butter cups are entirely dried and have a crunchy texture.

Rehydration (If desired):

While freeze-dried peanut butter cups can be enjoyed as a crunchy treat, if you wish to rehydrate:

Place the freeze-dried peanut butter cups in an airtight container.

Add a few moisture-absorbing packets (found in food storage sections or with certain food products). Do NOT add water.

Seal the container and let the peanut butter cups sit for several hours. The slight moisture from the packets will help soften the peanut butter cups.

Note: Keep in mind they will not return to their exact original state, but this method can help soften them if the crunchy texture isn't preferred.

Candied Ginger

SERVINGS: 4   **PREP TIME:** 20 MIN   **COOK TIME:** 30 MIN   **FREEZE-DRY TIME:** 15-25 HRS

Ingredients For Candied Ginger:

1 lb fresh ginger root
5 cups water (for boiling)
1 cup granulated sugar, plus more for rolling
1 pinch of salt

Instructions For Candied Ginger:

Prepare the Ginger: Peel the ginger and slice it thinly, about 1/8-inch thick.

Boil: Place ginger slices in a pot, cover with the 5 cups of water, and bring to a boil. Reduce heat and let ginger simmer for about 30 minutes.

Drain and Reserve Water: After simmering, drain ginger slices, reserving 1/4 cup of the ginger water.

Candy the Ginger: Return ginger slices to the pot. Add the reserved 1/4 cup ginger water, sugar, and a pinch of salt. Set the pot over medium heat and cook, stirring regularly, until the liquid is almost evaporated and turns syrupy (approximately 20 minutes).

Roll in Sugar: Let the ginger cool for a few minutes, then roll each slice in granulated sugar to coat.

Dry: Place the sugared ginger slices on a wire rack and let them dry for several hours or overnight.

For Freeze-Drying:

Arrange the candied ginger slices in a single layer on the trays of your freeze dryer, ensuring they aren't touching.

Run a standard freeze-drying cycle, typically lasting 24-36 hours depending on your machine and settings.

Once the cycle is complete, ensure the ginger slices are thoroughly dried and crisp to the touch.

Rehydration (If desired):

To be honest, rehydrating candied ginger might not restore its exact original texture, and it's usually enjoyed freeze-dried or as-is without rehydration. However, if you still want to:

Place the freeze-dried candied ginger slices in a bowl.

Spritz or sprinkle them with a small amount of water, just enough to moisten but not soak. Let them sit for a few minutes, then enjoy. Adjust moisture level as necessary.

Remember, while freeze-drying preserves most of the qualities of foods, certain textures, especially in sugary or syrupy items, might not be precisely the same post-rehydration.

Lemon Drops

SERVINGS: 4   **PREP TIME:** 20 MIN   **COOK TIME:** 30 MIN   **FREEZE-DRY TIME:** 15-25 HRS

Ingredients For Lemon Drops:

2 cups granulated sugar
1/2 cup water
1/2 cup light corn syrup
1/4 teaspoon cream of tartar
1/4 cup lemon juice (freshly squeezed)
2 teaspoons finely grated lemon zest
Yellow food coloring (optional)
Extra granulated sugar for coating

Instructions For Lemon Drops:

Prepare a Baking Sheet: Line a baking sheet with parchment paper or a silicone baking mat.

Cook Sugar Mixture: In a medium saucepan, combine sugar, water, corn syrup, and cream of tartar. Cook over medium heat, stirring occasionally until sugar has dissolved.

Boil without Stirring: Once sugar has dissolved, increase the heat and bring the mixture to a boil. Do not stir from this point on, but keep an eye on the temperature using a candy thermometer.

Add Lemon: When the mixture reaches 250°F (120°C), remove it from the heat and let it cool for a minute. Stir in the lemon juice, lemon zest, and food coloring (if using). Be careful as the mixture might bubble up when adding the juice.

Shape Drops: Using a teaspoon or a dropper, carefully drop small amounts of the mixture onto the prepared baking sheet. Let them harden and cool completely, which could take several hours.

Coat with Sugar: Once cooled, roll each lemon drop in granulated sugar to coat.

For Freeze-Drying:

Prepare for Freeze Drying: Once the lemon drops have cooled and are coated in sugar, arrange them in a single layer on the freeze dryer trays. Ensure they aren't touching each other.

Run the Freeze Dryer: Proceed with a standard freeze-drying cycle. Depending on the machine, the drying process could take between 24-36 hours.

Check Dryness: After the cycle is complete, check the lemon drops to make sure they are thoroughly dried. They should be hard and not sticky.

Rehydration (If desired):

Lemon drops are typically enjoyed as hard candies, and there's usually no need to rehydrate them.

However, if you decide to experiment:

Spritz or sprinkle the freeze-dried lemon drops with a minimal amount of water.

Let them sit for a few moments.

Test the texture and adjust moisture if necessary. Remember, the unique charm of lemon drops is their crisp sugar shell and intense flavor burst. Freeze-drying will preserve these characteristics, but rehydrating might alter the texture and experience. Enjoy your homemade lemon drops!

Chocolate Mint Wafers

SERVINGS: 4   **PREP TIME:** 20 MIN   **COOK TIME:** 30 MIN   **FREEZE-DRY TIME:** 15-25 HRS

Ingredients For Chocolate Mint Wafers:

1/2 cup unsalted butter, softened
3/4 cup granulated sugar
1 large egg
1 teaspoon mint extract (or peppermint extract, based on preference)
1 and 1/2 cups all-purpose flour
1/4 cup unsweetened cocoa powder
1/2 teaspoon baking powder
1/4 teaspoon salt
Green or blue food coloring (optional, for a minty look)

Instructions For Chocolate Mint Wafers:

Cream Butter and Sugar: In a large bowl, beat the butter and sugar until light and fluffy.
Add Egg and Mint Extract: Beat in the egg and mint extract until smooth. If desired, add a few drops of food coloring to give a hint of minty color.

Dry Ingredients: In a separate bowl, sift together the flour, cocoa powder, baking powder, and salt.

Combine Mixtures: Gradually add the dry ingredients to the butter mixture, beating until well combined.

Shape Dough: Roll out the dough between two sheets of parchment paper to about 1/4-inch thickness. Using a cookie cutter or the rim of a glass, cut out wafer shapes.

Bake: Preheat the oven to 350°F (175°C). Place the wafers on parchment-lined baking sheets. Bake for 8-10 minutes or until they are set. Allow to cool on the baking sheets for a few minutes before transferring to a wire rack to cool completely.

For Freeze-Drying:

Prepare for Freeze Drying: Once the chocolate mint wafers have cooled completely, arrange them in a single layer on the freeze dryer trays. Ensure they aren't touching each other.

Run the Freeze Dryer: Use a standard freeze-drying cycle. The process could take between 24-36 hours, depending on the machine.

Check Dryness: Once the cycle is complete, check the wafers to ensure they're thoroughly dried. They should feel light and crisp.

Rehydration:

Chocolate mint wafers are typically enjoyed as crispy treats. However, if you decide to experiment with rehydration:

Moistening: Lightly spritz the freeze-dried wafers with water using a spray bottle. Don't oversaturate them.

Wait and Check: Allow the wafers to sit for a few minutes. Test for desired texture and adjust moisture if necessary.

Remember, the beauty of chocolate mint wafers lies in their crispy texture combined with the rich flavor of chocolate and coolness of mint.

Freeze-drying preserves this essence, but rehydrating might change their texture. Enjoy your homemade wafers!

Jelly Beans

SERVINGS: 4 **PREP TIME:** 20 MIN **COOK TIME:** 30 MIN **FREEZE-DRY TIME:** 5-10 HRS

Ingredients For Jelly Beans:

- 1 cup sugar
- 1 1/2 cups corn syrup (light)
- 2 1/4 cups water, divided
- 2 packages (1/4 ounce each) unflavored gelatin
- 2 packages (1.75 ounces each) fruit-flavored pectin (like Sure-Jell)
- 1 teaspoon lemon juice
- Assorted food coloring (optional)
- Assorted flavor extracts or oils (like vanilla, almond, orange, cherry, etc.)

Instructions For Jelly Beans:

Sugar Syrup: In a large saucepan, combine the sugar, corn syrup, and 1/4 cup of water. Cook and stir over medium heat until sugar is dissolved, then bring to a boil. Reduce heat and simmer, uncovered, until a candy thermometer reads 230°F (110°C).

Gelatin Mixture: Meanwhile, in another saucepan, sprinkle gelatin over 1/2 cup water; let stand for 1 minute. Heat over low heat, stirring until gelatin is completely dissolved.

Combine: Gradually add the gelatin mixture to sugar mixture, stirring constantly.

Pectin Mixture: In a small saucepan, combine pectin and the remaining water. Bring to a boil over medium heat, stirring constantly. Cook and stir for 1 minute. Gradually stir into the sugar/gelatin mixture. Add lemon juice and bring to a full rolling boil, stirring constantly.
Remove from the heat; skim off foam.

Flavor and Color: Divide the mixture among several bowls if making multiple flavors/colors. Add food coloring and corresponding flavor extracts/oils to each bowl and stir until well combined.

Shape: Using a clean eyedropper, drop mixture into bean shapes onto waxed paper-lined baking sheets. Let stand at room temperature overnight or until dry to the touch.

Finish: If desired, roll jelly beans in additional sugar to coat.

For Freeze-Drying:

Prepare for Freeze Drying: Once the jelly beans are fully set and dried, place them in a single layer on the freeze dryer trays. Ensure they aren't touching each other.

Run the Freeze Dryer: Use a standard freeze-drying cycle. The process might take between 20-30 hours, depending on the machine and humidity conditions.

Check Dryness: After the cycle is complete, ensure the jelly beans are thoroughly dried. They should feel very lightweight and brittle.

Rehydration:

Jelly beans are typically enjoyed in their original state, and freeze-dried jelly beans may be enjoyed as a crunchy treat. If you wish to rehydrate them:

Place in a Bowl: Put the freeze-dried jelly beans in a bowl and cover them with a light mist of water using a spray bottle.

Allow to Sit: Let the jelly beans sit for a short period. Monitor closely, as they can quickly turn from rehydrated to mushy.

Consume Promptly: Rehydrated jelly beans should be consumed quickly, as their texture will degrade over time.

Please note that freeze-drying jelly beans will change their texture, but it can be a unique and fun way to enjoy this classic candy. The freeze-drying process preserves the flavors but offers a crunchier version of the treat. Enjoy!

Caramel Popcorn

SERVINGS: 4   **PREP TIME:** 20 MIN   **COOK TIME:** 30 MIN   **FREEZE-DRY TIME:** 5-10 HRS

Ingredients For Caramel Popcorn:

12 cups popped popcorn (about 1/2 cup unpopped kernels)
1 cup unsalted butter (2 sticks)
2 cups packed light brown sugar
1/2 cup corn syrup
1 teaspoon sea salt
1/2 teaspoon baking soda
1 teaspoon pure vanilla extract

Instructions For Caramel Popcorn:

Preheat Oven: Preheat your oven to 250°F (120°C). Line a large baking sheet with parchment paper.

Popcorn Preparation: Ensure your popped popcorn is free of unpopped kernels. Place the popcorn in a large mixing bowl.

Caramel Sauce: In a saucepan over medium heat, melt the butter. Stir in brown sugar, corn syrup, and salt. Bring the mixture to a boil while stirring consistently. Allow it to boil for 4-5 minutes without stirring.

Add Baking Soda & Vanilla: Remove the saucepan from the heat and carefully stir in the baking soda and vanilla extract. The mixture will bubble up.

Coat Popcorn: Pour the caramel sauce over the popcorn gradually, stirring to ensure even coating.

Bake: Transfer the coated popcorn to the prepared baking sheet in an even layer. Bake for 45 minutes, stirring every 15 minutes to ensure even coating.

Cool: Remove from the oven and let the caramel popcorn cool on the baking sheet. Once cooled, break it into pieces.

For Freeze-Drying:

Spread on Trays: Place the cooled caramel popcorn in a single layer on the freeze dryer trays.

Freeze Dry: Use a standard freeze-drying cycle. The process will likely take between 20-30 hours depending on the machine and conditions.

Check for Dryness: Ensure that the caramel popcorn is completely dry before removing it from the freeze dryer. It should feel light and very crisp.

Rehydration:

For caramel popcorn, rehydration isn't typically necessary. Freeze-dried caramel popcorn can be enjoyed as a crunchy, sweet treat straight from the freeze dryer. If you wish to reintroduce some moisture:

Light Mist: Using a clean spray bottle, lightly mist the freeze-dried caramel popcorn with water.

Allow to Sit: Let it sit for a few minutes. The caramel popcorn will quickly absorb any moisture, so use water sparingly.

Consume Promptly: Eat promptly after rehydration to experience the best texture.

Keep in mind that freeze-dried caramel popcorn can become too soft or mushy if over-hydrated. The goal should be to slightly soften it rather than make it wet. Enjoy your unique and delightful treat!

Almond Joyfuls

SERVINGS: 4 **PREP TIME:** 20 MIN **COOK TIME:** 30 MIN **FREEZE-DRY TIME:** 5-10 HRS

Ingredients For Almond Joyfuls:

3 cups shredded coconut, unsweetened
1 cup sweetened condensed milk
1 teaspoon pure vanilla extract
1/4 teaspoon salt
30-40 whole almonds
2 cups dark or milk chocolate chips
2 tablespoons coconut oil

Instructions For Almond Joyfuls:

Mix Ingredients: In a mixing bowl, combine shredded coconut, sweetened condensed milk, vanilla, and salt. Mix well.

Form Bars: Scoop out a tablespoon of the mixture and shape it into a small bar or rectangle. Press an almond (or two, based on size) onto the top of each bar.

Freeze Bars: Place the formed bars on a parchment-lined tray and freeze for about 20 minutes, or until they're firm.

Melt Chocolate: In a microwave-safe bowl, combine chocolate chips and coconut oil. Melt in 30-second intervals, stirring between each until smooth.

Dip Bars in Chocolate: Using forks or dipping tools, dip each frozen bar into the melted chocolate, ensuring all sides are coated. Place them back on the parchment paper.

Chill: Allow the chocolate-coated bars to set in the refrigerator for about 10 minutes or until the chocolate is firm.

For Freeze-Drying:

Place on Trays: Lay the Almond Joyfuls in a single layer on your freeze dryer trays. Ensure they aren't touching so they can dry properly.

Freeze Dry: Use your freeze dryer's standard drying cycle. The process can vary in time, but it might take around 24-30 hours, depending on the machine and specific conditions.

Test for Dryness: After the cycle, ensure the Almond Joyfuls are thoroughly dry. They should be brittle and have no noticeable moisture when broken in half.

Rehydration:

Since these are candies, the intent is not to rehydrate them like other foods. The freeze drying process is used to enhance their shelf life and give a unique texture. Simply eat them straight from their freeze-dried state!

However, if you ever feel the need to reintroduce a little moisture:

Mist: Lightly spray the Almond Joyfuls with a fine mist of water.

Let Sit: Allow them to sit for a few minutes to absorb the moisture.

Consume Promptly: It's best to enjoy them soon after rehydration to get the best texture.

Remember, freeze-dried candies can become too soft if over-hydrated. The aim is to slightly soften them, not to make them wet. Enjoy!

Fruit Leather Pieces

SERVINGS: 4   **PREP TIME:** 20 MIN   **COOK TIME:** 30 MIN   **FREEZE-DRY TIME:** 15-25 HRS

Ingredients For Fruit Leather Pieces:

4 cups of fresh fruit (berries, apples, pears, mangoes, etc.)
1/2 cup sugar (optional, adjust to your taste)
1 tablespoon lemon juice
Optional: Spices like cinnamon or nutmeg if desired.

Instructions For Fruit Leather Pieces:

Preparation: Wash and prepare your fruits. If using apples, pears, or any fruit with seeds or tough skins, peel and core them.

Cook the Fruit: In a saucepan, combine the fruit, sugar, and lemon juice. Cook over medium heat, stirring occasionally until the fruit is soft. This usually takes about 10-15 minutes.

Blend: Once the fruit mixture is soft, let it cool slightly, then puree in a blender or food processor until smooth.

Spread: Pour the fruit puree onto a parchment-lined baking sheet. Spread it out evenly, ensuring it's not too thin (about 1/8 to 1/4 inch thick).

Dry: Place the baking sheet in an oven set to its lowest setting (around 140°F or 60°C). Let it dry for 6-8 hours or until the fruit leather is slightly tacky but not sticky. The drying time can vary depending on the fruit and oven.

Cut: Once dried, remove from the oven and let cool. Use scissors or a sharp knife to cut them into desired shapes or strips.

For Freeze-Drying:

Place on Trays: Lay the cut fruit leather pieces in a single layer on your freeze dryer trays. Ensure they aren't touching to allow for proper drying.

Freeze Dry: Use your freeze dryer's standard drying cycle. This might take around 20-24 hours, depending on the machine and specific conditions.

Test for Dryness: After the cycle, ensure the fruit leather pieces are thoroughly dry. They should be brittle and show no signs of moisture when broken.

Rehydration:

Rehydration is Optional: Fruit leathers are often enjoyed in their freeze-dried state for a crunchy texture.

For Traditional Texture: If you prefer them with their classic, chewy texture, lightly mist the fruit leather pieces with water and seal in a ziplock bag for 10-15 minutes.

Enjoy: Once they've regained some moisture, they should have a more flexible and traditional fruit leather texture.

Store the freeze-dried fruit leather pieces in airtight containers with desiccant packs to ensure they remain dry until you're ready to enjoy them!

Candy Apple Slices

SERVINGS: 4   **PREP TIME:** 20 MIN   **COOK TIME:** 30 MIN   **FREEZE-DRY TIME:** 10-20 HRS

Ingredients For Candy Apple Slices:

3 large apples
1 cup white sugar
1/2 cup light corn syrup
1 cup water
1/4 teaspoon red food coloring (optional)
1/2 teaspoon cinnamon flavoring or vanilla extract (optional)

Instructions For Candy Apple Slices:

Prepare Apples: Wash and core the apples. Slice them into 1/2-inch thick rings or wedges, depending on your preference.

Cook the Candy Coating: In a saucepan, combine sugar, corn syrup, and water. Stir and bring to a boil over medium-high heat. Continue cooking without stirring until the mixture reaches the hard-crack stage (about 300°F or 149°C on a candy thermometer).

Add Flavoring and Color: Once the syrup has reached the correct temperature, remove from heat. Carefully stir in the food coloring and flavoring, if using.

Dip Apples: Using tongs or a fork, carefully dip each apple slice into the candy mixture, ensuring they are fully coated. Lay them on a parchment-lined tray, ensuring they aren't touching each other.

Cool: Allow the candy apple slices to cool and harden completely at room temperature. This can take from 20 minutes to an hour.

For Freeze-Drying:

Pre-Freeze: Place the candy-coated apple slices in the freezer for about 1-2 hours.

Arrange on Trays: Lay the pre-frozen slices in a single layer on your freeze dryer trays.

Freeze Dry: Run your freeze dryer's standard cycle for fruit with a sugary coating. Depending on the thickness of the apple slices and the machine, this might take around 24-28 hours.

Check for Dryness: Once the cycle completes, ensure the apple slices are completely dry. They should be light and not have any soft or cold spots.

Rehydration:

No Rehydration Needed: Candy apple slices are best enjoyed in their freeze-dried state for a unique crunchy texture. Rehydrating them would not restore their original texture and might make the candy coating sticky.

Store the freeze-dried candy apple slices in airtight containers with desiccant packs to keep them dry until you're ready to savor them!

Yogurt Drops

SERVINGS: 4   **PREP TIME:** 20 MIN   **COOK TIME:** 30 MIN   **FREEZE-DRY TIME:** 25-35 HRS

Ingredients For Yogurt Drops:

2 cups of your favorite yogurt (full-fat varieties work best)

Optional: Fresh fruit puree, honey, or vanilla extract for flavoring

Instructions For Yogurt Drops:

If you're adding any flavorings like fruit puree, honey, or vanilla extract, mix them into the yogurt until well combined.

Line a baking sheet with parchment paper or a silicone baking mat.

Use a spoon or a piping bag to create small drops of yogurt on the prepared sheet. They should be about the size of a chocolate chip.

Place the baking sheet in the freezer for about an hour or until the yogurt drops are firmly frozen.

For Freeze-Drying:

Once the yogurt drops are frozen solid, transfer them to freeze-drying trays.

Follow the freeze-drying instructions specific to your machine.

Rehydration:

No rehydration is needed. The freeze-dried yogurt drops can be consumed directly as a crunchy, tangy snack. They're excellent on their own, or you can sprinkle them on cereals, fruit bowls, or desserts.

Nut Clusters

SERVINGS: 4   **PREP TIME:** 20 MIN   **COOK TIME:** 30 MIN   **FREEZE-DRY TIME:** 25-35 HRS

Ingredients For Nut Clusters:

2 cups mixed nuts (e.g., almonds, walnuts, cashews)

1 cup semi-sweet chocolate chips

Instructions For Nut Clusters:

Melt the chocolate chips in a microwave or on a stovetop double boiler.

Once melted, fold in the mixed nuts until they're coated evenly.

Using a spoon, drop clusters of the nut and chocolate mix onto a tray lined with parchment paper.

Allow to cool and harden.

For Freeze-Drying:

Place the nut clusters on freeze-drying trays.

Follow your freeze dryer's standard procedure. Once done, the clusters will be crunchy and can be stored for a long time.

Rehydration:

No rehydration needed.

Fudge Cubes

SERVINGS: 4   **PREP TIME:** 20 MIN   **COOK TIME:** 30 MIN   **FREEZE-DRY TIME:** 25-35 HRS

Ingredients For Fudge Cubes:

3 cups semi-sweet chocolate chips
1 can (14 oz) sweetened condensed milk
Pinch of salt

Instructions For Fudge Cubes:

In a saucepan, melt the chocolate chips with the sweetened condensed milk and salt. Stir continuously until smooth.

Pour into a square dish lined with parchment paper.

Allow to cool and set, then cut into cubes.

For Freeze-Drying:

Arrange the fudge cubes on the freeze-drying trays.

Follow the standard freeze-drying process.

Rehydration:

No rehydration needed.

Candy Cane Bites

SERVINGS: 4   **PREP TIME:** 20 MIN   **COOK TIME:** 30 MIN   **FREEZE-DRY TIME:** 10-15 HRS

Ingredients For Candy Cane Bites:

Candy canes

Instructions For Candy Cane Bites:

Simply break candy canes into bite-sized pieces.

For Freeze-Drying:

Lay the candy canes on the freeze-drying trays.

Follow the standard freeze-drying procedure.

Rehydration:

No rehydration needed.

Orange Peels

SERVINGS: 4 **PREP TIME:** 20 MIN **COOK TIME:** 30 MIN **FREEZE-DRY TIME:** 25-35 HRS

Ingredients For Orange Peels:

Peels from 3-4 oranges

Instructions For Orange Peels:

Using a peeler or knife, remove the orange part of the peel, leaving behind the white pith.

Cut into thin strips or desired shapes.

For Freeze-Drying:

Lay the orange peels on the freeze-drying trays.

Follow the standard freeze-drying procedure.

Rehydration:

No rehydration needed.

Gummy Bears

SERVINGS: 4   **PREP TIME:** 20 MIN   **COOK TIME:** 30 MIN   **FREEZE-DRY TIME:** 5-10 HRS

Ingredients For Gummy Bears:

1 cup fruit juice (your choice, but clear juices like apple work well as a base)

2 tablespoons honey or agave nectar (adjust to taste)

2 1/2 tablespoons unflavored gelatin (about 3 packets)

Instructions For Gummy Bears:

Prepare the Mold: Ensure your gummy bear molds are clean and dry. If you don't have a gummy bear mold, you can use ice cube trays or other candy molds.

Mix Ingredients: In a small saucepan, combine the fruit juice and honey/agave nectar. Stir well.

Add Gelatin: Sprinkle the gelatin powder over the fruit juice mixture. Let it sit without stirring for a few minutes until the gelatin has been soaked up by the juice. The mixture will look slightly wrinkled on the surface.

Heat the Mixture: Warm the saucepan over low heat. Stir constantly until the gelatin and honey/agave have dissolved completely. This usually takes about 5 minutes.

Pour into Molds: Remove the saucepan from the heat. Carefully pour the mixture into the gummy bear molds using a dropper (which often comes with the mold) or a small jug.

Set the Gummies: Place the molds in the refrigerator for about 2 hours or until fully set.

Unmold: Once the gummies have set, gently push them out of the molds.

For Freeze-Drying:

Pre-Freeze: Transfer the gummy bears to the freezer and freeze for at least 4 hours or overnight.

Place on Freeze Dryer Trays: Arrange the gummy bears in a single layer on the freeze-dryer trays, ensuring they aren't touching each other.

Freeze Dry: Run your freeze dryer's standard cycle. This may take between 20-24 hours, depending on the machine and the moisture content.

Check for Dryness: The gummies should be completely dry and should have a crunchy texture.

Rehydration:

Direct Consumption: Freeze-dried gummy bears can be enjoyed directly from the freeze-dryer for a crunchy texture.

Rehydration: To return them to their original gummy texture, mist the gummy bears lightly with cool water and let them sit for a few minutes. Be cautious not to use too much water, or they could become soggy.

For Baking or Incorporating into Desserts: It's recommended to use them without rehydration.

Store in airtight containers with oxygen absorbers to maintain their crunchy texture. Enjoy these fun, freeze-dried gummy bears!

Raspberry Jellies

SERVINGS: 4   **PREP TIME:** 20 MIN   **COOK TIME:** 30 MIN   **FREEZE-DRY TIME:** 10-20 HRS

Ingredients For Raspberry Jellies:

2 cups fresh raspberries
2 1/4 cups granulated sugar, plus extra for coating
2 tablespoons lemon juice
2 packets (1/2 ounce total) unflavored gelatin
1/2 cup cold water

Instructions For Raspberry Jellies:

Prepare the Raspberries: In a blender, puree the raspberries until smooth. Strain the puree through a fine-mesh sieve to remove the seeds, yielding about 1 cup of raspberry juice.

Gelatin Mixture: In a small bowl, sprinkle the gelatin over the cold water and let it stand for about 5 minutes.

Cook Raspberry Mixture: In a saucepan, combine the raspberry juice, sugar, and lemon juice. Bring to a boil over medium heat, stirring constantly. Once boiling, continue to cook for an additional 2 minutes.

Add Gelatin: Remove the raspberry mixture from the heat and stir in the gelatin mixture until completely dissolved.

Pour & Set: Pour the mixture into a lightly greased 8-inch square pan. Allow it to set in the refrigerator for at least 4 hours or until firm.

Cut into Shapes: Once set, turn the raspberry jelly out onto a cutting board dusted with sugar. Cut into desired shapes using a sharp knife or cookie cutters. Toss the pieces in granulated sugar to coat all sides.

For Freeze-Drying:

Pre-Freeze: Place the raspberry jellies on a parchment-lined tray and freeze for about 1-2 hours.

Arrange on Trays: Lay the pre-frozen raspberry jellies in a single layer on your freeze dryer trays.

Freeze Dry: Run your freeze dryer's standard cycle for candy or sugary items. This might take around 20-24 hours.

Check for Dryness: Once the cycle completes, ensure the raspberry jellies are completely dry. They should be lightweight and not have any soft or sticky spots.

Rehydration:

No Rehydration Needed: Raspberry jellies are meant to be enjoyed in their freeze-dried state for a crunchy and sweet texture. Rehydrating them would alter their texture and could make them soggy.

Store the freeze-dried raspberry jellies in airtight containers with desiccant packs to keep them dry and crunchy until you're ready to enjoy them!

Peanut Butter Morsels

SERVINGS: 4   **PREP TIME:** 20 MIN   **COOK TIME:** 30 MIN   **FREEZE-DRY TIME:** 15-25 HRS

Ingredients For Peanut Butter Morsels:

1 cup creamy peanut butter
1/4 cup powdered sugar
1/4 cup honey
1/2 tsp vanilla extract
Pinch of salt
Optional: 1/4 cup finely chopped roasted peanuts for added crunch

Instructions For Peanut Butter Morsels:

Mix Ingredients: In a medium-sized bowl, mix together peanut butter, powdered sugar, honey, vanilla extract, and a pinch of salt. If desired, fold in the finely chopped roasted peanuts for added crunch and texture.

Shape Morsels: Use a teaspoon to scoop out small amounts of the mixture. Roll them into balls and place them on a parchment-lined baking sheet.

Chill: Put the baking sheet in the freezer for about 1-2 hours or until the peanut butter morsels are firm.

For Freeze-Drying:

Pre-Freeze: Keep the peanut butter morsels in the freezer until you're ready to place them in the freeze dryer.

Arrange on Trays: Lay the frozen morsels in a single layer on your freeze dryer trays.

Freeze Dry: Run your freeze dryer's standard cycle for creamy or fatty items. This might take around 20-24 hours.

Check for Dryness: Once the cycle completes, ensure the peanut butter morsels are completely dry. They should be lightweight and crunchy to the touch.

Rehydration:

Direct Consumption: Freeze-dried peanut butter morsels are best enjoyed as a crunchy snack without rehydration.

Rehydration (Optional): If you wish to rehydrate them for some applications (like in baking), simply sprinkle them with a tiny amount of warm water and let them sit for a few minutes. However, keep in mind they might not regain their original creamy texture.

Store the freeze-dried peanut butter morsels in airtight containers with desiccant packs to keep them dry and crunchy. They make a perfect addition to cookies, brownies, or as a standalone snack!

Cherry Cordials

SERVINGS: 4   **PREP TIME:** 20 MIN   **COOK TIME:** 30 MIN   **FREEZE-DRY TIME:** 15-25 HRS

Ingredients For Cherry Cordials:

30 maraschino cherries with stems
3 tbsp maraschino cherry juice (from the jar)
2 cups semi-sweet chocolate chips
2 tbsp unsalted butter
1/4 cup heavy cream

1 cup powdered sugar
1/4 tsp almond extract (optional for enhanced flavor)
Pinch of salt

Instructions For Cherry Cordials:

Prepare Cherries: Gently pat dry the maraschino cherries with paper towels to remove excess liquid. Retain the cherry juice for the filling.

Make Filling: In a medium bowl, combine powdered sugar, 3 tbsp of cherry juice, almond extract (if using), and a pinch of salt. Stir until a smooth paste forms.

Dip Cherries: In a small saucepan, combine chocolate chips, butter, and heavy cream. Heat over low-medium heat, stirring constantly until melted and smooth. Allow to cool slightly. Dip each cherry into the chocolate using its stem, ensuring it's completely coated. Let the excess drip off and place them on a parchment-lined tray.

Fill Cherries: Using a pipette or a small spoon, carefully fill each chocolate-coated cherry with the prepared filling. Seal the hole with a little extra melted chocolate.

Set: Refrigerate for 1-2 hours or until the chocolate is firm.

For Freeze-Drying:

Pre-Freeze: Once the cherry cordials have set in the refrigerator, transfer them to the freezer for at least 4 hours or overnight.

Arrange on Trays: Place the frozen cherry cordials in a single layer on the freeze dryer trays.

Freeze Dry: Run your freeze dryer's standard cycle. Depending on the machine, it may take 20-24 hours.

Check for Dryness: Once the cycle is complete, ensure the cherry cordials are fully dried. They should feel lightweight.

Rehydration:

Direct Consumption: Freeze-dried cherry cordials can be eaten straight from the freeze dryer, offering a unique and delightful crunch.

Rehydration: To restore a more traditional cordial texture, lightly mist them with cool water and allow them to sit in an airtight container for several hours. However, they may not fully return to their original gooey consistency.

For Baking: If using in baked goods, directly incorporate them into your recipe without rehydration.

Store in airtight containers with oxygen absorbers to ensure they remain dry and retain their texture. Enjoy your cherry cordials in a completely new and exciting way!

Dulce de Leche Bites

SERVINGS: 4   **PREP TIME:** 20 MIN   **COOK TIME:** 30 MIN   **FREEZE-DRY TIME:** 10-25 HRS

Ingredients For Dulce de Leche Bites:

1 can (14 oz) of sweetened condensed milk OR ready-made dulce de leche

Sea salt flakes (optional)

1 cup semi-sweet chocolate chips (optional for coating)

1 tbsp coconut oil or butter (optional if coating with chocolate)

Instructions For Dulce de Leche Bites:

To Make Dulce de Leche from Sweetened Condensed Milk: (Skip if using ready-made dulce de leche)

Pour the sweetened condensed milk into a pie plate or shallow dish. Cover tightly with aluminum foil.

Place the dish inside a larger roasting pan and fill the roasting pan with water until it's about halfway up the side of the pie plate.

Bake in a preheated oven at 425°F (220°C) for about 1.5 to 2 hours. Check occasionally and add more water to the roasting pan if needed.

Once the sweetened condensed milk has turned into a thick, caramel-colored dulce de leche, remove from the oven and whisk until smooth.

Forming Bites: Once the dulce de leche is cooled, use a spoon or a melon baller to scoop out small amounts and roll them into bite-sized balls. Place them on a parchment-lined tray. If desired, sprinkle a tiny amount of sea salt flakes on top of each ball. Freeze the balls for about an hour to make them firm.

Chocolate Coating (Optional): Melt the chocolate chips with coconut oil or butter. Dip each dulce de leche bite into the melted chocolate, ensuring it's completely coated. Place them back on the parchment-lined tray and let them set.

For Freeze-Drying:

Pre-Freeze: Once the dulce de leche bites (with or without chocolate) are set, transfer them to the freezer for at least 4 hours or overnight.

Arrange on Trays: Place the frozen dulce de leche bites in a single layer on the freeze dryer trays.

Freeze Dry: Run your freeze dryer's standard cycle. Depending on the machine, it might take 20-24 hours.

Check for Dryness: Once the cycle is complete, ensure the bites are fully dried. They should feel lightweight and not sticky.

Rehydration:

Direct Consumption: Freeze-dried dulce de leche bites can be eaten straight from the freeze dryer, offering a delightful crunchy texture.

Rehydration: While freeze-dried dulce de leche bites can be lightly misted with cool water to rehydrate, it's recommended to enjoy them as-is for the unique texture. They may not fully return to their original creamy consistency when rehydrated.

For Baking: If using in baked goods, incorporate them directly without rehydration.

Store in airtight containers with oxygen absorbers to ensure they remain dry and maintain their texture. Enjoy this sweet treat with a unique twist!

Berry Bites

SERVINGS: 4   **PREP TIME:** 20 MIN   **COOK TIME:** 30 MIN   **FREEZE-DRY TIME:** 25-35 HRS

Ingredients For Berry Bites:

2 cups mixed berries (strawberries, blueberries, raspberries, blackberries)
1 cup Greek yogurt
1 tablespoon honey (optional)

Instructions For Berry Bites:

Berry Prep: If you're using strawberries, cut them into small bite-sized pieces. Leave other berries like blueberries, raspberries, and blackberries whole.

Mixing: In a mixing bowl, combine the Greek yogurt and honey, if using. Gently fold in the berries until they're all coated with the yogurt mixture.

Placing on Tray: Drop spoonfuls of the yogurt-covered berry mixture onto a baking sheet lined with parchment paper. Aim to have individual clumps of berries rather than one big mass.

Freezing: Transfer the baking sheet to the freezer and allow the berry bites to freeze solidly, about 2-3 hours.

For Freeze-Drying:

Once the berry bites are frozen, place them onto your freeze dryer trays without the berries touching one another. Start the freeze-drying process according to your machine's guidelines.

Storing:

After freeze drying, store the berry bites in an airtight container with an oxygen absorber or vacuum-sealed bag for optimal shelf life.

Rehydration:

These berry bites are delicious as a crunchy snack right out of the bag and don't need rehydration. If you wish to return them to their original consistency, you can leave them out at room temperature for a short period, or spritz them lightly with water.

Raspberry Chocolates

SERVINGS: 4   **PREP TIME:** 20 MIN   **COOK TIME:** 30 MIN   **FREEZE-DRY TIME:** 25-35 HRS

Ingredients For Raspberry Chocolates:

Fresh raspberries
High-quality dark chocolate or milk chocolate (as per your preference) - about 200g (7 oz)
Optional: white chocolate for drizzling

For Freeze-Drying:

Clean and dry the raspberries thoroughly.

Place the raspberries on the trays of your freeze dryer, ensuring they're not touching.

Run the freeze dryer cycle according to your machine's instructions for berries. Once complete, you should have crisp, freeze-dried raspberries.

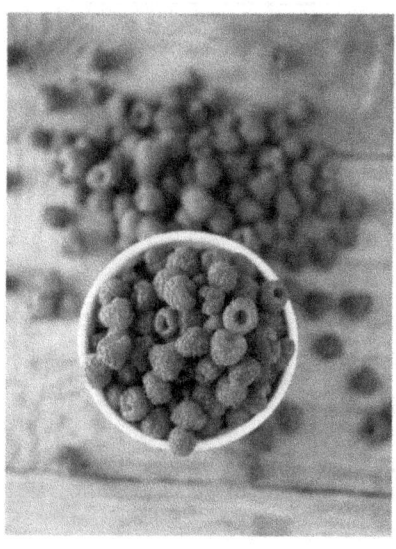

Making the Raspberry Chocolates:

Slowly melt your chosen chocolate using a double boiler method. This involves placing a bowl with chocolate pieces over a pot of simmering water, ensuring the bottom of the bowl doesn't touch the water. Stir constantly until it's smooth and completely melted.

Once melted, remove from heat. Let it cool slightly but ensure it remains liquid.

Gently fold in the freeze-dried raspberries, ensuring they are evenly distributed but not crushed.

On a baking sheet lined with parchment paper, drop spoonfuls of the chocolate-raspberry mixture to form clusters.

Optional: For an added touch, melt some white chocolate using the double boiler method, transfer it to a piping bag or a small Ziploc bag (and snip a tiny corner), and drizzle over the top of the chocolate clusters.
Let the raspberry chocolate clusters set and harden in a cool place or refrigerate for faster results.

Once set, enjoy immediately or store in an airtight container.

Note: You can also place individual freeze-dried raspberries into chocolate molds and pour melted chocolate over them for a different presentation.

Tutti Frutti Candy

SERVINGS: 4   **PREP TIME:** 20 MIN   **COOK TIME:** 30 MIN   **FREEZE-DRY TIME:** 25-35 HRS

Ingredients For Tutti Frutti Candy:

- 1 cup granulated sugar
- 1/2 cup corn syrup
- 1/4 cup water
- 1 tsp lemon juice
- Natural fruit flavor extracts (like orange, cherry, pineapple, etc.)
- Food coloring (matching with your chosen flavors)
- Citric acid (optional, for a tangy flavor)

Instructions For Tutti Frutti Candy:

In a heavy-bottomed saucepan, combine the sugar, corn syrup, water, and lemon juice.

Cook over medium heat, stirring until the sugar has dissolved.

Once the sugar is dissolved, increase the heat and bring to a boil. Do not stir from this point onwards.

Using a candy thermometer, boil the sugar mixture until it reaches the hard-crack stage (about 300°F or 150°C).

Remove the saucepan from the heat and let it stand for a moment to allow the bubbles to subside.

Divide the mixture into different bowls for each flavor/color you're using.

Quickly stir in the respective fruit flavor extracts and a pinch of citric acid (if you want a tangy flavor) into each bowl.

Add food coloring to match the flavor (e.g., red for cherry, yellow for pineapple, etc.).

Pour the colored mixtures into silicone molds or onto a silicone mat. You can also drop them with a spoon to create small droplet candies.

Let them cool and harden completely.

For Freeze-Drying:

Once the candies have completely hardened, remove them from the molds or silicone mat and place them on the freeze dryer trays in a single layer.

Run your freeze dryer according to the machine's instructions for candy.
After the cycle is complete, the candies will have a unique, crispy texture and intensified flavor.

Storing:

Store your freeze-dried Tutti Frutti Candy in an airtight container to maintain its crispy texture.

Toffee Crunch

SERVINGS: 4 **PREP TIME:** 20 MIN **COOK TIME:** 30 MIN **FREEZE-DRY TIME:** 20-30 HRS

Ingredients For Toffee Crunch:

- 1 cup unsalted butter
- 1 cup granulated sugar
- 1/4 cup water
- 1/4 tsp salt
- 1 tsp pure vanilla extract
- 1/4 tsp baking soda
- 1 cup semi-sweet chocolate chips
- 1/2 cup chopped nuts (like almonds, pecans, or walnuts)

Instructions For Toffee Crunch:

Line an 8x8-inch pan with parchment paper, ensuring the paper extends over the sides for easy removal later.

In a heavy-bottomed saucepan, combine the butter, sugar, water, and salt. Cook over medium heat, stirring constantly, until the mixture comes to a boil.

Continue to cook, stirring occasionally, until the mixture reaches a temperature of 295°F (146°C) on a candy thermometer. This is known as the "hard-crack stage."

Once the desired temperature is reached, remove from heat and quickly stir in the vanilla extract and baking soda. The mixture will bubble up.

Pour the hot toffee mixture into the prepared pan and spread it out evenly.

Sprinkle the chocolate chips on top. After a few minutes, the chocolate will have melted from the heat of the toffee. Spread the melted chocolate evenly over the toffee layer.

Sprinkle the chopped nuts over the melted chocolate, pressing them lightly into the chocolate.

Allow the toffee to cool and harden for several hours.

For Freeze-Drying:

Once the toffee is completely set, break it into smaller pieces.

Lay these pieces on the freeze dryer trays in a single layer, ensuring they aren't touching.

Follow your freeze dryer's guidelines and run the machine on a setting suitable for candy or chocolates.

After the freeze-drying process, the Toffee Crunch will have a unique crispy texture while retaining its rich flavors.

Storing:

Store the freeze-dried Toffee Crunch in airtight containers or vacuum-sealed bags to maintain its crispness.

Mocha Bites

SERVINGS: 4　　**PREP TIME:** 20 MIN　　**COOK TIME:** 30 MIN　　**FREEZE-DRY TIME:** 30-40 HRS

Ingredients For Mocha Bites:

1 cup dark chocolate chips
1/4 cup strong brewed coffee, cooled to room temperature
1/4 cup unsweetened cocoa powder
1 tbsp instant coffee granules
1/2 cup powdered sugar
1 tsp vanilla extract
A pinch of salt
1/2 cup almond flour or finely ground almonds
Optional: 1/4 cup chopped nuts (like walnuts or pecans) for added crunch

Instructions For Mocha Bites:

In a microwave-safe bowl, melt the chocolate chips in 20-second intervals, stirring in between until smooth.

To the melted chocolate, add the brewed coffee, cocoa powder, instant coffee granules, powdered sugar, vanilla extract, and a pinch of salt. Mix until well combined.

Gradually fold in the almond flour (or ground almonds) until the mixture is dense and holds together. If you're adding chopped nuts, fold them in now.

Using your hands or a spoon, form small bite-sized balls from the mixture and place them on a tray lined with parchment paper.

Freeze the mocha bites for about 1 hour, or until they are firm and set.

For Freeze-Drying:

Once the mocha bites are set, arrange them on the freeze dryer trays, ensuring they aren't touching.

Follow your freeze dryer's instructions and set it to the mode suitable for chocolates or candy.

Once the freeze-drying process is complete, the Mocha Bites should be crispy yet still rich in flavor.

Storing:

Store the freeze-dried Mocha Bites in airtight containers or vacuum-sealed bags to maintain freshness and crispness. They can last for months if stored properly!

Honey Almond Candy

SERVINGS: 4 **PREP TIME:** 20 MIN **COOK TIME:** 30 MIN **FREEZE-DRY TIME:** 25-35 HRS

Ingredients For Honey Almond Candy:

1 cup raw almonds, roughly chopped
1/2 cup honey
2 tablespoons butter (or coconut oil for a vegan version)
A pinch of sea salt
Optional: 1/2 teaspoon vanilla extract or almond extract for added flavor

Instructions For Honey Almond Candy:

In a medium saucepan, combine honey, butter (or coconut oil), and a pinch of salt. Heat the mixture over medium heat, stirring occasionally.

Once the mixture starts boiling, let it simmer for about 5 minutes, until it thickens slightly.

Add the roughly chopped almonds into the honey mixture, ensuring all the almonds are well-coated. Continue cooking and stirring for another 2-3 minutes.

Remove from heat and stir in the vanilla or almond extract if using.

Pour the mixture onto a parchment-lined baking sheet, spreading it out evenly.

Allow the mixture to cool and harden. This could take a few hours at room temperature, but you can speed up the process by placing the tray in the refrigerator.

For Freeze-Drying:

Once the honey almond mixture has hardened, break it into bite-sized pieces.

Arrange the pieces on your freeze dryer trays, ensuring they aren't touching.

Follow your freeze dryer's instructions, setting it to the mode suitable for candies.

After the freeze-drying process is complete, the Honey Almond Candy should have a light, crispy texture while retaining its sweet and nutty flavors.

Storing:

Store the freeze-dried Honey Almond Candy in airtight containers or vacuum-sealed bags. They can remain fresh and crispy for months if stored properly.

Maple Pecan Treats

SERVINGS: 4   **PREP TIME:** 20 MIN   **COOK TIME:** 30 MIN   **FREEZE-DRY TIME:** 35-45 HRS

Ingredients For Maple Pecan Treats:

1 cup pecan halves
1/2 cup pure maple syrup
A pinch of sea salt
1/2 teaspoon vanilla extract (optional)
Optional: A pinch of cinnamon for added warmth

Instructions For Maple Pecan Treats:

In a medium skillet or saucepan, heat the maple syrup over medium heat until it starts to simmer.

Add the pecan halves to the simmering maple syrup. Stir continuously, ensuring all pecans are coated with the syrup.

Allow the pecans to simmer in the syrup for 4-6 minutes, or until most of the syrup has been absorbed and the mixture has thickened.

Stir in the pinch of salt and optional vanilla extract or cinnamon.

Once the mixture is well combined, remove from heat and spread out the pecans on a parchment-lined tray, ensuring they are in a single layer.

For Freeze-Drying:

After allowing the maple-coated pecans to cool and the syrup to harden slightly, transfer the pecans to your freeze dryer trays.

Make sure the pecans are spread out evenly and not touching each other.

Follow your freeze dryer's instructions, setting it to the mode suitable for candies or nuts.

Once the freeze-drying process is complete, the Maple Pecan Treats should be crisp with intensified flavors of maple and pecan.

Storing:

Store your freeze-dried Maple Pecan Treats in airtight containers or vacuum-sealed bags. They can remain fresh and retain their crisp texture for months when stored properly.

Vanilla Bean White Chocolate Truffles

SERVINGS: 4   **PREP TIME:** 20 MIN   **COOK TIME:** 30 MIN   **FREEZE-DRY TIME:** 30-40 HRS

Ingredients For Vanilla Bean White Chocolate Truffles:

8 oz (about 1 cup) high-quality white chocolate, chopped
1/4 cup heavy cream
1 vanilla bean, split and seeds scraped
1/4 cup unsalted butter, softened
White chocolate or cocoa powder for coating (optional)

Instructions For Vanilla Bean White Chocolate Truffles:

Preparing the Truffle Mixture: In a heatproof bowl, combine the chopped white chocolate and the seeds from the vanilla bean.
In a small saucepan, heat the heavy cream over medium heat until it just begins to simmer.

Pour the hot cream over the white chocolate and vanilla seeds. Allow it to sit for a minute and then stir until the chocolate is completely melted and the mixture is smooth.

Add the softened butter to the mixture and stir until it's fully incorporated.

Cover the bowl with plastic wrap and refrigerate for about 2-3 hours or until the mixture is firm enough to shape.

Shaping the Truffles: Using a small scoop or your hands, shape the mixture into small balls, roughly the size of a cherry.

Place the shaped truffles on a parchment-lined tray.

If you're coating them, roll each truffle in melted white chocolate or cocoa powder before placing them on the tray.

For Freeze-Drying:

Once the truffles are shaped (and coated, if desired), arrange them on your freeze dryer trays, ensuring they aren't touching each other.

Set your freeze dryer to the mode suitable for chocolates or dairy products.

After the freeze-drying process is complete, the truffles should be dry and light but will still melt in your mouth with an intense burst of vanilla and white chocolate flavor.

Storing:

Store your freeze-dried Vanilla Bean White Chocolate Truffles in airtight containers or vacuum-sealed bags. They can stay fresh for a very long time when stored properly.

These truffles offer an incredible experience, giving you the rich taste of white chocolate and the aromatic essence of vanilla in a texture that's unlike any traditional truffle. Enjoy!

Pistachio Brittle

SERVINGS: 4   **PREP TIME:** 20 MIN   **COOK TIME:** 30 MIN   **FREEZE-DRY TIME:** 35-45 HRS

Ingredients For Pistachio Brittle:

1 cup granulated sugar
1/2 cup light corn syrup
1/4 teaspoon salt
1/4 cup water
1 cup shelled pistachios
2 tablespoons unsalted butter, softened
1 teaspoon baking soda
1 teaspoon vanilla extract

Instructions For Pistachio Brittle:

Line a large baking sheet with a silicone baking mat or lightly greased parchment paper. Set aside.

In a large, heavy saucepan, combine sugar, corn syrup, salt, and water. Cook over medium heat, stirring until the sugar dissolves.

Once the sugar has dissolved, increase the heat to medium-high and bring the mixture to a boil. Insert a candy thermometer.

Without stirring, let the mixture cook until the thermometer reads 250°F (120°C).

Stir in the pistachios and continue cooking until the thermometer reaches 300°F (150°C).

Immediately remove from heat and carefully stir in the butter, baking soda, and vanilla extract. The mixture will bubble up.

Pour the mixture onto the prepared baking sheet and spread it out using a spatula. Allow it to cool completely.

For Freeze-Drying:

Once the brittle is cooled and set, break it into smaller pieces.

Distribute the pieces on your freeze dryer trays, making sure they don't overlap.

Set your freeze dryer to the mode suitable for candy or high-sugar content items.

After the freeze-drying process is complete, the brittle will be super crispy and will retain its natural flavor but have an added crunch from the freeze-drying process.

Storing:

Store your freeze-dried Pistachio Brittle in airtight containers or vacuum-sealed bags to ensure it remains fresh and crisp.

This Pistachio Brittle, when freeze-dried, offers a unique texture and intensified flavor, making it an extraordinary treat! Enjoy!

Batch Logs & Worksheets

The Importance of Using Batch Logs and Worksheets When Freeze Drying Food

Freeze drying, also known as lyophilization, is a meticulous process of preserving food that involves removing the moisture content while maintaining the food's structure and nutritional value. This method of food preservation is superior in many ways to traditional drying or canning, as it can maintain the color, taste, and nutritional content of fresh food for extended periods. However, with such a delicate process comes the need for precision, and this is where batch logs and worksheets play an indispensable role. Using batch logs and worksheets when freeze drying food can mean the difference between a successful preservation and a wasted batch.

Here are several benefits of using these tools:

1. **Consistency in Quality**: One of the primary reasons for using batch logs and worksheets is to ensure that every batch of freeze-dried food meets consistent quality standards. By documenting specific details about each batch – such as the type of food, its initial weight, drying time, and final weight – one can replicate successful batches in the future and avoid repeating mistakes.

2. **Tracking Variations**: Different foods have unique requirements when it comes to freeze drying. For instance, the time required to freeze dry strawberries might differ significantly from that of meat. By maintaining logs, users can note the specific parameters used for each type of food and refine them over time, achieving optimal results.

3. **Safety Assurance**: Freeze drying food is not just about preserving taste and nutrition; it's also about ensuring the food is safe to eat. Incomplete drying can result in the growth of harmful bacteria or mold. With worksheets, one can ensure that the food has been dried for the appropriate amount of time and at the correct temperature to guarantee safety.

4. **Efficient Problem-Solving**: Should an issue arise with a specific batch of food, having detailed logs allows users to quickly identify what might have gone wrong. Whether it's a malfunction in the freeze dryer, an inconsistency in the food's preparation, or an error in the drying process, batch logs provide invaluable data for troubleshooting.

5. **Cost Efficiency**: Freeze drying, while effective, can be energy-intensive. By using worksheets to optimize the process, users can ensure that they're not wasting electricity on overly long drying times or on batches that don't turn out correctly. Over time, this can result in significant cost savings.

Batch logs and worksheets are essential tools for anyone serious about freeze drying food, whether for personal consumption or commercial purposes. They offer a methodical approach to the process, ensuring that each batch is of the highest quality, safe to consume, and made in the most efficient manner possible. In the world of freeze drying, documentation isn't just paperwork—it's a vital component of the preservation journey.

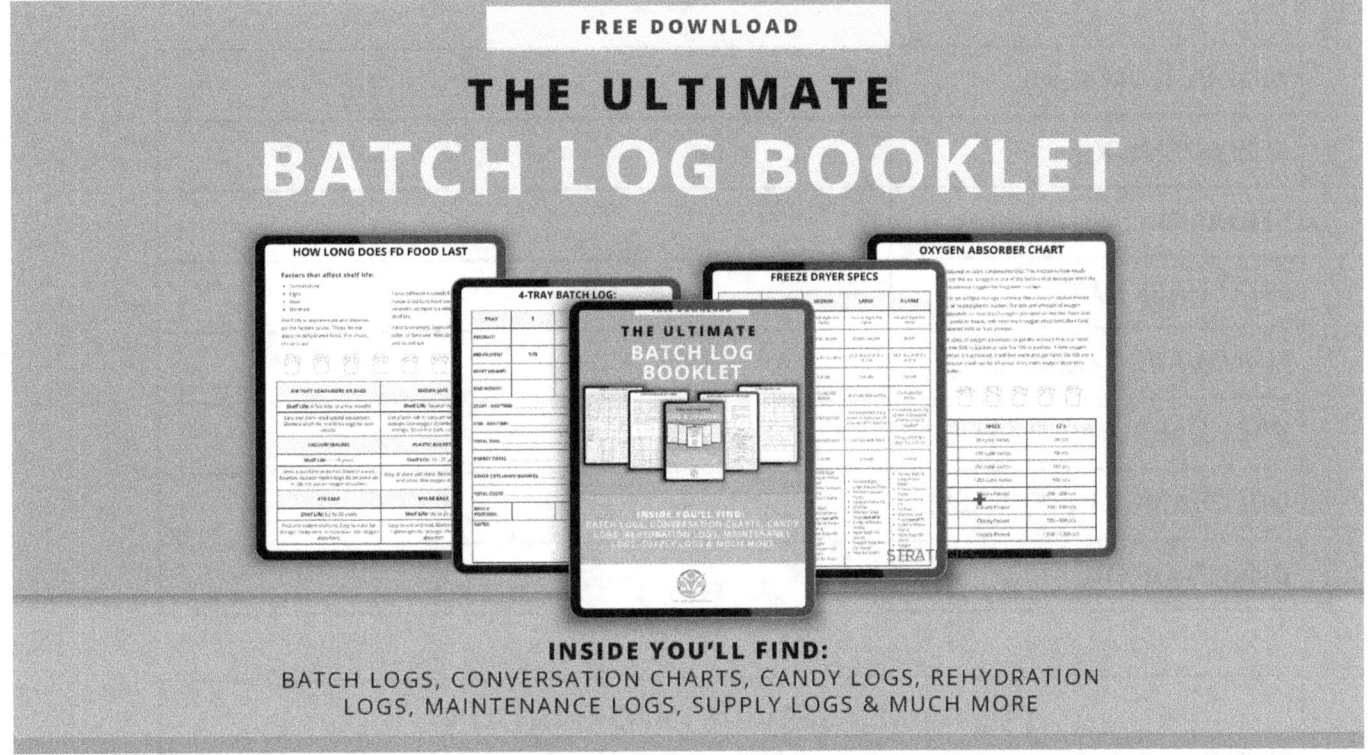

ABOUT MY FREEZE DRYER:

MODEL NUMBER:	
SIZE (S/M/L/X):	
SERIAL No:	
PURCHASE DATE:	
FIRMWARE VERSION:	
VACUUM PUMP TYPE:	
OIL CHANGE INTERVALS:	
BRAND OF OIL:	

CUSTOMER SERVICE INFORMATION:	
NAME:	
PHONE:	
EMAIL:	

NOTES:

REHYDRATION INFORMATION

Do not rehydrate if:
- You'd like to preserve the crunchy texture of your snacks.
- If you'd like to convert some of your freeze dried fruit or veggies into powers.

WATER LOSS CALCULATOR

For each tray, subtract the post-freeze-drying weight from the pre-freeze-drying weight. This gives you the weight of the water removed.

Water Loss per Tray = Pre–Freeze – Drying Weight - Post-Freeze-Drying Weight

Example:

If Tray 1 weighed 1000g before freeze-drying and 800g after, then the water loss is 200g.

*** You will add back about 200g

MEALS: 5-20 min	Add hot water, let it sit and allow it or put it in the over, add hot water and bake it for 10 min or until fully reconstructed.
COOKED MEAT: 5-60 min	Add enough hot water to cover the meat. Don't add more to prevent meat turning mushy.
RAW MEAT: 30 min-3 hrs	Place it in a dish, add cold water and let it sit in your fridge overnight. Pat it dry and cook normally.
FRUIT & VEG: 1-10 min	Lay it out on a tray, spritz it with cold water, wait a few minutes and repeat. Add more moisture as needed.
EGGS: 1-2 min	To rehydrate your eggs, add 2 tablespoons of egg powder to 2 tablespoons of cold water, stir and allow it to sit. Cook.
DESSERTS: 5-10 min	You can eat these crunchy or wrap them in a moist paper towel and allow it to sit until desired consitatncy.
CANDY:	Eat as is! :)
CHEESE & DAIRY: 5-10 min	You can either wrap it in a moist paper towel or sprits with cold water and let it sit. If shredded, you can add to meals.

REHYDRATING YOUR FOOD

FOOD:	DRY WEIGHT:	WATER AMOUNT:	HOT/COLD WATER:	TIME:
			H/C	
NOTES:				

FOOD:	DRY WEIGHT:	WATER AMOUNT:	HOT/COLD WATER:	TIME:
			H/C	
NOTES:				

FOOD:	DRY WEIGHT:	WATER AMOUNT:	HOT/COLD WATER:	TIME:
			H/C	
NOTES:				

FOOD:	DRY WEIGHT:	WATER AMOUNT:	HOT/COLD WATER:	TIME:
			H/C	
NOTES:				

FREEZE DRYER SPECS

SPECS	SMALL	MEDIUM	LARGE	X-LARGE
MANUFACTURER:	Harvest Right Pro Home	Harvest Right Pro Home	Harvest Right Pro Home	Harvest Right Pro Home
PRICE:	$2,495 - $2,695	$3,195 - $3,395	$3,895 - $4,095	$5,095
DIMENTIONS:	17.4" W x 21.5" D x 26.8" H	19" W x 25" D x 29"H	21.3" W x 27.5" D x 31.3"H	24.3" W x 37.4" D x 35.6" H
WEIGHT:	91 LBS	119 LBS	143 LBS	265 LBS
AVERAGE YIELD:	6-10 LBS PER BATCH	10-15 LBS PER BATCH	18-27 LBS PER BATCH	12-16 LBS PER BATCH
POWER:	110 VOLT OUTLET	110 VOLT OUTLET	110 Volt (NEMA 5-20) outlet. A dedicated 20 amp circuit is required	110 Volt (NEMA 5-20) Outlet. A dedicated 20 amp circuit is required
TRAY SPACE:	434 SQUARE INCH	675 SQUARE INCH	1,107 SQUARE INCH	7 Trays (10.9" W x 29.5" D x 0.75" H)
WARRANTY:	3 YEARS	3 YEARS	3 YEARS	3 YEARS
WHAT'S INCLUDED:	<ul><li>Harvest Right Small Freeze Dryer</li><li>Premier Vacuum Pump</li><li>Vacuum Pump Oil</li><li>Oil Filter</li><li>Stainless Steel Trays **(set of 4)**</li><li>Guide to Freeze Drying</li><li>Mylar Bags (50 count)</li><li>Oxygen Absorbers (50 count)</li><li>Impulse Sealer</li></ul>	<ul><li>Harvest Right Medium Freeze Dryer</li><li>Premier Vacuum Pump</li><li>Vacuum Pump Oil</li><li>Oil Filter</li><li>Stainless Steel Trays **(set of 5)**</li><li>Guide to Freeze Drying</li><li>Mylar Bags (50 count)</li><li>Oxygen Absorbers (50 count)</li><li>Impulse Sealer</li></ul>	<ul><li>Harvest Right Large Freeze Dryer</li><li>Premier Vacuum Pump</li><li>Vacuum Pump Oil</li><li>Oil Filter</li><li>Stainless Steel Trays **(set of 6)**</li><li>Guide to Freeze Drying</li><li>Mylar Bags (50 count)</li><li>Oxygen Absorbers (50 count)</li><li>Impulse Sealer</li></ul>	<ul><li>Harvest Right X-Large Freeze Dryer</li><li>Premier Vacuum Pump</li><li>Vacuum Pump Oil</li><li>Oil Filter</li><li>Stainless Steel Trays **(set of 7)**</li><li>Guide to Freeze Drying</li><li>Mylar Bags (50 count)</li><li>Oxygen Absorbers (50 count)</li><li>Impulse Sealer</li></ul>

HOW LONG DOES FD FOOD LAST

Factors that affect shelf life:

- Temperature
- Light
- Heat
- Moisture

Shelf life is approximate and depends on the factors below. These do not apply to dehydrated food. If in doubt, throw it out.

These different methods for storing freeze-dried food have several variables, so there is a wide range of shelf life.

If the food smells, looks off, has lost color, or feels wet, then discard it and do not eat.

AIRTIGHT CONTAINERS OR BAGS	MASON JARS
Shelf Life: A few days to a few months	**Shelf Life:** Several months
Easy and don't need special equipment. Shortest shelf life. Use thick bags for best results.	Use plastic lids or vacuum seal for longer storage. Use oxygen absorbers for longer storage. Store in a dark, cool location.
VACUUM SEALING	**PLASTIC BUCKETS**
Shelf Life: 1 - 10 years	**Shelf Life:** 15 - 25 years
Need a machine to do this. Store in a dark location. Vacuum sealed bags do let some air in. Do not use an oxygen absorber.	Easy to store and stack. Resistant to rodents and pests. Use oxygen absorbers.
#10 CANS	**MYLAR BAGS**
Shelf Life: Up to 25 years	**Shelf Life:** Up to 25 years
Pest and rodent resistant. Easy to stack for storage. Equipment. is expensive. Use oxygen absorbers.	Easy to use and seal. Blocks light and air. Lightweight for storage. Use an oxygen absorber.

OXYGEN ABSORBER CHART

Oxygen absorbers are measured in cubic centimetres (CC). This measures how much oxygen they can absorb from the air. Oxygen is one of the factors that decrease shelf life of food, so it's important to remove oxygen for long-term storage.

You should only use them in an airtight storage container like a vacuum-sealed mason jar, mylar bag, or #10 can, or sealed plastic bucket. The size and amount of oxygen absorbers that you need depends on how much oxygen you need to remove. Food that has a lot of air space, e.g., pasta or beans, will need more oxygen absorbers than food that is powdered, like powdered milk or fruit powder.

You can combine different sizes of oxygen absorbers to get the amount that you need. For example, you can use one 500 cc packet or use five 100 cc packets. A new oxygen absorber will be flexible. When it's activated, it will feel warm and get hard. Do not use a spent oxygen absorber because it will not be effective. Keep extra oxygen absorbers sealed using an impulse sealer.

CONTAINER	SPACE	CC's
Pint	30 cubic inches	20 cc's
Quart or Liter	120 cubic inches	50 cc's
1 Galon	250 cubic inches	100 cc's
5 Galon	1250 cubic inches	500 cc's
#10 Can	Closely Packed	200 - 300 cc's
#10 Can	Loosely Packed	300 - 500 cc's
5 Galon Bucket	Closely Packed	700 - 900 cc's
5 Galon Bucket	Loosely Packed	1,000 - 1,200 cc's

MAINTENANCE & REPAIR LOG

DATE:	PART/SERVICE:	COST:	NOTES:

SUPPLIES

DATE:	COST:	PRODUCT:	BRAND:

RECIPE:			
PREP TIME:	COOK TIME:	# OF SERVINGS:	STORAGE DATE:

INGREDIENTS:

FREEZE-DRYING INSTRUCTIONS:

REHYDRATING INSTRUCTIONS:

4-TRAY BATCH LOG:

TRAY	1	2	3	4
PRODUCT:				
PRE-FROZEN?	Y/N	Y/N	Y/N	Y/N
START WEIGHT:				
END WEIGHT:				

START - DAY/TIME: _____ / _____

END - DAY/TIME: _____ / _____

TOTAL TIME: _____ HRS _____ MIN

ENERGY COSTS: _____

OTHER COSTS (MAINTENANCE): _____

TOTAL COSTS: _____

BAGS x PORTIONS:				

NOTES:

CANDY 4-TRAY BATCH LOG:

TRAY	1	2	3	4
PRODUCT:				
PRE-FROZEN?	Y/N	Y/N	Y/N	Y/N
START WEIGHT:				
END WEIGHT:				

START - DAY/TIME: _____ / _____

END - DAY/TIME: _____ / _____

TOTAL TIME: _____ HRS _____ MIN

ENERGY COSTS: _____

OTHER COSTS (MAINTENANCE): _____

TOTAL COSTS: _____

BAGS x PORTIONS:				
NOTES:				

BATCH PLAN:

DATE OF PURCHASE:	PRODUCT:	PRE-FROZEN?	BATCH PLANNING DATE:	NUMBER OF TRAYS:
		Y/N		
		Y/N		
		Y/N		
		Y/N		
		Y/N		
		Y/N		
		Y/N		
		Y/N		
		Y/N		
		Y/N		
		Y/N		
		Y/N		
		Y/N		
		Y/N		
		Y/N		
		Y/N		
		Y/N		
		Y/N		
		Y/N		
		Y/N		
		Y/N		

FREEZE DRIED FOOD

PRODUCT	EXPIRY	QUANTITY

FREEZE DRIED MEALS

PRODUCT	EXPIRY	QUANTITY

FREEZE DRIED CANDY

PRODUCT	EXPIRY	QUANTITY

FREEZE DRIED DESSERTS

PRODUCT	EXPIRY	QUANTITY

FREEZE DRIED _____

PRODUCT	EXPIRY	QUANTITY

Publisher

HarvestGuard Publications is a leading brand specializing in comprehensive and accessible resources for freeze-drying novices. Our mission is to demystify the art and science of freeze-drying, making it approachable and practical for everyone—from homemakers wanting to preserve food to hobbyists interested in freeze-drying flowers or other items.

At HarvestGuard Publications, we recognize the diverse applications and potentials of freeze-drying technology. That's why our books range from introductory guides to more specialized texts that dive deep into specific freeze-drying techniques and their uses in various industries like food preservation, pharmaceuticals, and even space travel.

Our educational materials rely on a foundation of evidence-based research and hands-on experience in the field of freeze-drying. We focus on simplifying complex concepts and methodologies, ensuring that our readers can easily comprehend and apply the information. Our guides prioritize safety and efficiency, offering step-by-step instructions, tips, and tricks that have been vetted by experts in the field.

By adopting a straightforward and user-friendly approach, HarvestGuard Publications aims to make freeze-drying not just a highly specialized technique but a practical skill that can be mastered and enjoyed by all. We believe that with the right information and guidance, anyone can benefit from this amazing preservation method, making it a valuable addition to households and businesses alike.

Resources

Chapter 1

- Villazon, L. (2022, March 4). How does freeze drying work? BBC Science Focus Magazine. https://www.sciencefocus.com/science/how-does-freeze-drying-work

Chapter 3

- Harvest Right. (2019, July 30). FAQs. Harvest Right | Home Freeze Dryers | Freeze Dried Food Storage. https://harvestright.com/faqs/

Chapter 4

- Harvest Right Oil Pump – https://harvestright.com/product/oil-free-pump-pre-order/

Chapter 6

- Assistant Secretary for Public Affairs (ASPA). (2023). Cook to a safe minimum internal temperature. FoodSafety.gov. https://www.foodsafety.gov/food-safety-charts/safe-minimum-internal-temperatures

Chapter 7

- Preparing your Freeze-dryer – https://www.familycanning.com/freeze-drying-posts/food-temperature-monitor-take-1/
- Assistant Secretary for Public Affairs (ASPA). (2023a). Cold food storage chart. FoodSafety.gov. – https://www.foodsafety.gov/food-safety-charts/cold-food-storage-charts

Chapter 8

- Mylar Bags – https://www.uline.ca/BL_3123/Clear-Stand-Up-Barrier-Pouches

Chapter 10

- Harvest Right. (2023, September 26). Customer support. Harvest Right TM | Home Freeze Dryers | Freeze Dried Food Storage – https://harvestright.com/support/

- Starr, K. (2023, April 24). Harvest Right Freeze Dryer Software: A complete guide. Backyard Homestead HQ - https://backyardhomesteadhq.com/harvest-right-freeze-dryer-software-a-complete-guide/

Chapter 11

- Harvest Right. (2017, September 28). Helping those in need. Harvest Right TM | Home Freeze Dryers | Freeze Dried Food Storage -https://harvestright.com/blog/2017/helping-those-in-need/

- Wells, S. (2022). Harvest Right: How to Freeze-Dry Food, at home! Our Best Bites - https://ourbestbites.com/harvest-right-how-to-freeze-dry-food-at-home/comment-page-4/

- USDA local food directories. (n.d.). https://www.usdalocalfoodportal.com/#directories

ADDITIONAL RESOURCES

- Mylar Bags in Canada – www.72hours.ca

- Candy Bags – www.Uline.com

- Fixing / Troubleshooting your freeze-dryer – https://www.fixmyfd.com/?aff=152&fbclid=IwAR2t44wVgIQEObXi_M0RPhu9yqVc-qVKgMGRjO4Sktz7U1_6eKbFe_n4YgI

- Harvest Right Instructions – https://www.earthtechproducts.com/freeze-dryers-for-home-use.html

www.ingramcontent.com/pod-product-compliance
Lightning Source LLC
Chambersburg PA
CBHW081108080526
44587CB00021B/3497